This new anthology "CALLED HOME" [Book Two] and the earlier work "TWO WORLDS: Lost Children of the Indian Adoption Projects" are very important contributions to American Indian history. The editors Trace A. DeMeyer and Patricia Busbee, both adoptees, found other Native adult survivors of adoption and asked them to write a narrative. In the part one of Called Home, adoptees share their unique experience of living in Two Worlds, feeling CALLED HOME, surviving assimilation via adoption, opening sealed adoption records, and in most cases, a reunion with tribal relatives. Adoptees who wrote in Two Worlds provide updates in part two. In part three, adoptees still searching for their families share their birth information, date and location. Recent history about the Supreme Court case involving Baby Veronica and The New Normal: DNA is also covered.

The new anthology CALLED HOME offers even more revelations of this hidden history of Indian child removals in North America, their impact on Indian Country and how it impacts the adoptee and their entire family. These unforgettable accounts of Native American adoptees will certainly challenge beliefs in the positive outcomes of closed adoptions in the US and Canada and exposes the genocidal policies of governments who created Indian adoption projects.

CALLED HOME

CALLED HOME

BOOK TWO: LOST CHILDREN OF THE INDIAN ADOPTION PROJECTS

PATRICIA BUSBEE, TRACE DEMEYER

Blue Hand Books
Greenfield, Massachusetts

Adoption Anthology/American Indian History

for the lost birds, lost ones, lost children and splitfeathers

© 2014 Patricia Busbee and Trace A. DeMeyer

All rights reserved under International Copyright Conventions. No parts of this book may be reproduced, stored in a retrieval system, or transmitted in any form or by any means (electronic, mechanical, photocopy, recording or otherwise) without the express written consent of the copyright holders with the sole exception of the fair use provisions recognized by laws. Fair use includes brief quotations in published reviews.

Library of Congress: On File

DeMeyer, Trace A. [1956-]

Berdan-Busbee, Patricia [1958-]

ISBN-13: 978-0692245880 (Blue Hand Books) (paperback)

First Edition

Book Cover Design: KIM PITMAN Firefly Inx.com

Formatting and Pre-Press: PressBooks

MEDIA BLOG: http://lostchildrencalledhome.blogspot.com/

FACEBOOK PAGE: https://www.facebook.com/pages/Called-Home-Lost-Children-of-the-Indian-Adoption-Projects-book

Cover Photo: Lost Children (by permission of participants in book)

Publisher: Blue Hand Books, 442 Main St. #1061, Greenfield, MA 01301

Website: www.bluehandbooks.org

Published in the United States

QUOTES

The Indian survived our open intention of wiping them out. And since the tide turned they have even weathered our good intentions toward them, which can be more deadly." —John Steinbeck, America and Americans

By the end of the 19th century, writes David E. Stannard, a historian at the University of Hawaii, Native Americans had undergone the "worst human holocaust the world had ever witnessed, roaring across two continents non-stop for four centuries and consuming the lives of countless tens of millions of people."

In the judgment of Lenore A. Stiffarm and Phil Lane, Jr., "there can be no more monumental example of sustained genocide—certainly none involving a 'race' of people as broad and complex as this—anywhere in the annals of human history."

The lesson (is) to realize the value of an alternative perspective. And that is why we are here. That is why the Creator allowed some of us to remain, in spite of all the attempts to destroy us... —Tall Oak (Everett Weeden), Wampanoag/Pequot, 500 Nations video

Contents

PREFACE   xiii
The Resilience of Lost Birds
TRACE A. DEMEYER *(Tsalagi-Shawnee-Euro)* CO-EDITOR

INTRODUCTION   1
THE ACT OF DOCUMENTING
PATRICIA BUSBEE *(Shawnee-Cherokee)* CO-EDITOR

HISTORY: Split Feather Syndrome   xi

Part I. Called Home

1. The Indian Wars are Not Over   15
   LAWRENCE SAMPSON *(Delaware, Eastern Band Cherokee)*

2. Sooner or Later, All Lost Birds Come Home   21
   MITZI LIPSCOMB/ROSEMARY BLACKBIRD *(Walpole Bkejwanong First Nations)*

3. Caught in the Middle   25
   JANELLE BLACK OWL *(Mandan, Hidatsa, Turtle Mountain Chippewa and Lakota)*

4. Two Families   29
   DOUGLAS LIBRETTI LITTLEJOHN *(Roseau River Anishinabe)*

5. Blue Bear   31
   JANELL LOOS

6. In Search of Julio   39
   LYNN GRUBB

7.	Finding the Truth MARK O. HEISER	45
8.	5 Siblings—Found in the Wind MAZI, later ELIZABETH BLAKE	51
9.	White Earth Adoptee…Who am I? TERRY NISKA WATSON (White Earth Anishinabe)	59
10.	Maybe El Reno… Somewhere Near Oklahoma City KIM SHUCK (Sauk and Fox, Cherokee)	67
11.	Split Feathers STARLA BILYEU (Eastern Band Cherokee Indian)	75
12.	Welcomed MARY CHARLES (St. MARTIN) (Koyukon Athabascan)	79
13.	Josie/She's There In My Bones C SUZANNE ZAHRT MURPHY (Cherokee)	85
14.	It's a Wild World SAMANTHA FRANKLIN	89
15.	When Love Cannot Conquer A 60s Scoop Adoptee's Journey from Reserve to Mainstream Society Back to the Reserve KAREN KAMINAWAISH M.A., M.S. (Anishinawbe)	93
16.	Michelle's Spirit Can Now Rest PATRICK QUINTON YEAKEY (Sugpiaq)	109
17.	On the Red Road THAYLA BARRETT (Cherokee)	113
18.	I am Cynthia with Two Birth Certificates CYNTHIA LAMMERS (Lakota)	119
19.	Wolf Clan JESSE STONEFIELD (Cherokee)	125
20.	Lost Bird Jefferson KAREN ANN (Wounded Cougar) JEFFERSON (Choctaw)	129
21.	Baby V TRACE A DEMEYER (co-editor)	141
22.	The Holocaust Self LEVI EAGLE FEATHER (Lakota/Dakota)	147

23. History: Project Papoose *The Editors*	159
24. History: The Rainbow Project *The Editors*	163

Part II. Updates TWO WORLDS adoptees

25. Finding Our Meaning JESSE FASTHORSE FLOYD NEUBERT *(Lakota)*	169
26. UUTUQTUA, COMING HOME ANECIA TRETIKOFF O'CARROLL *(Alutiiq)*	173
27. Family Gatherings ALICE DIVER *(Mi'kmaq)*	183
28. Lost and Now Found GAIL HUGGARD *(Rocky Boy Chippewa-Cree)*	191
29. Eleven Months/Eleven Years SUZIE/CRICKET SMITH-FEDORKO *(Anishinabe)*	195
30. Unringing the Bell: Annulling My Adoption BEN ANI CHOSA *(Lac du Flambeau Anishinabe/Menominee)*	199
31. Seven Year Cycles MESCHELLE LINJEAN *(Tsalagi)*	203
32. Finding Peace, Coming Home DEBBY PRECIUS POITRAS *(Cree)*	219
33. "Home at last, Thank God I am home at last" THOMAS PIERCE *(Menominee)*	225
34. Knowing You Are Not Alone JOAN KAUPPI *(Red Lake Anishinabe)*	227
35. Lost ANDY MILLER HILL *(Mohawk, Pawnee, Shawnee, British Isles ancestors)*	231
36. She Went Home EVELYN RED LODGE *(Sicangu Lakota)*	235
37. I Am Home LELAND P. MORRILL KIRK *(Navajo Nation Citizen, Many Goats Clan)*	239

38. Fresh Flesh: Ronni and me TRACE A. DEMEYER (CO-EDITOR) (Tsalagi-Shawnee-Euro)	247
39. The Path from Separativeness to Oneness JOHNATHAN BROOKS (Cheyenne/Cree)	255

Part III. SEARCHING

40. Brit Reed	265
41. Kim Dupre	267
42. Catie Ransom	271
43. Drew RedBear Rutledge	273
44. Karla Mena	275
45. Lisa Bos	277
46. Michael Pintozzi	279
47. Marylyn Jean Chrismer	281
48. Doreen Evelyn Sinclair	283
49. Mary Thompson	285
50. Amelia Cagle	287
51. DNA: The New Normal	289
Image Credits	293
Acknowledgments	295
About the Authors/Editors	297
Come Home JUDI BRANNAN ARMBRUSTER	301

PREFACE

The Resilience of Lost Birds

TRACE A. DEMEYER (Tsalagi-Shawnee-Euro) CO-EDITOR

In my dream I'm on a mountainside with an elder who tells me to look at all the tiny lights flickering as far as the eyes could see. He tells me, "…those are new souls coming to be with us, coming soon, and many will be adopted out. Some will be lost birds like you. Some will need help. Some will have to find their way home like you. No matter who raises them, we still dream in Indian…"

That dream stayed with me for months.

No matter who adopts us, new parents will **never** erase our blood, ancestry, DNA or our dreams… No matter how much I want to believe things have changed for the better in Indian Country and in our world, the reality is there is still an "adoption-land" waiting to scoop up more children and more children who need healthy moms and dads. These books will be their roadmap.

This is why Patricia and I chose the title CALLED HOME for the new anthology. There are many adoptees called home, who are back living on tribal lands and they are a testament to the courage needed to be in reunion as adult adoptees, as survivors who were part of the government plans to rid the world of Indigenous and First Nation People. Adoption didn't kill our spirit but it hurt it deeply.

After ten years of researching the topic and history of adoption, sadly, states like South Dakota and South Carolina are still violating federal law called the Indian Child Welfare Act of 1978 when Native children are supposed to be placed with family, close kin, a relative, or with a different tribe. "Stranger adoptions" with non-Indian parents is supposed to be the absolute last resort or rare occurance. How it can still happen, read the chapter on **Baby V.**

Let's face it: With a shortage of Native adoptive and foster homes in the US and Canada, children will be lost and later called Lost Birds, adoptees and *Stolen Generations*. Indian Country as a whole is still impoverished, living with daily reminders of broken treaties, remote reservations, soul-crushing poverty, and generations who are dealing with post-traumatic stress after centuries of war, residential boarding school abuse and neglect. Since so many are still subjected to Third World conditions, Indigenous children will continue to be taken and placed into foster care and adoptions. (Wasn't this the plan?) Native American moms and dads can still lose their child (or all their children) in courtrooms ruled by non-Indian judges and social workers steeped in their bias of white privilege and cultural insensitivity.

On a visit to Brock University in 2014, my co-editor Patricia Busbee and I learned how foster and adoptive parents are invited to bring their Native child to First Nations Friendship Centres in the Niagara, Ontario area. Children are invited to hear stories, learn their language and songs, while their new parents can participate in activities, too. The entire family is welcome and nourished in this cultural exchange.

Indian Country needs to look to its northerly neighbors in Canada and start its own US-wide "Truth and Reconciliation Commission," and reinvent and redesign its own child care protection systems for the sake of its own future generations.

After many adoptees contacted me wanting to find their first families, I can say with certainty adoptees are CALLED HOME, called in dreams to be reunited with family members and their many nations. These adoptees do find a way to reconnect despite difficulties with archaic laws, a clueless public, biased lawmakers, closed adoptions, sealed court documents and falsified birth records.

It's long overdue that North America opens their closed adoption files. When this happens, **if** this happens, the entire world will finally comprehend how adoption was actually colonization and child trafficking of Indigenous Indian children by the "Nation Builders" who call themselves America and Canada. We in North America are literally educated to be **ignorant** of the true history of our colonization, by the nation builders who use it and what really happened here. Hiding it only perpetuates continued racism and intolerance.

The fog is lifting now and it's time we shine a light on the hidden history of the Indian Adoption Projects and Programs like ARENA, Operation Papoose and Project Rainbow. You will read about these programs in this book.

For the writers in this book, adoption was the tool of assimilation, erasing our identity and sovereign rights as tribal citizens, intending it to be permanent.

Who profits from pain? Are the people who invented and keep the adoption machine going unaware or aware that it causes great harm? Does this have to do with money?

Little regard has been given to parents and children separated by adoption and the long-term health effects on their minds and bodies. It may hit you as it did me that "adoption" is really about money and jobs, not about children.

> "...If we look at 2014, child "protection" is one of the biggest businesses in the US. We spend **$12 billion** a year on it. The US Department of Health & Human Services (DSS) administers Child Protective Services. That money goes to tens of thousands of a) state employees, b) collateral professionals, such as lawyers, court personnel, court investigators, evaluators and guardians, judges, and c) DSS contracted vendors such as counselors, therapists, more "evaluators," junk psychologists, residential facilities, foster parents, adoptive parents, etc.
>
> With the implementation of the Adoption and Safe Families Act, President Clinton tried to make himself look like a humanitarian who is responsible for saving the abused and neglected children. The drive of this initiative is to offer cash "bonuses" to states for every child they have adopted out of foster care, with the goal of doubling their adoptions by 2002, and sustaining that for each subsequent year. They actually call them "adoption incentive bonuses," to promote the adoption of children. The way adoption bonuses work is that each state is given a baseline number of expected adoptions based on its population. For every child that DSS can get adopted, there is a bonus of $4,000 to $6,000." [1]

Someone hijacked adoption. Some children were sold like commodities and trafficked in other countries like Korea, China, Africa, Ireland and Guatemala and their babies were also trafficked to Americans. Adoption files are filled with falsehoods and lies to **SELL** a child to prospective adopters. Sealed documents hide an adoptee's identity, our name and ancestry, our parent's names. Concealing the truth legally, it ends any chance or hope for a reunion.

For too many of us, states still won't release our files to us, even as adults. What are they hiding? We have included a section in this book for adoptees who are still searching for clues after their closed adoptions.

As these books travel to new lands and new hands, I pray that adoptive parents accept that we cannot be the child they **want** us to be, or dream us to be, and that we are born with our own unique biology, ancestry and characteristics. We will dream in Indian. If you do adopt us, then never lie to us. Tell us the truth. It's your job as our loving unselfish guardians to tell us about our first parents and get us educated about our tribes. We need you to recognize the life-long health effects and fog of stress that we adoptees live under and endure. The primal wound and "genetic bewilderment" that being adopted creates is very real. Be a bridge for us, not a wall or weapon of assimilation.

Someday I hope the entire world will see how children feel like imposters in their adopted family. As an adoptee, I was posing as a DeMeyer, when I know the falsehood of that name was legally forced upon me.

There is one thing I am learning from other adoptees and that is, return to your tribe well, in a good way, with a good heart and a strong mind. With an epidemic of historical trauma, alcoholism and diabetes, the colonizer's poison, there are already enough broken souls on the rez and in our families. After they get to know you, become familiar with you, and know who you are, you will be welcomed home. This could take a long time. You might meet some relatives who accept you immediately! Other relatives, even our own mothers, may not accept us when we return. I know this is hard for some of you. I know it is hard because I never met my mother Helen.

Closed adoption left adoptees like me lodged between two worlds yet not quite fitting in any world.

So I dream a new world where children and their safety are top priority, **not** who adopts them. I dream we are now working harder to unify families, preserving family units, helping parents care for their own children, not separating them unless absolutely necessary. Children should never be placed with paying strangers or paid caretakers if there is kin, other family members who are willing.

The Truth and Reconciliation Commission of Canada has unearthed thousands of records of residential school abuses and documenting many of those survivors (including 60s Scoop Adoptees) who will finally and eventually receive settlements, reparations and an apology. [2]

These same practices affected thousands of American Indians in the US and someday I hope we will have our day in court and our records will finally be opened... Then there will be congressional hearings for the survivors of the Indian Adoption Projects, an investigation into the government's adoption policies and practices in the US, so adoptees can be given our original birth certificates, and our history will finally be acknowledged, known about and widely taught.

By writing these wrongs, in our own words, in the anthology TWO WORLDS and CALLED HOME, we ask that our own tribes create a Welcome Home for their adoptees, enroll us or re-enroll us, facilitate a reunion with our relatives, offer us a place to live, hold a naming ceremony, and reeducate us on own tribal history that we lost being adopted out.

For Lost Birds/adoptees coming after us, when they find this new book and the earlier anthology TWO WORLDS, adoptees themselves documented this history and evidence. We have created a roadmap, a resource for new adoptees who will wish to journey back to their First Nations and understand exactly what happened and why.

There is no doubt in my mind that adoption changes us, clouds the mind and steals years of our lives, but there is something non-Indians can never take and that is our dreams and the truth we are resilient!

> A new wave of discovery is upon us: THANKS to author Margaret D. Jacobs' new book in 2014 "A GENERATION REMOVED: THE FOSTERING AND ADOPTION OF INDIGENOUS CHILDREN IN THE POSTWAR WORLD." This shockwave will reach a new generation and change the world.

[1] DSS and affiliates rewarded for breaking up families, Nev Moore, Massachusetts News, *www.massnews.com/past_issues/2000/5_May/mayds4.htm*

[2] *www.trc.ca*

INTRODUCTION
THE ACT OF DOCUMENTING

PATRICIA BUSBEE (Shawnee-Cherokee) **CO-EDITOR**

a young Patricia and her adoptive mother Helen

Lately I have thought a lot about words spoken or written with intent. Words and sentences uttered across cities and countries over landlines and cell phones—over texts. I thought about all the people creating news feeds and why as humans we feel it is necessary to craft mini billboards that get our messages "out." I can bake a cake and the world can see it within seconds. It can even be viewed in its progression from mixing bowl to table.

I am especially interested in words written in diaries and journals—the act of documenting. I am acutely aware of what is left in and what is left out. Both a choice. I think about how Facebook has become an interactive diary of sorts that reflects a life lived—snapshots of moments. I wonder if my grandchildren or my daughters will comb thru my news feed, photos and posts in search of clues, in search of insight into who I was and what mattered to me after I am gone. I wish my ancestors had been FB subscribers. I wish they had Twitter accounts.

I have also been thinking about what I write, especially what I write when I am not worried about publication, when I'm not analyzing every comma, when I'm not concerned over how I or my writing will be perceived.

It is obvious my adopted mother, Helen Cotter, felt this way as well. Unlike mine, her diaries are very controlled. Every now and again she writes her true thoughts—she writes as a way to uncover how she feels about something but then she becomes aware of an invisible audience and she ends her writing abruptly, "And that is all I am going to say about that." This statement infuriates me. As an editor I catch the places where the writing has the potential to go deeper—to the bone. Raw speak is what I call it. Usually what happens is, the writing is perceived by the writer as being too revealing and the rawness gets aborted—hidden or decorated like a Christmas tree.

I've spent a lot of years, combing through documents, sentences, diaries and anything else I could get my hands on as a way to learn more about my life—the context of it. It's a strange feeling to read how other people perceived you as a child and the situations around your existence.

As odd as this might seem to some, my adopted family is just as much a mystery to me as my biological family. I never really knew who my adopted mother, Helen, actually was. Realities were very distorted. I would wake up to Helen holding an ice pack over a blackened eye and when I asked what happened, I was met with a blank stare. "What are you talking about? No, the police were not here last night." I learned that I could not trust what I saw and that I could not trust myself or any conclusions I came to.

Helen's diaries shocked me. What is written is very different from what I experienced. Her outward actions revealed nothing as to what was really going on inside her. Her outward life was muted by alcohol but her inner life provided some clarity as to how she perceived her world and how she perceived me.

Since my piece in Two Worlds a lot has happened. All the new information is still organizing itself internally.

I recently reread the part in my adoptive mother Helen's diary where my biological father, Ralph Watkins, called our house. He asked my adoptive father, Edmond, if he was harboring his child. This caused an uproar and Helen and I went into hiding. (I wonder if anyone considered my biological father's pain?) I have read and reread these words many times. I never considered what took place after this point. I was too busy comforting myself over the fact that my biological father wanted me. I usually stopped here. This time I focused on what happened after the call.

Helen and I traveled to upstate New York by train to derail a potential kidnapping. A month passes. Her writing is sporadic. We travel back-and-forth between Great Barrington, Massachusetts and Saratoga Springs, New York. My grandparents were in Great Barrington and Helen's sister was in Saratoga. My adoptive father, Edmond, was not with us. I notice that Helen's writing seems lighter, her days easier, even though she and I have gone into hiding. Does this indicate that her stress over a possible kidnapping has dissipated? Is she happy to be a way from Edmond? Their relationship was certainly intense. Her fear over my being taken has been replaced by an under-current of adventure. Our days are spent at the lake, baking and bike riding.

During my recent diary crawl I discover that Mrs. Ammes from Hardin County, Ohio, was in charge of the adoption decisions. Mrs. Ammes threatens Helen. She states that the other couples in her bridge club may not be approved for a baby if Helen doesn't do what she wants. One of the couples, Maryanne and Johnny, mentioned in Helen's diary, were promised the next baby.

Diary from 1958, November 18th
Mrs. Ammes and her daughter Pat, both pressure Helen into taking a fifteen-year-old girl named Lydia. Lydia was staying with Mrs. Ammes but she was not actually up for adoption. (I wish I knew more of her story.) On Tuesday November 20, 1958, (I was almost four months old) Helen tells Mrs. Ammes she has changed her mind. Helen explains that she does not feel up to taking an older child as she is still adjusting to a new baby. (My adoptive parents were married twelve years before they adopted me. My adoption was not yet official.) Mrs. Ammes became "quite nasty." Helen was so upset by her conversation with Mrs. Ammes that my adoptive father, Edmond was called home from work. Helen wrote that she was nearly hysterical. She is petrified that I may be taken from the home. A couple named Marcille and Chuck came rushing over to sit with Helen until my father came home. Several people called the next day to check on her. My adoptive father did not go to his classes at the college and he went into work late.

On November 25th 1958 the issue resolved itself. Maryanna and Johnny phoned to say that Mrs. Ammes had decided to let them have the next child. I have no idea what took place or how this decision was made. A few months later Helen writes briefly about how they were awarded two boys. This is stated in two lines. This couple was never mentioned again in her diaries. I find this unsettling, as this couple was very much involved with my adoptive parents. Weekly get-togethers were documented up until this point. Maryanna was a close friend. Helen's usual, "That is all I have to say about that," closed the door in my face. How did Mrs. Ammes arrive at this decision? What changed her mind? I find myself outraged by Mrs. Ammes and her daughter, Pat. Who were these women that ruled the adoption world in Hardin County? How many other bridge club mother's were awarded babies by this woman?

I am the oldest child. I never lived with my siblings. My sister Beth is the youngest. She is the only sibling I am close with. We are ten years apart. Our cousin adopted my sister, Beth, when she was three. Beth remembers our mother. She was adopted after our mother died in a car accident. Mo and Lena, my other siblings, were older and were not put up for adoption. All my siblings were placed in a children's home after my mother's death. Beth was kept in a different wing of the children's home. She was not allowed to interact with her siblings as she was soon to be adopted. Not only did Beth lose her mother in a traumatic way she was not allowed to be with her siblings. What sort of monsters reinforced these rules? Mo and Lena grew-up in a children's home within miles from where I was raised.

I remember my parents being asked if they wanted to take my siblings. They were told that my brother and sisters had recently been orphaned. I remember my adoptive father, Edmond, wrestling with this information. I was close to thirteen at this time. Helen was very clear. She did not want any more children.

Beth still does not know who her father is. Mo and Lena know their father. Beth's father most likely had hemophilia. Beth's son Scotty has hemophilia. There is a small chance that the gene mutated with my sister. When we are able I think we should comb thru hospital records. Her father had to be treated at some point. Family members told her that her father was Native and that he was a "bad man." My sister is dark-skinned. Not knowing her father has caused Beth extreme pain.

This past winter Beth attended the funeral of our Aunt. She was the wife of my mother's brother, Sonny. I did not attend. I wish this woman well in the afterlife but she was not kind to me in this life. She told me to go back into the closet. She told me I was a skeleton and that she would never tell her children (my cousins) about me. I was in my late twenties when I was told this and it was extremely hurtful at the time. I allowed this to shut down my searching. I am working through my issues regarding my Aunt as she did eventually connect me with my sister, Beth. For this, I will always be grateful.

Beth met a woman attending the funeral that knew my mother. She knew my entire story. This woman announced to my sister that my mother actually knew my adopted family and she visited me. She knew where I was. I have not fully explored this knowledge but I plan to in the near future.

In June of 2013 a matriarch of the Cole family (my biological father's side) called and shared information. She told me that my parents paid a lot of money for me and that she knew my biological grandfather when he was alive. She used to visit with him. She told me he had another son. Who is this son? I discovered that my grandfather had his own church in West Virginia and that he began working in the coalmines when he was sixteen. My biological parents are third cousins and their family lines crisscross back and forth. I was told that my mother was placed in a reform school not an unwed mother's home. This might explain why I could never uncover which unwed mother's home my mother was in. I called and harassed every single one I could find. I was told that notes were packed a way in musty basements. "Find them," I said. "Find the fucking notes."

How is this possible? How can a sixteen-year-old be placed in a reform school when she is pregnant? My father was forty-four at the time of my conception. He had children her age. I want to bring him back—hold a séance—disturb his ghost and question him—question the relatives and the people that sent her away. I want to question the other women at the reform school—what was her day-to-day life like? I want to know.

I have been told I am lucky. I am. I do know more than most. I have stacks of papers—and lineages and a thesis about my family. But not knowing my mother—being separated—never seems to heal. I have not healed as I imagined. I once thought that healing meant everything was good—never bothered again, all behaviors gone—anger gone. This is not what healing has been for me—healing has been a journey—a circular process that goes round and round until I find myself back at square one but each time from a different perspective.

I try to remember that I do have more information than a lot of people but I am tired of feeling guilty because I want more. Often adoptees are told they should be grateful as adoption spared them from poverty or abuse. Yes, this is true but what is also true— being separated from the mother is traumatic. Not knowing your identity causes a multitude of problems. I will always want to know more. I am not ungrateful because I feel this way. My adoptive parents were not saviors. I don't owe them because they adopted me. Through the reading of Helen's diaries, therapy and ritual, I have let go of most of my anger. They just wanted a baby and they did the best they could. They were educated and I became educated. Helen was an artist. She taught me to see light in the most unusual places. She would drag me out of bed at four in the morning to go with her while she painted. I am grateful for these experiences. However, no amount of money, education or anything else can cover up the fact that separation from the mother is traumatic.

I have been thinking about my privileges in this lifetime. Only recently have I viewed myself as privileged. I saw myself as broken or as a victim. But I do have privileges. I have an education. I am a writer. I am a survivor. I can use these gifts in a way that is beneficial to other people.

My most recent shift took place at Brock University in late March of 2014. This is where Trace DeMeyer, and I first met in person. Meeting Trace was extremely healing. We were invited to Brock to speak about the book, *Two Worlds: Lost Children of the Indian Adoption Projects*. Adoptees from the community also attended. Hearing the adoptees stories was very different from reading and editing them. There was no way to buffer the pain. I suppose I could have left and ran screaming down the street, but I didn't choose that option. I chose to be present and to allow the stories to enter my heart. I detest crying in public. I spent a large portion of this trip in tears. I don't like crying because I fear if I start—I won't stop. I fear losing control. Reality is, I have never had control—not even over my own birth story.

Healing for me is in layers. It is an ongoing but never completed process. Sometimes it's joyous but often I feel like Sisyphus—pushing the boulder up the hill over and over with no relief. Most of the time I feel fragile—like the wind could knock me over.

My search for my mother got twisted up with my ideas about God. My adoptive parents had very different religions. They often fought over which church I should attend. Edmond was Catholic and Helen belonged to the First Presbyterian Church on the South end of town. Her church was upscale. My mother called my father's church pagan. She made fun of the statues and told my father that they would scare me. Actually I loved Mary. She was a mother. I wanted to understand what a loving mother was. My father referred to the attendees of her church as Rich Bitches in Floppy Hats. I experienced this as very confusing. I attended various churches with the neighborhood children. Each church offered a different perspective. I decided that God was schizophrenic. I grew up longing to know where I belonged.

I went to a Pentecostal Bible College in the 70s. I lived at an Outreach for Youth for over a year. (I was sent there for running away when I was thirteen by the courts. My adoptive parents said I was unruly. (Apparently I was following in my mother's footsteps) Out Reach for Youth had Pentecostal leanings. They believed in being filled with the Holy Spirit. I was taught that each person had a direct-line to God. I have since left the church and the narrow-minded-view points. It's not for me.

When I left Bible College I set off on a pilgrimage that continues. I studied branches of Buddhism and Hinduism. I studied Witchcraft and Goddess studies for over twenty-five-years. I learned how to connect with the energies of the moon—the turning of the seasons. I learned how to work with the elements. I led women's circles. I wrote a book of seasonal rituals. This book of rituals was crafted while I was attending Evergreen State College. Oddly my adviser was a Native woman, Yvonne Peterson. This was before I knew my ancestry. I asked her advice on crafting public ritual. This book is still on my desktop. I have been thinking about publishing it.

I leaned towards spiritual practices that were female based. I loved Buddhism but didn't really relate to the Buddha. I related to Tara—the 21 Tara's.

When my youngest daughter was in grade school I enrolled her in St. Mary's school. This school offered a really good education. I lied and said we were practicing Catholics. I knew enough from my father to get by. My daughter started having problems with The Holy Ghost. She was afraid it was going to show up unannounced. She developed a sleeping disorder. (My karma for lying to the nuns). I decided it was time she was introduced to other practices. I traveled to Woodstock, NY, to a Tibetan Buddhist Monastery, Karma Triyana Darmachakra. I wanted to take her to see the shrine room of the Twenty-One Tara's. Upon arrival I was told it was not yet open to visitors. I had to see the Tara's. My daughter and I crawled on our hands and knees down a long hallway. I glanced behind to make sure my daughter was following me. We looked like a small train. We crawled past the Llama's office and to the shrine room. The door was not locked. We sat on the floor in front of a massive shrine and gazed upon these awesome Deities. Each was housed in connecting glass shrines. I had never viewed all the aspects together. Viewing the Divine Feminine was healing for both of us. My daughter realized that there were other interpretations of God/Goddess. I left money on the table as an offering. Over the years I have exposed my daughters and my entire family to various forms of spiritual practices. My oldest daughter is now Muslim. She lived in Egypt for three years and felt at home in the mosques. She married and took on the religion of her husband. I worry how Islam is viewed in the west. She has studied Christianity and Hinduism extensively. I opened doors—now she must open her own and decide for herself where she wants to walk.

Over the years I have adopted many practices but they are not the practices of my ancestors. When I found out about my Native ancestry I wanted to understand how to pray—how to practice—what rituals were available to me? I remain an outsider. This doesn't sit very well with me. My entire life is filtered thru a spiritual lens.

Maybe this lens was created as a buffer—as a way to make sense out of my reality—as a way to cope—as a way to make sense out of the senseless. It's quite possible. Even so, it doesn't take a way the fact that my spirituality is very important to me. I feel pulled apart inside. I want to understand the ways of my ancestors. The image I have is of a wishbone. Except I'm not getting my wish. I do not have the keys to the Kingdom. I do not hold the understanding of how to connect to the Gods of my ancestors.

I have floor to ceiling altars to Ganesha, Lakshmi and Kali. I used to have a puja room (Ritual room.) Even though I am not a traditional Hindu I have been welcomed into the community. Most are excited that I prefer to wear saris and that I enjoy placing bindis, ceremonial red kum-kum and sandalwood paste on my forehead. I'm not seen as a poser. I'm not asked about my blood quantum. Maybe it is because I have taken the time to learn the traditions, rituals, chants, meditations and proper etiquette. People have been generous with their knowledge. Yet, I feel like something is missing. Maybe I am misinterpreting this feeling of loss. Maybe it is my birth mother I am missing. Maybe this sense of loss or not belonging is an adoptee wound that I am going to have to learn how to live with no matter what spiritual path I chose to walk. Maybe my spirituality cannot address this. I don't know.

There is no one to teach me the rituals and spiritual practices of the Cherokee or Shawnee. I know that fire was an integral part. I know that water is as well. I know about the four directions and I know some of the myths. I know about the Medicine Wheel and dreams. But maybe what I know isn't real. Maybe it's s shadow of the truth. I participated in a two-year Shamanic studies program with a group called, The Great Grey Owl Clan in Michigan. The focus was on journeywork. I have no idea if these teachings were valid or mixed with New Age. A white woman taught me. Supposedly she had a tribal elder that passed down information but this was never verified. I didn't know enough to ask. This was over twenty years ago. I don't know how to pray in the proper way. I know of Corn Mother. Her images are all over my office. I don't know how to approach her so I look at her. I hang her pictures as if they are prayer flags. There is no one to guide me. How do I get this information? How do I practice?

I have learned that discovering your ancestry is complex. For me, it's been like opening Pandora's box. It has a ripple effect—that continues. With answers came all sorts of other things—some painful and some healing.

I want to leave my stories for my daughters and grandchildren to read. I want them to know what I experienced. I want them to care about their lineage. I want them to find comfort in their spirituality. I don't have all the pieces. I pray that they will continue the work of healing—of connecting to their roots. I pray that they will feel compelled to have a voice in the adoption laws. At the very least it is my desire that they know I embarked on this journey not only for myself but for them as well. I believe that when we heal— the healing is generational.

May the women in my family heal from the generational wounds of losing their children. Women in my family have lost their children due to death, imprisonment, alcohol or the inability to care for them. May this wound be healed. May this disease not spread and fester. May my ancestors—the women in my family, take comfort from my prayers. May their wounds heal in the after-life. May my adoptive mother, Helen and my adoptive father, Edmond, find peace and healing in the Summerland's. When my children read my diaries, examine my Twitter feed and Facebook, may they discover that underneath all my pain, I was a Strong Woman.

An update to my update.
I felt compelled to include an update to my update. As soon as I sent my piece to Trace DeMeyer to look at I had a shift regarding my spirituality. A book was gifted to me, *The Bond Between Women,* by China Galland. This book had a section on child trafficking, missing children, death, dying, illness, environmental devastation and extreme poverty. Strong women were fighting these injustices and educating other women. I wanted to avert my eyes—look away and close the book. What kept me reading was the commitment that the women in this book made to educate and serve their communities. Some went through things I cannot even fathom. This book assisted me in turning the lens outward—off of my own pain. While the author is interviewing women she also visits temples and sacred Goddess sites. She wrote a lot about Kali and fierce aspects of the Goddess Tara. (I saw these images when I went with my daughter to the Tara shrine in upstate, New York.) The women worked with these Deities and had them as patrons because these wrathful Deities were protectors. Their imagery speaks to the marginalized and the oppressed. They reveal the shadow, not only on a personal level but on a global and collective level as well. These Deities are the patrons of the oppressed—they give voice to the voiceless. This helped me to understand how to bring my spiritual practices out of the ritual room—out of my head and into the physical world in a practical way.

I realized that my work with adoption was my spiritual practice. My work involves reading and listening to stories that are heartbreaking. I thought if these women and the adoptees have the strength to speak up then I can certainly edit their work. In Buddhism there is a precept that states, "Do not avert your eyes from suffering."

Many of the adoptees have suffered on levels beyond my imagination. Collectively the pain and sadness feels unbearable. Together we must bear it—expose it and figure out ways to heal and move forward.

Yes, I am a Native woman. I am a Native woman that has the fierce Hindu Goddess Kali as her patron. My spirituality will always be complicated and my beliefs complex as I try to make sense out of life and my place in it.

I welcome opportunities to learn about the practices of my ancestors but I no longer choose to be the girl outside the candy store peering through the window—hoping that someone will toss me a treat or invite me to the drum circle.

The Fierce Goddesses and what they represent is my spirituality—their imagery reminds me to walk in this world with Fierce Compassion. I see each adoptee in this book as a Warrior—Brave. Fierce. I will find my place at the campfire with other adoptees as we journey together to wholeness. They are my inspiration.

HISTORY: Split Feather Syndrome

SPLIT FEATHERS: A study conducted by Carol Locust, Cherokee Nation
Reprinted with the permission of the National Indian Child Welfare Association Inc. Originally published in Pathways, September / October 1998, Volume 13, Number 4.

The literature that does exist on adult Indians who have experienced out-of-culture placements as children, including the preliminary study conducted by this investigator on which this article is based, indicates that **nineteen (19) out of twenty (20) Indian adoptees have psychological problems related to their placement in non-Indian homes.**

This study has revealed that:

- placing American Indian children in foster/ adoptive non-Indian homes puts them at great risk for experiencing psychological trauma that leads to the development of long-term emotional and psychological problems in later life
- the cluster of long-term psychological liabilities exhibited by American Indian adults who experienced non-Indian placement as children may be recognized as a syndrome (Syndrome: a set of symptoms, which occur together. From Dorland's Medical Dictionary, 24th edition, 1965.)

The Split Feather Syndrome appears to be related to a reciprocal-possessive form of belongingness unique to survivors of cultures that have faced annihilation.

The Split Feathers themselves have identified the following factors as major contributors to the development of the syndrome, in order of their importance:

1. the loss of Indian identity
2. the loss of family, culture, heritage, language, spiritual beliefs, tribal affiliation and tribal ceremonial experiences
3. the experience of growing up being different
4. the experience of discrimination from the dominant culture
5. a cognitive difference in the way Indian children receive, process, integrate and apply new information—in short, a difference in learning style

PART I

Called Home

1

The Indian Wars are Not Over

LAWRENCE SAMPSON (Delaware, Eastern Band Cherokee)

Lawrence Sampson

January 25, 1973. My sixth birthday. I remember my mother, Mary Louise Thompson, a mixed blood Delaware, pulling me into her lap and telling me I was going to have to find a new mother. I remember giggling, laughing and saying no, I didn't want another mother. How could I have known the precipice my life stood on, the slim thread the world I knew was hanging from. One month to the day later, she was gone. My mother was dead. Everything I knew, everything my life should have been was about to change. As my mother's life ended, the Wounded Knee occupation in South Dakota began. These two events would be the most significant of my childhood.

My sister Dianne and I were scooped up by a family that had made my mother's acquaintance only months before. Supposedly at my mother's behest they hid me on a farm north of Houston, where my father wouldn't find me. My mother and father being separated, he didn't even know of my mother's death and by the time he found out, I was effectively hidden. The Sampsons claimed this was my mother's wish, for me and my sister to be kept together and away from my father. Dianne and I had different fathers but the truth of it was, my dad would gladly have raised the both of us. So the testimony given at my adoption hearing was that this woman they had just met asked them, begged them in fact to adopt her two children.

So while I was squirreled away on a farm, the first hearings of my adoption began. One day my sister arrived at the farm, to inform me my mother had died. Sitting on a hay trailer in a field of cows was how I learned. I don't think I ever really understood anything that was happening, I just remember the helpless feeling of not having any control over any of the events affecting me. One thing I do remember during that time, was seeing an Indian man on the news talking about changing life for Indian people. Many years later I would meet and become close to that man, Russell Means. He gave me the very first inklings of what I might call pride in being Indian. I had a vague awareness that I was Native, but still had no real concept of what that meant.

My formal adoption hearing was on the Monday after Christmas, the holiday falling on a weekend that year. My father discovered the goings on, only on the previous Thursday. He made the trip from Houston to his mother's home in Tennessee to get my birth certificate and was in the courtroom on Monday morning. By the time the case was settled, falsified documents were presented with my father's signature on them saying I wasn't his son. The Sampson's attempts to muddy the waters of my paternity, as much as their tales of my father's abusive nature, succeeded in my being taken away from the only remaining adult I knew. With the ongoing occupation of Wounded Knee as a backdrop, I was like so many Native American children—taken from all I knew and what was rightfully mine. I was thrust into a world of abuse and denial of who I was.

The Sampson were a Caucasian family of English descent, very fair in complexion and devout in their Southern Baptist beliefs. Mr. Sampson was even an ordained minister, though a carpenter by trade. I immediately was forced to work in the family business which was primarily roofing houses in the Houston heat. I routinely worked well past midnight, and never got a weekend off. The hard work turned my already olive skin very dark, making me stand out distinctly from the Sampsons. Routinely they were asked about me and my origins, standing out as I did. They were clearly uncomfortable with these questions and my whole ethnicity.

I was early on told not to tell anyone I was Indian. If I was ever to admit to anything but being white, at least say I was Mexican. Apparently that was better than being Indian in their eyes. Race was frequently discussed in our household, as I learned early what "wetback" and "nigger" meant. Moreover, it was expressed to me just how disgusting my gene pool was, coming from an "Indian whore" mother and "crazy Indian" father. Mom was a beautiful woman with stunning black hair, dad identifiably Indian from the Eastern Band of Cherokee Indians of North Carolina.

I had been the baggage that came along with my sister. She was in the same age bracket as the other Sampson children. Very pretty when she was young, with beautiful waist length hair, she was seen as something as a prize I guess. Their Indian princess maybe. I was this bastard dark-skinned Indian that had to be a part of the deal. I was reminded often how I wasn't my adopted brother's "real" brother. *As though I wanted to be.* I was often told how it cost $10,000 to adopt me, a curious factoid that would present itself again years later.

I experienced my first beating within a few months. A beating for something I didn't do and then "lying" about it. This would be the routine. Eventually I learned either admit to something I didn't do and get beat, or tell the truth and get beaten worse. I can tell you from experience: how an end table, a phone receiver, a board, a belt, and a can of beans feels when it hits your bones, your flesh, or your skull. I was beaten so severely on a couple of occasions, I had to miss school so the marks would heal. Not that they had anything to fear, Mrs. Sampson's brother was the deputy police chief, and a highly decorated officer in the Pasadena, Texas police department.

I also know that words cut more deeply than any physical object bruises. The things I was told about my real parents were only the tip of the iceberg. I was routinely informed how stupid and worthless I was, and how I was likely to end up in prison. From my genetics, to my appearance, to my intellect, it was made clear to me how inferior I was. I could do their work, empty their garbage, wash their dishes, and do their manual labor on a roof, but I would never be one of them. Deep down, that was fine with me. I never identified with the Sampson. I didn't want to be like them.

This would be my life until I turned twelve. Mr. Sampson developed Melanoma and died a horrible drawn-out death. A few months later my father took a chance and found me through a private investigator. He had been told at the conclusion of my adoption to never contact me. Growing larger, and strong from manual labor, I think Ms. Sampson realized I needed a father figure. Or maybe she just wanted to get rid of me on the weekends. In any event I was enthralled by getting to see my father for brief periods of time. It was like stepping into a whole other reality. The atmosphere in his house was what was probably normal but which I had never felt: a home with love, especially for children.

These visits became yet another form of abuse, as Ms. Sampson routinely threatened to not let me see my father, and quite often carried through on the threat. By the time I was thirteen I'd had enough of the whole situation. I knew now life wasn't supposed to be filled with so much psychological and physical torture. Even if my father wouldn't or couldn't let me live with him, I chose to live on the streets rather than suffer any more abuse. One day after getting a radio slammed against my head something in me snapped. I was no longer a Sampson, I would no longer live with them. I would rather die on my own at 13 than live another second with them. Early one morning I walked away from the Sampson home as fast as my legs could carry me.

After a few days living on the street I contacted my father. He came for me immediately not knowing if it would cause him legal problems. I would finally be with someone who loved me and actually made an effort to care for me. At some point my father told me how a private investigator had turned up evidence the Sampsons had paid the judge $10,000 to approve the adoption, the same $10,000 I had been told about repeatedly when I was younger. Well they got my sister out of it, that's what they wanted. This little Indian boy was gone, never to be abused again.

My father was tall and he filled a room with more than his stature when he entered. He had a persona that outsized even his 6'5" frame. He had a tremendous sense of humor and could have a whole room laughing in no time. Yet, he had his demons, growing up in his generation, being made ashamed of his heritage, having his son taken from him. He had a fury about him that could emerge in a millisecond. But it wasn't born of hate, only the things he had also been denied. My father elicited love from everyone who met him. He was loved and admired by family, friends, and his business associates. Years later, on his passing, his funeral would be massive, with hundreds in attendance.

My father taught me the beatings and verbal abuse had not been my fault, the first time I had heard that. Slowly I developed pride in who I was and who I came from. Things between my father and I weren't always perfect, as we were frighteningly alike. But there was love there. Love to spare. I met my other relatives, who showered me with acceptance. I learned the first aspects of my heritage, and would later pursue them on my own to the point of speaking Cherokee and being active in the American Indian community and participating in events all over Indian Country.

I went to college, and finished my degree in the Army. I am the first member of my family to ever graduate high school and college. I jumped out of airplanes and went to combat multiple times. I became a decorated combat veteran. I took part in events that mattered. I wasn't a nobody and I mattered. I learned firsthand what it means to be Indian in this generation at this time in the United States. I learned how many in this country feel about Indian people and Indian rights.

Later, as I grew more politically aware and active, I took part in standoffs with the federal government on Indian land. I've been chased, shot at, and at times wanted for being an Indian that upheld the law. That little boy taken all those years ago, became an unidentified Indian male to law enforcement. But I am not unidentified. I am a human being. I am an American Indian. I am a Sundancer first pierced by Russell Means. I am of Delaware and Cherokee blood. I have earned the title of Warrior on the battlefield and in ceremony. I wear it proudly. I am not worthless.

Most importantly, I am a father now, and I know the importance of praising a child, and lifting children up to make them proud of who they are and who they come from. The welfare of American Indian children have become a focal point of my life. Even though the Indian Child Welfare Act (ICWA) was passed in 1978 to prevent the stealing and adopting of Indian children, we all have sadly learned in the years just prior to this writing, that these practices continue and ICWA is in dire need of strengthening. Obviously we cannot let down our guard. *The Indian wars are not over.*

And so I go forth as a writer, activist, and organizer in my community. I continue to battle the ghosts of years of abuse and neglect. For the most part I have been victorious but the war is never really won. Spending time in Indian communities are constant reminders of the policies born of colonialism and genocide. I'm 47 now and I still wake up from nightmarish remembrances that unleash themselves on my subconscious. These things are what have made me, for better or worse. It is up to me, it is up to all of us, to make sure they never repeat themselves.

2

Sooner or Later, All Lost Birds Come Home

MITZI LIPSCOMB/ROSEMARY BLACKBIRD (Walpole Bkejwanong First Nations)

Pregnant Mitzi and son

I woke in a sweat. I realized that my nightgown was in a knot around my waist. Suddenly I recalled the reason for all my anxiety as I removed my sopping gown and headed for the bathroom to slip into the shower.

The day before I had attended the funeral of my adopted uncle, but now, today, was "The Day"!!! My husband, my two-year-old son and I were making the trip across the St. Clair River into Canada on to the Walpole Island reserve to meet my birthmother and my oldest sister and her family.

As I showered I reviewed the past two months. Once again I was ready to resume the search for my birth family after a particularly nasty fight with my adopted father and eight weeks of working with a therapist. On the last visit, the therapist casually remarked that he thought I would find a lot of answers if I could find my birth family. I went home and shared this with Hubby.

Friday morning we picked up the papers that I had filed away from a previous search that hit a dead-end. We'd started with a phone call to the county's Department of Social Services. My Hubby talked with a clerk and shared our questions and stated that I was looking for something that would prove that I was Native American as I was planning to go back to school after the birth of my second child in a few months. I was asking for the name of my birthmother and father.

I was given a copy of a revised birth certificate from the state of Michigan, but I was old enough to remember at the age of 5 that my name had been legally changed at the time of adoption from Rosemary Blackbird to Mitzi Ann Inch. We used this to aid the clerk with information that she need to complete the search. She asked if we could call her back in 30 minutes. So we waited.

I was too nervous to make the call and so my hubby started the call. The clerk plainly stated that she was NOT supposed to give any identifying information but I would need to get all of this information in one sitting as she was not supposed to be doing what she was doing. She proceeded to give me the name of my birthmother. She also shared information regarding my history with Social Services. She stated that I had a long history in the file: being moved four times in less than three years because of physical abuse and sexual abuse including actual penetration. She took my physical address and actually mailed me an official copy of my original birth certificate that stated at the top "Live Birth of an Indian." I now had the "Smoking Gun" that I was after.

I thanked the woman without asking her name and thanked her profusely. Once again she cautioned me to be very careful with the information that she had given me as she could lose her job and stated that what she had done was against the law.

With the information we had just received, we began the second part of the search still stunned about what just had happened. Now we turned to directory assistance in Wallaceburg, Ontario, Canada, for the next leg. I mulled over what to ask for. I was struck to ask for all the single female listings of Blackbirds. I was given three names and numbers.

What should I say? How should I approach the subject? I was dialing before I really had time to think. The phone rang and rang with no answer. On to the second number. I dialed and someone picked up the phone on the second ring.

"Hi, my name is Rosemary Blackbird. I was born February 26, 1956. Does this date mean anything to you?" Immediately she asked if I was a twin. I stated, "No, not to my knowledge." I then began to tell her that I was adopted and searching for my birth family. She instructed me to to call the Indian band office and ask for "Records" and told me that they may be able to help me there.

She gave me the number and the extension of the number and wished me well, along with the comment, "Sooner or later, all 'lost birds' come home!" I hung up the phone to ponder what happened.

My Hubby and I exchanged a few comments and I could feel the baby stir in my ever-growing belly. We had begun to wonder if it was twins and were waiting for an ultrasound in the coming weeks. Now I was very concerned at her mention of being a twin.

Now we were onto something and felt that we really needed some answers. Now my mind was whirling with questions regarding the health and well-being of the baby that seemed to be carving it's initials on the wall of my uterus.

I picked up the phone and began the last leg of this journey. "Indian Band office, records, how may I help you?" I gave her the name that I was given at birth and my birthdate. She asked me to hold while she looked it up. My heart was pounding furiously in my ears and I was struggling to hear. It was just a moment and she picked up the phone. I could hear voices in the background. She began to rattle off information and I wrote quickly as I could: 4 living siblings, one deceased. Then the names of my maternal grandparents. No name listed as birth father. I guess that I was an immaculate conception.

As I hung up the phone I suddenly felt that I was a real person with a real birth certificate, with a real name and real brothers and sisters. For now I was satisfied and felt great relief. Now I could get on with my life and know that my children could have a chance for some financial help with their secondary/higher education.

That fateful day as I climbed back into bed, my Hubby asked me if I was OK.

"No," I answered, "I'm a train wreck."

The morning light grew in the eastern sky as we quietly talked. He was wise enough to make a plan that if things did not go well or if I was uncomfortable we would leave quickly to meet with the rest of my adopted family for dinner, even thought we had made open-ended plans.

It was a bright warm early summer day as we waited in Marine City along the St. Clair River to ride the ferry across to the Walpole Island First Nations reserve. My blond curly-headed 3 1/2 year old was floating a plastic red boat that we had purchased. He had it tied to a string and was watching the ferry leave the island and make it's way across the busy shipping channel to the US.

I could not believe that here was my whole birth family less than 25 miles from my home with my adopted mother and dad. All these years I had imagined that I'd be walking down the street and would look into a native face and see myself in their face. Early on I knew that I was adopted and knew I had older brothers and sisters. Every native woman's face that was close to my mothers age I gazed at intently, always asking in my mind, "Are you my mother?"

I once embarrassed my adopted mother by asking the pediatrician that she had taken me to see if he was my father. She asked me why I asked him that? I remember telling her that he treated me so lovingly I felt sure that he must have been my father. You can be sure that I was instructed that I should NEVER ask that question again to anyone, because she and Jack were now "Mother and Daddy!"

The ferry chugged it's way across the channel and docked. We drove onto the ferry as I tightly held the directions to my Aunties house. I looked down at my hands. My knuckles were white and my hands were trembling. "Breathe," I kept reminding myself. This was what I had been waiting for over 20 years. I remember promising myself that some day I would find them and now that "someday" was now.

It was a wonderful moment when my Aunt Gladys opened the door and took me into her arms and whispered into my ear, "Sooner or later, all Lost Birds come home." I knew then that it was she that answered the phone that fateful day!

Mitzi, right, with sisters Bonnie (left) and Linda (middle)

3

Caught in the Middle

JANELLE BLACK OWL (Mandan, Hidatsa, Turtle Mountain Chippewa and Lakota)

Janell and her sister

I was wandering aimlessly around Target, trying to clear my mind of all the things that were going through it, that had no answers or solutions, but just were. As I turned down the aisle, I saw three white women talking and laughing. As I got closer to them, I saw two little girls in jean jumpers, bright pink t-shirts, and white Keds. They were dark skinned with long black hair. They were holding hands and smiled at me as I walked by them. The woman closest to the oldest girl put her hand on the girls as she saw me walk by them. The little one stared at me with huge brown eyes that smiled. As I turned down the next aisle, I looked back and gave them a wave. Both were staring at me expressionless. I could not help but wonder what those girls were doing with that family. It seemed strange at first, and I said a silent prayer. I could not get them off my mind as the familiarity came back to me as I remembered when I was that little girl, holding my sisters hand.

I remember so many times seeing people who my childhood mind thought looked like me, and wondering if they were a part of me. I remember having a hand on my arm whenever a Native American woman would walk by us in a store as I stared at her and wondered. I wanted so much to look like someone, to be a part of something. I wanted the emptiness I felt to be filled, if ONLY to look like someone. I did not want people to look at me and wonder why I was with this family.

I am four tribes Native American (Mandan, Hidatsa, Turtle Mtn, Chippewa and Lakota),but am often mistaken for Chinese, Japanese, Vietnamese and Filipino. My sister is black and native but never mistaken for anything because she looks black. We were adopted into the same non-native family. They had two biological sons. They thought they were protecting us by not letting us associate with anything that was representative of our culture. They tried to make us be like them, and taught us the things they could accept. They took us to church and taught us "Christian" ways; they took us to their parents houses and tried to instill their Norwegian traditions in us. They had their prejudices and any problems that me and my sister encountered, according to them, was because we were Indian, AND we were adopted.

The more they tried to make us be like them, the more we rebelled against it, as we realized that our souls already carried the pain of our ancestors that were taken from their homes, religious and cultural traditions stripped of them because it was not "civil" or Christian enough; taken from the people they loved, and the land they called home. We struggled to fit into a culture we did not fit into. We were in a home that was supposed to provide us with our culture, but did the exact opposite. My black sister and my white brother became my strength, as I searched for myself.

When I was nineteen, I made the connections to my past and my future. When I first met them, the only thing that mattered to them, was that I was "back in the family." They never asked about my adoptive family, and I never told them. The emptiness returned as I realized standing in the midst of my bio family, that I did not belong here either. Just like my adoptive family, they had their prejudices. Based on what they knew, which was nothing, but everything they assumed, my life had been perfect because I had been raised by a white family. They started calling me their "Indian princess" and "white lady." The more I heard these terms, the more it made me sick. It created confusion and hurt I was never able to express. They could not understand what it was like to do what I did by leaving one family and coming into another, and not fitting into either of them.

My biological families became more a part of me as I learned about my ancestors, as I heard about the stories from my relatives about their boarding school experience. The more I learned, the more the reality of the government policies, that literally gave me life, yet stripped me of it, began to burn a hole in my heart.

My biological family gave me the sense of identity that has always been a part of me. My adoptive family taught me the kind of person, I did not want to be. My adoptive family could not accept me being Indian in their white family; my biological family could not accept me being Indian in their Indian family, because I was raised "white." They blame each other for decisions they made and for the decisions I made because of them. They have been angry with each other, while I have stood in the middle angry with both. I was caught in the middle of two cultures with many families, but neither could accept everything that is a part of me.

My name is Janelle A. Black Owl. I am Mandan, Hidatsa, Turtle Mountain Chippewa and Lakota. I have a BA in Social Work and have also done many, many years of teaching in child care settings. I currently work with an organization that provides Domestic Violence Services. I was adopted out when I was 1, after having lived with my bio mother and two sisters for a year. I was reunited with my bio family, both sides, when I was 19/20 years old. I am now 43. I have no contact with my adoptive family since I was 18 for many reasons. My sister that I write about is on the other side now. My brother that I write about I still keep in contact with. They were my everything. My goal in writing is to speak my truth and to help put an end to the continued trauma that our Native children, families and communities go through when one of our own is taken away. It is an honor to have you share in my life by reading this and I pray that you can help someone with it, or help yourself heal.

4

Two Families

DOUGLAS LIBRETTI LITTLEJOHN (Roseau River Anishinabe)

In doing research for my own book on the 60s and 70s Scoop, I came across the call for stories for this anthology: Called Home and I would like to share my story with you.

My adopted name is Douglas Libretti. My birth name is Douglas Littlejohn. I am from the Roseau River Anishinabe First Nation, in Southern Manitoba, where I currently reside. I keep my adopted name to honor the family that raised me. I was raised in a good home, in a loving family. I had a mother who stayed at home and a father that went to work every day. I was raised Catholic and went to Catholic grammar school and attended a Catholic University.

My life, growing up, was not perfect. I knew I was different but never felt it. I wanted to know why my parents didn't want me and gave me up. That is where my troubles began as a teenager. I was a blackout drinker from the get-go; I ran away from home several times; I attempted suicide; and I dropped out of high school. The one constant through all my struggles was my family: mom and dad, sisters and brothers, aunts, and uncles. They were always there.

While I was living in New York in 1988, I was contacted by Indian Affairs and offered a choice to make contact with my biological family under the Repatriation program that was happening at the time. I agreed and had several correspondences with my siblings and parents. In 1990, we agreed to meet. So at Christmas time, in 1990, I flew up to Sturgeon Falls, Ontario to meet one of my sisters and then we then took a bus to Winnipeg, Manitoba. My mother and sisters cried for several minutes in the bus terminal. I remember being nervous and scared.

One thing I could not do was to call my biological mother and father, "mom" and "dad." I explained that to them apologetically. I said it wasn't out of disrespect for them but respect for the people that raised me. They understood. I stayed for a week then.

I returned again in 1997, when my father, Wallace, passed away suddenly. His loss affected me more than I thought it would at the time.

In 2010, I learned that my mother, Esther, was suffering from dementia and her condition was worsening. So, in 2011, I decided to return to the reserve permanently. My reason for returning permanently was the feeling of love and family I felt.

I live in two worlds now, which creates inner turmoil at times. Sometimes, people will remind me that I didn't grow up on the reserve so I really don't know how it is. More importantly, I experience the cultural differences first hand.

Sometimes, I feel like I don't belong here, on the reserve, because my thinking is so different which causes inner turmoil. I have two families which are worlds apart, culturally. It's hard at times but I get through it.

I may not stay on the reserve for good. But I wouldn't change it for the world. It's made me who I am today.

5

Blue Bear

JANELL LOOS

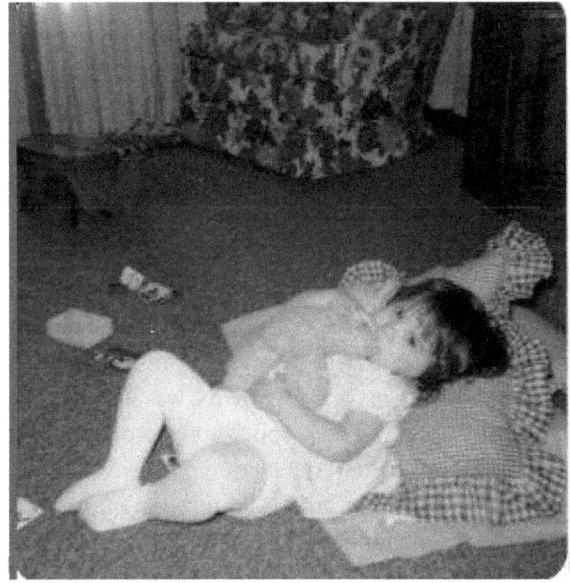

Janell with Blue Bear

I cannot remember a time when I didn't know I was adopted. I think I asked around four years of age. My adoptive mom told me. It was actually my "ah-ha" moment. It made sense. I can always remember feeling different. I feel horrible saying this, but I felt like they were my caregivers, not my family. They loved me and I love them. I couldn't connect with them though. I could never shake feeling like they were a family and I was separate. They had a connection to each other that I didn't. They never excluded me or gave me any reason to feel that way, but I did. It was lonely growing up.

My only security in my whole little world was a bear. Blue Bear was my family. I have Blue Bear still. He sits on the shelf in my four-year-old daughter's room. As I was growing up, I would have horrible dreams that someone would try to take away my bear, or I would leave him someplace and then I couldn't find him. Worse, in my dreams I would be presented with two Blue Bears. They looked identical in every way, but one was real and the other was fake. If I chose wrong, I would lose the one "person" in my life that loved me unconditionally and was always there for me. I would wake up crying and holding my bear tight.

My oldest a-brother has resented me since the day I was brought home from the hospital. He used to enjoy being cruel to me. He would tell me that I wasn't part of his family. He would tell me that no one really wanted me. He would also beat me up. He would purposely hit me in the stomach first so I couldn't yell for help. His favorite way to hurt me was hiding my bear or "hurting" him (ripping off Blue Bears legs, arms and ears, breaking his plastic eyes, dragging him around town by a rope tied to the end of his car, taking him into Chicago, dropping him from the tops of buildings and taking pictures). He would laugh and laugh and laugh at me when he did these things. We are older now. He has found new ways to hurt me and make me feel like I am not part of his family. As an adult, I can walk away from him knowing exactly what he is trying to do and not let it affect me.

There are other things that happened in my childhood, adolescence and adulthood that made me grateful that I did not have a biological connection to my family. All families are messed up in some way. Mine was more than others. Unfortunately, because I would not let anyone see when I was hurting, my parents took it as I was tougher, stronger. I knew about adult problems and their secrets as a child. I was the fica in the corner, the picture on the wall. Even though it was assumed I was too little to understand, I did. It wasn't until I go into my teenage years, did I become their confidant. I hated it. In essence, I was their priest who they confessed to. I would shut down my feeling and listen. I have a knack of being able to observe people and then become what they want me to be. It was easier to become what my a-parents wanted me to be, than to be myself...

I found that the only way I could be myself was to be alone. I would ride my bike to the country. I would spend all day climbing trees and explore fields. I would watch nature around me. I felt a connection. As for any abilities, I am spot on when it comes to instantly knowing a person's character. I used to think I was judgmental. For over forty-one years I continually hit the mark. This leads me to believe that this is my gift. I have an acute understanding of human nature as well. I think that has more to do with observing people over the years and attempting to become what they wanted me to be. If I became what they wanted, I would never be truly rejected. They would only be rejecting what I have projected to them.

I asked about my adoption, randomly, in small doses. I didn't want to make my a-mom feel bad. She would tell me that she wanted a little American Indian girl. She and my a-dad were denied by the public adoption agency, Christian Charities, so they hired a lawyer and proceeded with a private adoption—my adoptive mom could still have babies. My mom told me that a Cherokee woman from out of state in her late 20's, was giving birth to an Indian baby girl at a local hospital. My b-mom wasn't able to take care of me and my b-father was out of the picture. It was a "miracle." My a-mom told me that she didn't care that I might not be 100% Indian (they told my mom that I was ½ Cherokee & ½ Mexican). When I would ask for my b-mothers name, my adoptive mom would tell me that she blocked it out. She told me that their lawyer let them look at all of my birth mom's information at his office, but she could not remember any details.

I was told recently that my name was supposed to go to The Cradle Adoption Agency in Chicago, but my parent's lawyer was friends with the lady in charge of handling adoptions at the hospital where I was born. This administrator pulled my name and contacted my parent's lawyer so I could be adopted privately.

At about 18 years old, I started my search. I contacted my a-parents lawyer several times. He will not provide me with any information on my b-mom. He kept telling me "talk to the courts and petition your records." He told me that I probably wouldn't get anywhere. I talked with my a-grandma (my a-mom's mom). She told me that my b-mom's name was Phyllis Camp. She also told me that she could not believe that my a-mom would block her name from her mind. Then life happened. I went to college and met a guy. I got pregnant with my first child and got married to the father.

When I gave birth to my first child at age 21, I started to search for my birth family again. It was off and on. I was raising a family. My husband and I were newlyweds (he spent our first year of marriage overseas stationed in Japan) with a two-year-old son living on Camp Pendleton Marine Corps base.

I meet a wonderful woman named Anita Neilsen, an Ojibwe from Minnesota/Northern Wisconsin. I was in line at Navy Federal, when she came up to me asked what tribe I belonged to. I was shocked. No one ever thought I was Indian. I have been asked if I was Mexican, Italian, Asian, but no one ever thinks to ask if I am Indian. I was immediately intrigued. I told her Cherokee and she said, "No, you're not, you're Lakota." We continued to talk in line (she was actually ahead of me, but fell back to continue to talk with me). I asked her why I wasn't Cherokee. She said she has friends who are Cherokee and friends who are Lakota. She said, "You are Lakota. I can see it and I can feel it."

We stood outside Navy Federal for over 45 minutes talking while my son ran around in the grass. She told me she was Indian as well. She was a mix of Swedish and Ojibwe. She offered to help me search for my birth family. She had done her own research at the Mormon Center. She was kind enough to take me there to research. There seemed to be a million Phyllis Camp's. I was discouraged but she kept encouraging me in my search. I still have all the computer papers filled with Phyllis Camp's. Because of Anita I learned of the American Indian Movement in Carlsbad, CA and became a member.

I had never been around so many American Indians in my life! I was nervous and excited. I was raised in a small rural town that was 98% white. All I knew about Indians was in textbooks, Time Life Books and movies. Talking to the group about my life, growing up adopted and hearing their responses, opened my eyes. Had I felt objectified growing up? Yes. Had I been able to pinpoint the beginnings of why I felt this way? No. Not until I spoke with the members of AIM.

My a-mom wanted to educate the elementary school where she taught. Every year she would have a program on American Indians. At the end of her program, she would cart me out and basically say, "See? Indians still exist and here is my proof." I would smile for everyone and wave.

My a-mom also thought by giving me things it would make me happy. Janell is sad? Buy her some toys. Janell is upset? Buy her some clothes. This is what happened to me when I was in college. I was never a "big thing" at my high school, but I had security that I knew everyone and I was involved in absolutely everything and my parents had money—popular by default.

Since I was raised in a small rural town and we all grew up together, my friends essentially looked at me like a dark-skinned white girl. They never wanted to know about my adoption (possibly their parents told them not to ask me, I don't know.) I was sheltered. I played the part. I was so scared to go to college though. It was one thing to be surrounded by people you knew and feel alone, but to be surrounded by strangers AND feel alone? I isolated myself. There were too many people for me to try to study so I could become what they wanted. I felt like there was no way out of my loneliness. I tried to commit suicide. I remember staring out my dorm window at the corn fields and the trees. I felt so far away from the comfort and the peacefulness that they gave to me as a child. My roommate found me and I had to tell my a-mom. I will never forget what she asked me.

She asked me, "Janell, why would you do that?! I just bought you a dress."

I didn't need AIM to tell me that my a-mom saying that was wrong or that it was clear that I was a living doll to my a-mom. I was surprised how I never dealt with my feelings about being paraded around as a child.

When my ex-husband got out of the marine-corps, we headed back to IL. I put my search on hold. My son was diagnosed with ADHD and he needed a lot of help. Not so much that he needed an aid, but he had difficulties. Then I had two more children. After my youngest was born, I decided to find my b-mom full force.

I petitioned the court. I got the court records. My ex is a cop and he got an arrest record of Phyllis Camp. He also ran all Phyllis Camps in the US with the information on the arrest record. Nothing turned up with that info. My uncle is a lawyer so I asked for his help. He contacted the *guardian ad litum* for me. She had passed away but her daughter was willing to help. Her suggestion turned out to be one of my key searches. She suggested that I check the newspapers around the time of my birth—back in the 70's; newspapers still listed patients that were discharged from the hospital. Two days after I was born, Mrs. William Camp was discharged from the hospital that I was born in. I had all this new found information and I was so close!

Then my world ended. My husband confessed that he was leaving me for a friend of mine. The details are so heartbreaking that I won't include them. Needless to say, I tried to take my life again. My a-mom said I was stupid for trying it again. On that point, she was right. My ex wasn't worth it. At the time, I felt like I was being abandoned. I could barely breathe. I felt that everyone that I loved had left me. I couldn't bear the fact that I keep getting left behind. My search was put on hold again.

About a year and a half ago, my a-mom passed away. I have spent much time trying to forgive her and understand that she was trying her best. I was provided with love, clothes, education and monetary help along the way. I do miss her. She is all I had. I want to think that her motivations originated from her love for me. I am so different from her. In her eyes, I was independent, stubborn and inquisitive. I had a profound understanding of human nature and a bond with all things nature. I was a complete puzzlement to her. I wish she would have realized that I was not cold-hearted. She accused me of that more than once as I wouldn't cry in front of her. That is my one regret. I never got to explain to her why I acted that way. Although even today if she was still here, I may not be able to tell her. It might hurt her feelings. It has everything to do with vulnerability. I couldn't open up. I tried a couple of times growing up and my a-mom didn't like it. She wanted the little girl that I "acted" like.

Even though my a-dad was kinda mad, I started my search again a couple of months after my a-mom died. My best friend hired a private detective who was getting nowhere. My b-mom's trail let to North Carolina and the local police stopped him in his tracks. I then was searching on Facebook and found Trace DeMeyer. I emailed her and asked for her help. She put me in contact with Soaring Angels, a Yahoo group that does free searches for adoptees and they found her! All roads have lead to North Carolina. It has to be her. I found her on Facebook and was "following" her page for a couple of months. My best friend suggested that I send her a private message. I was too nervous to do it, so he did it for me. I was also too nervous to check out her page. I waited to Mother's Day to see if she replied. I typed in her name and nothing came up on my search. I looked through my "followed" folder and she was not there.

What was going on? It was on Mother's Day I found out that my b-mom blocked me from her page. I broke down. Why would she reject me twice? I didn't understand. Trace was kind enough to console me.

I love my best friend, he is the most amazing man I have had the honor of knowing, but sometime you need to have someone who knows firsthand what you are going through emotionally.

I took five months off and decided on a different approach. I needed my original birth certificate to verify all the facts that I have found. My b-mom has every right to block me if she wants. Well, maybe not, but I need to respect her wishes if she does not want any contact with me. I can't let it end there. I was told that my b-grandma accompanied my b-mom when she gave birth to me here in IL. I have family. I have sent down to the State of IL for a copy of my original birth certificate three times.

The first time, I was so excited that I forgot to include the filing fee. The second time, I included the filing fee, but they do not accept bank counter checks. I am still waiting on my third time. This time I got a certified check from the bank. I asked two times if this was considered a "real check." I had to make sure. I have less than one week to go. There's nothing more exciting and scarier than finally being able to hold the key to your past in your hands. I've been checking my mail box every day like a little kid looking for birthday cards these past two weeks.

UPDATE:

I received a copy of my original OBC. I held it in my hands shaking. I had solid proof that Phyllis Camp is my mom, I have a beginning. I needed to find the story of my parents. I needed to find my family. Once again, I contacted Soaring Angels. They were wonderful. They gave me a list of many possibles in the area. As I anxiously called each number, I found out that one by one, they were all disconnected. Now what? After a couple of deep breaths, I decided that This time, I wasn't going to be discouraged. This time, I wasn't going to let life sidetrack my efforts. I will push through. Then an advocate friend of mine, contacted me on Facebook. **She. Found. My. Mom.** She was living in the same town I was living in… I can't figure out how to explain how that made me feel and continues to make me feel. I walked into my daughter room, grabbed Blue Bear off the shelf, held him and cried.

Nothing is ever as it seems. I underestimated my a-parents lawyer. He lied to them. He lied to me. My mom did not travel from out of state to give birth to me. She moved when she was a child. She has remained in Illinois ever since. She is not 100% Cherokee. She is also Irish. The only truth that he told my a-parents was that my Dad was Mexican and that he was out of the picture. These are the answers I was given when I went to the nursing home to meet my mom. She has been at one time or another in the past 16 years only about **three** miles away from me. She worked at the college I attended as a janitor. There is a strong possibility I had spoken with her. Her sister, my aunt, has worked in the bakery at the local big box store for years. She has waited on me when I would get birthday cakes for my children. My uncle works at a local restaurant that I have gone to many times. When an article was written about my adoption search in the local paper, I had a lady with the name Camp contacted me on Facebook. We had been talking For Months. Unbeknownst to me, the details about my adoption were incorrect, so she didn't think we were related. It wasn't until I was re-reading my grandmother obituary for the ump-teenth time did a detail jump out at me. My grandmother Camp loved her dachshunds. My friend with the last name of Camp, loved and owned dachshunds. She even had a photo of them on her Facebook page. Hmmmm… Never hurts to ask a question, right?

After that pm, my second cousin, let the whole family know about me. I have a Huge family. In the midst of friend requests and messages, I finally found Home. They are amazing. And even though I look nothing like them, I sure do have their sense of humor, their kindness and their love.

My search is not over though. I will find my dad. We will meet, even if it is only once.

Janell (second from left) reunited with her birth family

6

In Search of Julio

LYNN GRUBB

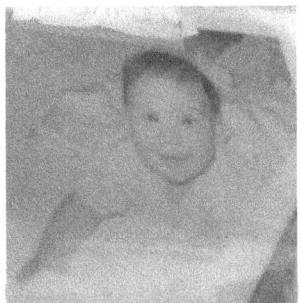

Baby Girl Unger aka Lynn

When I entered into the strange land of reunion with my maternal family in 2006, I never envisioned beforehand what was to follow. In my rainbow and fairy tale mindset, I pictured an Oprah moment: my mother and I hugging and crying. I would be told that I was loved, I was missed and this tall, dark and handsome man would enter the scene holding flowers, eager to meet his long-lost daughter. It never even occurred to me that when I would finally locate my mother—the woman I had longed to know for 40 years—that she would tell me that she did not know who my father was.

This was revealed to me on day two of our reunion sitting on the beaches of Ocean City, Maryland. This new reality did not register in my brain right away. Of course she knew. She was there!! She was a young, beautiful college graduate from Naperville, Illinois. Upon her recent graduation from Kent State University in Northeastern Ohio, her family had moved back to the Chicago area, this time settling in Aurora, Illinois where she met my father.

The details are sketchy at best and conflicting depending on who you ask, but one thing is for sure: I am living proof of their union. My mother was 23 years old at the time of my birth—not your typical teenage girl. She had a college degree, came from an upper-middle class family, was an artist, and had good job prospects. The problem was that she was pregnant with me by the wrong man and not married in 1965.

During one phone conversation we had, my mother confided that had my father been her high school sweetheart, she would have kept me. Apparently, the original plan was to marry her high school beau but a wrench was thrown into the plan: he got another girl pregnant when he was away at college. My mother, being single, with very little support from her own mother, decided to place me for adoption at The Cradle Adoption Agency in Evanston, IL. I like to call this the "Great Experiment" because during the 60s, the experiment had reached an all-time high for numbers of babies relinquished by their mothers due to the stigma of being unmarried.

The experts at the time believed that you could swap a child from one family to the next, and everything would be just like in a biological family. The thinking of the time was also that post-relinquishing mothers could just move on with their lives and forget about the child they placed, marry and have more children. The Great Experiment both succeeded and failed. It succeeded in finding homes for children; however, many of those children were raised with very little understanding of the true way in which adoption would affect them and their adoptive families. Collection of ancestral information and medical history was poor, if not non-existent. Many biological mothers were encouraged to lie about the identity of the birth father.

I often wonder if my parents considered getting married. They were both in their 20s and according to my adoption paperwork, my father was also a college graduate. I would like to believe they were in love. There is little evidence of this fantasy being a reality but considering I still don't know the actual true story, anything is possible.

I have come to believe because my father was from an undesirable race or culture, I was not the baby that the Ungers were hoping for. A shotgun wedding was out the question and abortion was illegal and undesirable to my mother. I came at the wrong time and definitely with the wrong paternal history. This paternal history is "Mexican" according to my mother.

The revelation that my father was "unknown" was a hard pill to swallow, but I am somebody who appreciates the truth over fluffy lies. There are no support groups I am aware with for "Women With Unknown Fathers." It's a painful thing to have an unknown father and many keep it a deep dark secret for there is shame in this knowledge. If my grandparents and mother would have given me a chance, they would have later seen that I was very much like them in both looks and talents. Little did I know before reunion that racism played a part in whether I would remain with my biological family.

In 2013, I decided to embark on DNA testing after I read and reviewed Richard Hill's Book, Finding Family, for the Lost Daughters blog, about his successful search for his own father using the latest DNA technology. I eagerly sent my DNA to both Family Tree DNA and 23 and Me. At that time, 23 and Me was still offering health information and I received an extensive outline of all my health risks, including Alzheimer's, Parkinson's, Ovarian and Breast Cancer. The results contained information on markers for high blood pressure, diabetes, most known diseases and even told me my eye color and that my hair was curly!

But the real reason I decided to do DNA was because I wanted any paternal information I could get my hands on. Without a father's name, DNA seemed to be my only hope in finding my paternal roots. My results at Family Tree DNA showed that I am 30% Native American, with Mayan roots in Central America and some Jewish roots. My mother is White (German/Scottish) so the majority of my cousin matches (about 85%) are from the U.S. and European places with English sounding names.

Birthmom and Lynn, both in our 20s

Then the other 15% of my DNA cousins have Mexican and Spanish names. I attribute this to the fact that more of my maternal relatives are in the database than my paternal relatives. In speaking with one of my cousins through Gedmatch.com (a database you can transfer DNA results to, and can match cousins on the "X" chromosome), I learned that I am related to her father's mother's side. Below is the only information currently in my possession of where my

Native ancestors originate. The following information was contained in an email from my cousin:

My cousin's father's mother:
Rosa Romero 1918-1995, New Mexico
Father's maternal grandparents:
Santos Tapia 1895-1936.
"She was born in Mexico. I do not know where specifically, but she was also mostly Native American. I'm not sure which tribe, possibly **Chiracahua** or some form of **Apache**."

Antonio Romero 1879-1949. "He was born in northern New Mexico and I believe his family has been in New Mexico for several generations. I do not have more information about him that is confirmed. Many of my DNA matches at the other websites seem to have similar family names and **Romero** is involved."

As you can see, I don't have a huge amount to go on, but I have consulted with a psychic who has seen the letters **AR** and **G** as part of my father's name. I don't think it is coincidence that Antonio Romero fits in with the AR that was predicted before I got this information. I believe that his line is a strong clue to my paternal history.

Below is a profile created by my brilliant DNA search angel and 7th cousin:

Your father was born about 1938, graduated high school around 1956, graduated college 1960, and had been working in advertising for approximately five years when he and your mother met in March or April, 1965 in Chicago, and shortly after she was hired at Foot, Cone & Belding Inc. (an advertising agency). He's likely Latino, second generation American, and may have been married at the time of the affair. I'm convinced he's the source of Native American DNA you share.

After five years, he may also have been promoted to a mid-level advertising position or higher and was in a position of status in 1965. It is possible he served in the Vietnam war between 1965-1975, perhaps as an officer since he allegedly was a college graduate. If the ages in your documents are true, he would have been about five years older than his peers due to his post college career. Today, if he's alive, he's likely 75 years old, retired and perhaps has grandchildren and great-grandchildren.

Other clues to my father: He is likely Colombian, Peruvian or Mexican and his father may have worked in government in Chicago in 1965. His first name may be **Julio**.

I continue on in my search for my paternal roots and I have no plans of giving up anytime soon. I look forward to the day where I can embrace a complete version of my ancestry, my tribe, my lost culture and my people.

Lynn Grubb is a Baby Scoop Era adoptee, a stepmother, biological mother and kinship adoptive parent. She lives in a suburb of Dayton, Ohio with her kind and patient non-adopted husband, Mark, and their two children. Lynn is a paralegal and is active in adoptee rights with the Adoptee Rights Coalition. She is a published author in several adoption anthologies, a former CASA/Guardian ad litem and enjoys reading, playing the keyboard and writing at Lost Daughters and at her blog, No Apologies for Being Me.

7

Finding the Truth

MARK O. HEISER

Young Mark

In 1958, my birthmother Christine Josephine Harry delivered me and she named me Francis David Harry. She had me out of wedlock, I found out, which is why I don't have information on my birthdad.

My bmom Christine is from SeaBird Island (in British Columbia) and had moved to Bremerton, Washington with her two sisters in 1956. My bmom didn't want me or something, so my aparents adopted me. Later I asked why they picked me and adoptive dad's reply was, "because you made the other children cry and then you were happy." Go figure.

As I was growing up, my sister always picked on me. (LOL—Laugh Out Loud) Later I found out why. She told me I was *in* her space, and she didn't want a brother.

We grew up together and over the years we moved a lot. We started out in Bremerton, Washington then moved to Portland, Oregon—all because father worked for the U.S. Government's National Park Service. Me and my asister really got to see lots of neat parks and caves.

Then we lived in Fresno, California and I saw Yosemite National Park, the

Redwoods and even the Grand Canyon. We also lived in Reno, Nevada; Tucson, Arizona; then Tupelo and Jackson, Mississippi; and then Richmond, Virginia. I loved it in Richmond and started school there and had my first kiss. I think I was maybe six years old. I'll never forget the girls name either: Lisa Buttons. So after third grade in Richmond, we moved to Omaha, Nebraska. I was ten years old by this time.

Now, as I was growing up I remember some kids asking me if I was Indian, so I asked my adoptive dad if I was.

He said, "No, you're French-Canadian," so I grew up BELIEVING I was French Canadian, like Donny Osmond. (LOL) As a young kid, I liked him.

Throughout the years of childhood, I was picked on, singled out and always last to be picked in games and told I STINKED… *talk about HURT FEELINGS*.

But you know something INSIDE me felt as if I was Native, Indian; it was a very STRONG feeling I had. I always loved Native drawings, the art and culture.

By grade school, I knew our amom was an alcoholic. She and father seemed to always have an argument or fight. I remember one time I was in my room and heard mother yelling, then my father came running down the stairs—so I opened up my door and told him to come in. When he did, here comes a lamp—BANG against the wall. (LOL) Those were the days.

Eventually we all went to counseling for their divorce and then came the day where my amom came to ask me to live with her. My sister stayed with my father.

I was always getting beat up at school so I went to live with my amom in a different state even, so I moved to Iowa to live on a farm. It was very peaceful there. I started going to a country school and got along with everyone. WOW. I thought this is great. I went out for football, track, loved to run. Go figure. I fell in love with a cheerleader, got dumped; fell in love with the high school famous girl but that didn't last long either. (LOL)

My first car was a 1966 Ford Mustang—289 three-speed on the floor—why do I say that?? Because living on the farm I first started to drive a 1948 Chevy pickup…the one with the starter button next to the accelerator (long skinny foot thingy) and had three on the tree. I was 12 when I learned to drive and I also learned to operate D-6 cat and D-8 cat down to D-4, the smallest—I had a dream to operate the mighty D-9 but it never happened.

I learned to plow and disk with a John Deere Model B tractor then after a few years we got a 5020, bigger than the 4020. I had a vision one night that the cabs on the John Deeres were going on the Cats like the D-9; only a couple years later, BAM, there they were—just like the vision I had, same thing with the tracks on the Cats. UGH, if only I said something to someone back then.

Anyways, I didn't finish high school. I joined the Army. "What?" you ask. I did because my sister did and was stationed in Jersey and that's where I went for Basic Training. I didn't finish that either, like one day before graduating I drift. It seemed like my world was in a LOST state, dazed. NO job. NO sense of Responsibility. NONE whatsoever—and I did what I wanted.

So, fed up with that life, I went to the Job Corps in Chadron, Nebraska in 1979. Yup, you guessed it. I didn't finish that either—was there maybe nine months. I moved in a house, got a job washing cars at a dealership, fell in love with a redhead and married that redhead and had two BEAUTIFUL girls, then in 1983, too WILD at heart, I didn't finish that either—got divorced. (I wanted to party and stuff.)

After the divorce I got a job at KDUH TV station as a switch operator, and loved that job, then the station moved to Scottsbluff and I moved as well. I was working for KDUH TV 4 as a switch man (switching buttons for the commercials you see on TV— that's what I did. I ran commercials maybe three, four years.) Now get this—my boss was Lakota—and I grew with him, a great guy. I soon lost that job over a romantic fling. So I moved to Chadron, Nebraska and opened up my own business as a vehicle detailer. I did a lot of business with the railroad vehicles, then others.

Then I moved to Gordon, Nebraska and met a Native girl. Oh man, I LOVED her and it was there I LEARNED from her and many other people. I shall NEVER forget the sweat lodge, the faces when I sang songs—the look on their faces said a lot to me. Today I still sing the songs, to myself, of course. I can't explain the feelings, but they are very very happy feelings.

Soon the girl told me that I need to move back to Omaha but I didn't want to leave her. I asked the spiritual leader holy man, if I could marry her, and he told me that he could BUT she wouldn't be happy and he asked me, "Do you want her to be happy?"

I said, "Yes, nothing but the best for her," and that's when he told me I should follow her advice.

The next day I called my adad and asked if I could move back home, but I didn't have money for the move, so he wired me some to get a bus ticket and a motel room—BAM, back in Omaha.

I went to the University of Nebraska-Omaha (UNO) for two years. Get this: I married the girl next door. (LOL) Now keep in mind she was looking HOT. She also went to UNO and was working at a hospital. I worked at Sears in the shipping/receiving area. One thing led to another and I **did** marry her and we had a son and were married for five years. Woohoo, not bad—BUT wait there's more.

That didn't last. Go figure. Why??? Because I went out and bought a Harley and hung around all the WRONG peeps, got in trouble, thanks to great person, even though she still denies it. I say she turned me in to the LAW. So I got probation for two years and I lost my three Harleys, wife, house, but did that stop me? Hell, no....

I got a job at Firestone, started out changing tires, doing oil changes then moved up to sales, then up to service manager. Then I moved to Denver, Colorado and worked at Firestone for about a year. Yep, didn't finish that. I got a DUI there—ugh, so back to Omaha I went.

After all that I went back to school to learn computer programming and received a diploma but never pursued the field. By this time in life I was around 32 years old.

After I got a grant for school, my adad said, "You should have allowed me to look at the grant application because you're Indian."

I thought, "WHAT???" After all this time you've been lying to me??? I'm not sure if he wanted me to ask that question.

Yeah, he told me that he had all papers downstairs at the house. Funny but he never found them. So, out of respect I waited until both my aparents changed worlds to start my search, with the help of my adopted sister.

Now comes the fun part: the test of patience. I got the birth certificate(s). Yes, both— one with my real name on it and the other amended one with my adopted name, and the court papers too—which are all LIES.

I noticed on the original with me and my bmom, it stated she was INDIAN from British Columbia and the amended birth certificate has my new name and race that said I was WHITE!!

Later I learned that my bmom had jumped out of a third-story window to elude two or three guys. To this day I wish I could find out why they were after her; at that time she was married.

I also found out that I have an uncle still living in the SeaBird Island area but as of now, I haven't been in contact with him due to a DNA test. I'd like to find out for sure which Tribe/Band my bmom was in.

But I did find out something from my asister. Come to find out she told me that she and I are really cousins—I'll wait for the DNA test for sure now. Now I have a lot more to say but it would be like the unabridged dictionary thick (LOL) so for now we have to wait for the DNA test to come back.

While I was in Gordon, Nebraska, I had stayed with a Lakota Family. They took me in and many people told me that I looked like someone there.

(I can't tell the name, hope you understand.) I did the Wounded Knee Walk in 1983. That was a great experience I'll never forget and I did the pow wows in Pine Ridge. I felt accepted by the Lakota people.

As for visions—I had one BAD vision—I changed worlds all by myself. I was on a beach sitting on a bench all alone and changed worlds….and I accepted that, took me awhile but I came to accept it.

I haven't really had a good strong relationship with anyone—I want to, but it's hard for me. Yes, I am shy, love movies, going out to eat, but now I'm going it alone and I hate REJECTION—so I don't ask anyone out.

You know thinking back on my life, I made a very nice ribbon shirt; it was black silk with beautiful colors and I made a few chokers as well. Even today I make chokers. "Creator I LOVE BEING Native!!!!"

What do I do these days? I load trucks with steel at a building company, been working there five years now. I have learned a lot over the years. Now I'm waiting to hear from Canada about what band I'm from. As for my bdad, I haven't found one. Like a gentleman once told me, I was born under a rock….

I am First Nations—my birth mother was born in British Columbia and I miss her with ALL my heart. She was 20 years old when she delivered me. I always wondered why I loved the oceans, the tropics and Florida. My adad showed me pictures of me standing next to a beached whale, and he told me how I would walk down the beach and eat raw oysters.

Mark (2014)

In 2009, my adad passed away—he was always there to help me one way or another. I can still hear him saying, "You know I won't be around forever."

I told him, "Yes, he would be," so talk about wishful thinking. After he passed I started looking to see if by chance my birth mother is/was out there somewhere. Even my sister helped me — and I gained ALOT of new friends on Facebook who helped as well — but it wasn't until someone told me about SEARCH ANGLES. They were awesome and **quick**, too.

So after getting my **hopes** high enough, only to be shot down just as fast, I found out my mom Christine passed away when I was maybe 10. I learned she passed in 1968 at the age of only 30. Holy crap, I thought. It seemed like my whole life just went out from under me. Then someone told me to breath—just breath.

So would I ever change anything in my life or do anything over again? Yes. Only some things.

8

5 Siblings—Found in the Wind

MAZI, later ELIZABETH BLAKE

Elizabeth

Childhood Revisited

When I was a child, I always knew I was adopted. My family told me from the time I was young. Born in Minneapolis, it took a long time to piece together, but I was the first of five children born to our birthmother. When she was 18, she developed schizophrenia and has spent most of her life in group homes or mental health housing. She was married for many years, but because of her illness, she could not raise any of us siblings.

After my birth, I lived in foster care for many months. It could be that families were reluctant to adopt me because of my birthmother's history. I don't know. So those early months are blank. No pictures, and too early for memories.

When my adoptive parents went to an adoption agency, they already had a child by birth that was eight years older than me. He was also blind, and very smart. They told the agency that they wanted to adopt a child because they didn't want my brother to be an only child. Also my adoptive mother had insulin-dependent diabetes, which was brittle. They hoped to have a child who could help around home, as they had many needs around home. They also told the agency they wanted a daughter, so someone could care for them when they got old.

The social worker asked that they think of at least one reason that was for the benefit of the child. My adoptive father told this as a humorous tale and said, "Well, we had a home to offer and love." As it turned out they were better at offering a home than love.

When things were good at home, my father would say, "My beautiful little Indian Princess." I think this was because my skin would get very brown in the summer. I always could relate to being Indian. I don't know if I was told that I had any Indian heritage.

Throughout childhood my place of peace and refuge was my grandmother's apartment. She was not demonstrative in her love, but I was always aware that I was loved and cared for with her. I spent lots of time with her, learning to sew on an old treadle sewing machine, making doll clothes, mending, and learning to crochet and cook. She also had a grown blind daughter, my aunt, who lived with her. Part of my time spent there I would go shopping with my aunt, help her crossing streets safely, describing foods in the store, and pulling the wire cart back home. Aunt E. was very independent though, and as an adult, I knew she could navigate her way to and from work and to the store on her own. She would ask the grocery store clerks to help her find foods at the store when grandma or I were not along.

The other place I found solace was outdoors, where life was so quiet and peaceful. For that reason I loved belonging to Girl Scouts, so I could go camping and be in the woods of Minnesota with friends who also loved nature.

We lived in a fine house with a beautiful and bountiful garden. But life inside was punctuated with abuse. There were probably times I did wrong and needed correcting, but the worst of times were when my brother or I were unjustly accused. A few times during my childhood, my father would wake me in the middle of the night, and take me to the living room to be interrogated. The goal was to have me confess that I had done whatever deed he suspected.

I'm sure I made many mistakes as a child, but strangely on these occasions at night, I was innocent of his accusations.

My mother was mostly distant. My father, unsure I had seen the signals told me many years later, just before her funeral, "She just couldn't love you." But in his own way, I think my father did. I'm grateful for having a much more stable home than my birthparents could have offered.

From the time I was 4, as my father left for work, he would say, "Remember to watch that your mother is okay." He worried about her having an insulin reaction. She tended to have quite a few—and sometimes to the point of unconsciousness. It could be that because of caring for those in my family, I decided to become a nurse later, even though I loved art and wanted to be an artist.

My grandmother was really my salvation. I feel that if I had not had her nurturing as a child, I may have had many more problems in life. She had faith in me and loved me. It was clear to my cousins also, that I was special to our grandmother. At a family Thanksgiving dinner, a cousin taunted me with, "You are Grandma's favorite, and you are not even REAL!" The comment was meant to hurt me, but it really made me happy.

I had years of taking the bus by myself to grandma's. And years of feeling nurtured. Then, when I was 14, my grandmother died of a heart attack. I was devastated. I loved her dearly, and now would not have her apartment as a respite. My sweet, gentle grandmother, wise with few words, gone. Kind and humble, gone. Comfort and respite, gone. We all have probably lost someone close whose presence we miss to the depth of our soul, and for me, it was Grandma Marie.

When I was 17, I graduated from high school. My parents told me that I would need to pay rent as soon as I graduated. I knew I couldn't go to college or trade school without some savings, so I got a job full-time. I graduated on a Thursday, and started a full-time clerk-typist job on Monday. I did pay them rent for a month, but then realized it was much cheaper to rent a room than live with them, with all the good and bad of being free from family at 17.

Becoming emancipated minor was necessary. In those days, I think you needed to be 21 to sign for your care and be responsible for your debts. Being totally independent was both a little scary and a way to grow up quick. It is not an easy way, but I think young people need to know they can do it all alone if they need to. Just keep trying! Imagine yourself, as you want to be.

For 15 months I worked full-time, saved money, then quit my job to go to nursing school. LPN school was the quickest way I knew to have a job that I could support myself. It took many more years and three degrees to become a pediatric nurse practitioner.

As we walked to school, my friend Kat turned off at Minneapolis College of Art & Design. I smiled and waved, and inside my heart sank, knowing I could not afford to go to art school. Just recently I was able to take art school courses in illustration. It felt like home.

Native Guiding Spirit

Margaret was a dear friend, Anishinabe, Ojibwe teacher and guiding spirit. She helped me find a connection to the culture that felt like home. I took classes and lessons from her on Ojibwe language for most of seven years. She took me along like a daughter to powwows and events in the community. Always I hoped that at these community gatherings I would see someone who looked enough like me that I would know it was a mother, sister, brother, aunt or uncle. I will never know if any of these faces were my close relatives, but they all welcomed me as family. I was blessed to have Margaret show me the way back, and teach me to live life as a verb. She said, "You will notice that most of our words are verbs. We have very little use for nouns. They are the words of solid, stagnating things, not of life, which is always moving." Miigwetch Margaret for bringing me home, and Miigwetch Gitchi Manido for Margaret and my sense of belonging.

Finding Family

When I had my daughter, I began to think how important having a child was, and realized that my birthmother would probably not forget this experience. I wanted to respect her privacy and whatever life she had now. So I contacted the adoption agency to do a search for birth family. The social worker asked the reason I wanted information and I said mainly, I wanted to know family medical history, and also more about their family history. They said they could give non-identifying information that was about 27 years old, but that might help. The social worker put my file on her desk, and did not let me look at it, and read, "Your birthmother had you when she was 21. She had serious problems with mental health." At the same time, she was dictating this so that I could have a solid piece of information that I could read again and again, trying to make three-dimensional people from these words and non-identifying descriptions of events. That was all I had for about three years, and it seemed to be enough for a while. She was unable to raise a child, so she made a plan. At some point either the social worker or my parents told me she had schizophrenia and had needed electroshock treatment at some time. She had been a good student in high school, but at age 18 she developed this illness. Her condition was not very good during the pregnancy. The record noted that when she came back for counseling after my birth, she had cared for her hair and appearance and looked better.

They also said that one aunt was a fashion illustrator, and an uncle was an artist. A smile came across my face to think that being an artist could be genetic. It worried me about her mental health issues however. What if the "s" word was genetic too? I couldn't speak it, or tell anyone. It scared me for years, until I realized it was not happening to my daughter or me.

At the time in Minnesota, finding birth family was not easy, but possible. First I contacted the adoption agency and they spent six months trying to find my birth mother. During that time they did find an aunt who would not share any information without knowing why. The search was officially closed.

A friend told me about a woman who did searches for adoptees. I called her and told her I knew my birth name and mother's maiden name. She agreed to do the search for $50 to start. If it took longer than she expected, she would charge more for her time. She called me within a few hours and told me that she had spoken to my grandmother and that I could have her phone number to learn more about my mother. It gave me chills to think of real birth family found. The conversation was full of information about the whole family, and she also told me that I had two more siblings, sisters, who were several years younger than me, and had also been adopted when they were toddlers. It was a shock, but I was determined to find them.

Soon afterward I was able to meet my birthmother at a group home for women with schizophrenia. Sad and poignant when she told me, "I am an artist. Would you like to see my work?" "Yes!" I thought, another Van Gogh possibly. She brought me into her shared bedroom, opened a drawer and showed me pages in her Mickey Mouse coloring book. I tried to hide my tears.

Since then I have seen her once. She seems happy, and even caring, but in a very childlike state. At this time, I think she is still living. We write occasionally.

Now the mystical part began. A couple of weeks later, the woman who did the search called me again. She said, "You'll never believe this, but I talked to your brother, and he called looking for family. He grew up in foster care."

"No, that couldn't be MY brother. My grandmother said there were just two other children. Two sisters who are younger than me."

She said, "Yes, he has the same unusual last name as your birth name. He never lost his birth name because he was in foster care. Call him and find out more."

Frank

This was Frank. Soon afterward we met, he had arranged to get his birth certificate and I now had mine. I expected to see his and find out that he had a different birth mother. It was as much of a shock to see that he was my brother as to see that he had a strong Indian appearance. He said he grew up with many other Native American foster brothers. He was mainly in two foster homes: one from birth—seven, one after that short-term, and another for the rest of his childhood and adolescence.

The first ones he felt were his "real" parents. He was shocked one day when he came downstairs and saw his suitcase packed, his shoes at its side. His mother, the only one he knew, said he was going to another home to live. It took him a long time to get over that.

In his final foster home, he said the foster children were expected to eat meals at a table in a different room from their family. He never felt he was really part of that family. His other foster brothers were lost to him as an adult, and now he wanted to find his real family and his birth parents.

Frank had a seizure disorder that was not well-controlled with the medication he took. His neurologist tried lots of things including a research trial medication. Nothing stopped the seizures. He died at age 38 of status epilepticus, a very long seizure and swelling of his brain. It was so hard to lose him. I was devastated.

I'm thankful that he was able to spend time with our birth mother on and off before he died. He told me once that he had never had a relative who needed him for anything, and so with mixed feelings, he would help her with errands and to get things she needed.

Jody & Terry

In the next few years I also met my sister Jody. She and Terry were adopted together as toddlers. It gave me peace to know that they had each other. These were the two children that our grandmother told me about. When I had asked her about Frank, she said, "There were many years I didn't have much contact with (Dolores) and so she probably had Frank during those years. She didn't tell me everything you know."

At that time I didn't have a chance to meet Terry. Their adoptive parents did not really approve of Jody meeting another sibling, and I heard were somewhat disbelieving of our existence. (Terry Niska Watson is also sharing her story in this book.)

Linda

Years passed, and I went to live in Europe with my husband. One day, the phone rang, and I was surprised to hear someone speaking English say, "Hi, I'm Linda, and I'm your sister."

"No, I told her," I already know about all my siblings. I have two sisters and a brother." I thought it must be a mistake; there couldn't possibly be more. She assured me that the state department of human services had helped her locate me because of a medical problem. Her son possibly had a neurological problem and the state helped her locate me in Europe so she could learn about my medical history, which would help the physician diagnose her son. As it turned out, the condition she mentioned was one I had been checked for too. She was my sister. And I was devastated to think there were more of us with similar medical problems.

She shared that she had gone to art school, and that was her primary work; another artist in the family. We kept in contact for several months, and then drifted apart. Her last name is common, and I couldn't find her again.

Terry

Beautiful Terry. I'm so grateful to know her. There are amazing coincidences in our lives. We are both nurses. She works in ICU and is also in school for advanced practice nursing and I'm a pediatric nurse practitioner. We are both artists too. As we have exchanged information, we also learned we both have the same severe allergy to latex. So that must be genetic too. Like Frank, she has a great sense of humor. It is such an amazing story of how similar we have all been, though raised in many different families.

Frank (1957-1996)

My Hope

In life, my hope is that I can help a child to learn that being unique is good and we all belong to one world family. First we need to learn about belonging in our families of so many kinds and our community, no matter how apart they seem.

Thoughts that comforted me as a child, still give me peace today: The wonder of life in all its forms; the mystical connection to people we may never meet in life; the air we breathe being the breath of all life; the gentle kindness that humans often share; the beauty of nature and the Universe that surrounds us.

It's possible there are two more siblings. Someday we may find them, or they find us. Whether we meet or not, we are connected. If only they had a chance to meet our sweet and gentle Frank.

Elizabeth lives with her husband in the Pacific Northwest and is often found with her daughter and four young grandchildren. She is a pediatric nurse practitioner with a special interest in children with disrupted families who may have attachment problems. She is the author of GreenBean: True Blue Family, a story of differences and belonging. You can find her though her website, http://elizabethblake.us

9

White Earth Adoptee…Who am I?

TERRY NISKA WATSON (White Earth Anishinabe)

EARLY MEMORIES

A deep blue sky with a few fluffy white clouds, warm summer air scented with the smell of fresh cut grass, wind whipping in my ears, I swung ever higher in the squeaky chain suspended swing. I was imagining that I was flying, I suppose, because I still remember the sound of the light plane flying overhead as I flew faster and faster hoping to attain Everest-like heights. I was hopelessly, deliriously happy basking in the warm  summer air in my favorite place on earth, the outdoors. This was my first memory, as a young child, living in a foster home in the suburbs of Minneapolis, Minnesota and it remains in my mind as a pleasant one, primarily because of the feeling of freedom and carefreeness of childhood. It is with all likelihood that I had already faced very traumatic events, due to my removal from the only home I had ever known or perhaps it was the loss of my mother and father, but on that stellar day of swinging, I was happy and as free as a bird. I am not sure how old I was, where I lived, where my family was, and there are no photos to commemorate that day. Today, after almost fifty years, I cling to these cloudy memories as one might hold onto a tattered faded photo of a loved one from days gone by. These are the only things I have left from my childhood, an entire chapter torn from a book that can never be rewritten, gone.

I long for reinforcement to my scattered memories, looking at old faded photos when I was being evaluated for adoption around age three or four. Is that an address I see in the background of the grainy 1960's photo? I examine it with a magnifying glass, I search the internet and it is all in vain. Is there some

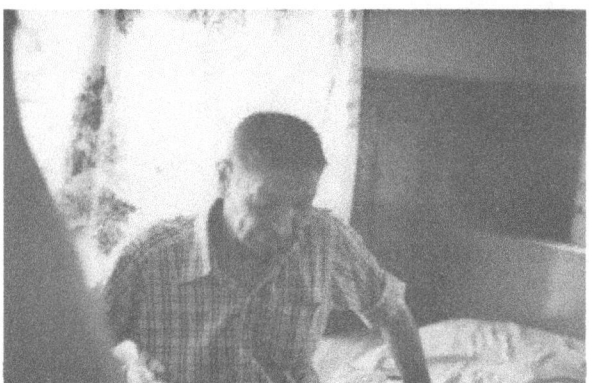

The only picture I have of my father, Louis Thomas Murray, courtesy of E.Blake/sister

tiny particle of the child I was, lurking there in the few mementos I have gleaned from my foster home days? Who was I? Where did I come from and WHO did I come from? These are things that many people may take for granted, the cute soft baby birth photo, photos of the beaming parents holding the newfound joy or photos of first steps, new shiny baby teeth or visits to Santa. As an adoptee, those things are locked up, sealed, destroyed and removed from our lives forever, but like a missing puzzle piece, and it leaves many like me feeling different and incomplete. But, one thing that can never be taken away is who we really are, the bloodlines we came from and the right to have distant and yes, pleasant memories of who we used to be before we were given to someone else.

Who am I?

What is a deceptively simple question turns into one of confusion and sometimes pain for the adoptee. I have spent years wondering who I was, aside from the simple facts such as I am a woman, with dark brown hair, dark brown eyes, olive skin and a pot belly, thank you middle age! I wondered if my sister, adopted with me, was really my sister. We were dressed alike, had the same boxy 1960's hair styles, one that looked like a bowl had been placed over our heads, but could I be really sure? After all, my adoptive mother told me a lot of things about myself over the years about my biological family, my history, and the fact that I was adopted. Many stories were conflicting, causing me great confusion as a child. I found myself being torn between loyalty to my adoptive parents and the desire to know who my birth parents were, who I was forced to become and who I was, and what I was expected to be and who I became.

Fifty some years later (2013)

I was drawn to the peacefulness of the woods and loved the sound of the wind murmuring in the pines. I would often find myself sitting under a big pine tree on a bed of soft needles, looking up at the sky and it helped me find my peace, my center. This place brought me peace when I was hurting and allowed me to feel like somehow I was connected to the earth, the wind and everything that nature had to offer. Was this a way of my ancestors, were they watching over me, like guardian angels? I may never know, but what I do know, is that to this day, I am still drawn to those Minnesota woods and the peace that they give me.

My life

I was born in 1961 to a Norwegian woman, Dolores Stolson Murray and her husband, Louis Thomas Murray in Minneapolis. According to the history I was given by the Children's Home Society & Family Services, I lived with my mother and father in the Minneapolis area until March of 1963. According to my sister Elizabeth, our maternal grandmother drove by to check on my sister Jody and I and found that we were sitting on the curb unsupervised on a busy street. Apparently, she notified the county and we were taken away, due to our parent's inability to take care of their children. Earlier, my sister Elizabeth and my brother Frank were also removed and put up for adoption. We also have another sister whose whereabouts are unknown at this time.

Seated, from left, my sister Jody who was adopted along with me and my birthmom, Dolores. Terry, standing. (2013)

I was adopted by a nice white family from the suburbs of Minnetonka, who were relatively new to suburban living. Both of my adoptive parents where from a humble background, raised in a traditional way, which could be viewed as very strict by today's standards. My dad's name was Harvey, he was 100% Finnish, strong and tall, stubborn but gentle as a kitten. I spent many hours alongside my dad, watching him in his workshop, honing his skills as a carpenter. He worked long hard hours to provide for his family as a union finish carpenter, but he always seemed to have energy enough to spend showing me some new project he had built. He taught me about basic carpentry, loading ammunition, hunting, cleaning fish and my favorite thing in the world, fishing. I spent many hours on Palmer Lake, near Park Rapids, Minnesota, sitting in an aluminum boat, not having to say a word, just at peace with the world fishing with my dad. Overall, I am proud to say that my adoptive dad taught me many things that I still enjoy today and instilled strong values, a great work ethic and a sense of family that I still carry with me today. My adoptive dad passed away not so long ago and I still miss him; he was the father my natural father couldn't be. Although many adoptees have suffered at the hands of their parents, I can say with all certainty that my father was heaven sent and a true blessing in my life.

My mother, Charlotte, was the polar opposite of my adoptive dad. She was strong, opinionated, domineering and sometimes downright mean. She picked on my older sister, Jody, and was convinced that my sister was pure evil. Due to the fact that my adoptive mom knew that my birth mother was schizophrenic, my mother did everything she could to convince herself and others that my sister just wasn't right in the head. She really expected nothing but pure perfection from her kids and she tried to control everything we did. Needless to say, once I got to the age of experimentation, I did a lot of really stupid things, like drinking and driving, drugs, and I can't even discuss my love life. I was so bent on trying everything that mom forbade us to do, that I am probably lucky to be alive.

I married in my mid-twenties, I think just to get out of the house, and it failed miserably at six months, due to my partner's infidelity prior to marriage. When I found out, I left him and set out on another search for Mr. Right. It was then that I met Mr. Wrong and lived twelve horrible years under his abusive reign. I had a wonderful son, who I cherished and eventually left the marriage to obtain my RN, so that I could care for him properly and remove him from a horribly dysfunctional family life. After a period of time had passed, I healed enough to meet and marry my husband, who is my soul mate and best friend. We were blessed with another child, my son William, who keeps me young and alive, so my life has improved vastly over the early years.

My Birth Family

My birth mother was born schizophrenic and never worked, according to my adoption records. She was from a large Norwegian family and much of the family history has been researched by sister, Elizabeth Blake. My father is more of a mystery, but from what I do know, he was an enrolled member of the White Earth Chippewa tribe of Minnesota, Mississippi band. He was raised by a paternal great aunt and her husband, who I assume had the Murray surname. Apparently his mother, Josephine (Rice) Murray/ Maydwayausung died young and his father, George Murray could not take care of him. He had a brother, whose name I do not know either, but I am investigating every lead I can get.

My father worked in the CCC camps and then joined the Army in 1950 and served until 1954, where he received a Korean Service ribbon, United Nations Service medal, Army of Occupation (Germany), Defense service medal and a Meritorious Unit Commendation. He was a paratrooper part of the time and he reenlisted in 1955, according to adoption records, but no military service records reflect this. He also received monetary compensation as a disabled veteran and this carried over into our lives as adoptees, as we got some financial help with school for a few short years. It is unfortunate that apparently, my birth father became an alcoholic, what led up to this, I will never know.

I have gleaned some information from the Children's Home Society paper-work which states "the birthfather reluctantly concluded that he and the birthmother could not care for their children and that the best plan for them would be commitment as wards of the state. He was most unwilling to think in terms of adoption and could not discuss this rationally. He became depressed and denied that the problem had to be solved that way." The same paperwork goes on to elaborate, "It appeared to the caseworker that the birthfather could accept guardianship just as he had the foster home placement simply because he recognized that his children needed care. But he wanted to believe that he could still call them his own and that he was their father." I find this very sad and disheartening to think that my father tried to be a father and was told he couldn't. Because of my birthmother's confirmed schizophrenia and inability to care for us, he lost his will and his right to father his own children—was this what made him dive deeper into the drink? One can never be sure and this bothers me: *I am so sorry, Father.*

Conclusion

What one can take away from my story is that I may have been deprived of a relationship with my birth parents, but I believe I am relatively unscathed. I don't abuse drugs; yes, I have thoughts of suicide earlier in my life; I do drink wine to excess sometimes; but overall, I am pretty intact mentally and physically. I have gotten over my abandonment issues, feelings of low self-worth, and codependent behavior, and none of it was easy, but I feel stronger for having lived such a life. I have talents that my parents gave me, like artistic talents, a compassionate heart, a passion for living well, not just existing but being happy and bringing joy to others. I love to laugh, be silly and enjoy what God has given me and I appreciate life.

I know my father still watches over me; I think about him often—who he would have been had circumstances been different. He gave me life and the native blood that runs through my veins and nobody can take that away. Yes, I am wanting to rejoin my tribe, but I am afraid, I don't know where I belong. I am hoping to be welcomed with open arms someday and be taught the traditions I was deprived of. These answers and many more are waiting for me and many of the other split feathers.

So I leave you with this illustration I painted years ago when I was in a very dark place in my life. This is a painting of a subject matter that has always drawn my interest that is the Native life and the beauty of tradition, family and nature. As my sister, Elizabeth, said about this painting that still hangs on my wall, when she stated, "the most interesting part is that the face is not visible. That is how it is when you do not know your birth family."

I also have a blood relative on my dad's side that I have met; her name is Vera Murray. She invited me to a Pow Wow so that is an important step.

I also look forward to meeting my wonderful sister, Elizabeth Blake (Chapter 8 in this book) in person this fall. My goal is to help her become enrolled as a rightful member of the White Earth Anishinabe. She has been denied that right, due to the fact that she was born before our parents were legally married. This is another injustice that I hope we can overcome.

10

Maybe El Reno... Somewhere Near Oklahoma City

KIM SHUCK (Sauk and Fox, Cherokee)

At that point I think that she was Patricia Elliott or maybe Evelyn Elliott. Last name Elliott anyway.

My grandmother is an amazingly difficult subject for a creative non-fiction piece. It's not the creative part of the writing that causes the problems, there is more creativity in her life story than in most; it's the non-fiction that makes things difficult. You may notice that I haven't started the piece with her name. The trouble begins there. Over the span of her life my grandmother had more than one name, almost like entry stamps in a passport, and just like those stamps they marked the places she'd been. I am going to ask readers for a favor. I need you to be gentle with my grandmother. Think kindly of her. She was a storyteller and I think that she got that way filling in the blanks for herself. There are many things about my grandmother that remain unknown, not because she was prone to a smoke and mirrors show that would have dazzled audiences far and wide, she was certainly that but the confusion is because there is often no paperwork or limited paperwork to tell us things we could call facts. That was the world she lived in, one with catastrophically interrupted personal mythology. It ends well, this story.

She lived a long life that gave her children and grandchildren and great grandchildren. Maybe most importantly it gave her a man who loved her in all of her chaotic and sometimes unreasonable and brilliant and hard working and bizarre and competitive glory. My grandma caused a great deal of pain but she also had other moments. I may not have forgiven her for some of her actions but those things aren't part of this story so you should just hold her gently in your thoughts. Make a little space between the ideas of truth and fact, pour yourself a beverage of your choice and imagine that we are playing scrabble at a kitchen table in Oklahoma in August and I'll tell you pieces of a story. Now be glad she isn't playing with us because she would have won and at any cost.

I'm already lying to you. Just by being in this book I'm lying. I need to make something clear. We have no real proof that grandma was Native. In her stories she was German or Sauk and Fox or Cherokee or maybe even Irish which I've denied for cause all these years but who knows? The circumstances involving her adoption, as explained to me, sound so profoundly shady in parts I can't imagine her being anything but Native, but again we're walking in the dark here. My grandfather, her husband, was career army. When he was on the brink of being stationed in Germany as part of the occupation forces after World War 2 my grandma needed a passport so that she and the kids could go with him. Other adoptees may well be laughing at this point. Good luck with the official documentation. There was a full rummage with backpressure from the army to find her birth certificate. There was just none to be found and then... there were two. They were both actual unadjusted birth certificates, they were different and both had, in some context, been offered up as the one belonging to the girl adopted by my grandma's adoptive parents. Crazy huh? Is this starting to sound shady to you yet?

It's entirely possible that Evelyn Grey was born somewhere in the area of Oklahoma City on September 22 in 1921 or 1922. This was new news to me as of about ten minutes before this writing I thought she'd been born in Ohio or Illinois. It is at this point in the writing my father and I realized that we weren't telling my grandma's story of trying to find her family. My father and I were trying to tell our story of finding her. We had a series of amazingly difficult conversations. In the middle of a rather funny/sad/strange part of a phone call and after a very long silence my father said, in a version of his voice I've never heard before, "Maybe doing this we can fill in some of the missing pieces for me." Hmmm. I decided at that point that any further talks with dad would need to be in person, over a table and with oodles of time to fill because I had just found a sore place. It's also at this point that I wondered if I have some of those sore places too. I didn't think that this would upset me but then, I hadn't thought it would upset dad either.

I originally found out that my grandmother was once Evelyn Grey from my partner. We'd been talking about family and I almost always call my dad's mom 'grandpa's wife'. I know, it's not nice but... When I call her by a name I use 'Pat' because it's what my besotted grandpa called her, because it's what my dad called her and because I had no idea anything but her last name had ever changed. My partner asked me what her name was and I said Patricia Shuck. I don't blame Doug for needing a detailed score card when it comes to my family. Both my father and I tell endless family stories, we're related to some profoundly interesting people who have done dangerous and useful and brave and just plain sociopathic things. In light of all of these stories Doug had started asking me for a family tree so that he could keep track. Doug is from one of those large and tumbling families that have enough information about each other that they could generate trading cards. Doug thought that a family tree would be, oh, maybe some work but not too much.

Well, my father's family consists of Evelyn/Pat and the oldest of a snarl of Cherokee boys from North Eastern Oklahoma. Grandpa Leroy was related by marriage or lineage to almost every Cherokee I've ever heard of and any time I deny a relationship the tribal expert should really be consulted because, well, I'm often wrong. I'd attempted a family tree in school... as a biology assignment... the tree structure is, um, let's say insufficient for charting my Native family. Not only was I taught to call many people cousin without any information about possible genetic relationships, but some people show up in more than one area on the chart. In High School I developed an unreasoning antipathy to people with straightforward family trees because of this assignment. I dodged his request. Doug took my grandma's name and my grandpa's name and came back a week later with a question about 'Evelyn'. "Who is Evelyn?" I asked. He explained. The Internet, who knew?

There are one or two things that I know came from grandma's adoptive status. One is that she was obsessively interested in my grandfather's family and her adoptive family. The family who adopted her were wealthy Oklahoma City folk whose last name was Elliott. They were of Scots descent, border people. The Elliott's have a storied past in the history of England and Scotland, and my grandmother told stories and stories about them. They were evidently good parents and I know that they were good grandparents because my dad adores their memory to this day: Lovell and Ida Elliott. At some point grandma made them profoundly angry and they disowned her. One version is that they didn't like her marrying my grandpa. I don't know if that's true or not but my father spent a few years living with them and, as I say, has nothing but good memories.

Grandma's interest in my grandfather's family could almost qualify her for Indian Groupie status but for one thing: she wanted nothing to do with being Native. I bead, make items for dance, finger-weave and tell traditional stories. I used to pick the brains of any people who could tell me old stories whenever and wherever I found those people. Let's be honest I practically mugged people for them. Grandma hated this… hated it. She didn't want to go to dances. She wouldn't learn to speak Cherokee, though my great grandma wanted her to, she wouldn't go out with great grandma in public and called her 'that old Indian woman'. In light of this attitude I nearly fell over one afternoon when she told me that she actually had tracked two possible candidates for her father and both were Native. On her birth certificates her father was clearly named; her parents were married, there was no confusion. The problem is that the name Grey is amazingly common. A man with her father's name appears on the enrollment lists of the Sauk and Fox people. There is also a man on the Cherokee rolls who has the same name. She has an official birth certificate, her dad's name is on the Dawes rolls, which makes her enrollable as Cherokee. She has similar qualifications to be Sauk and Fox. I couldn't believe it when she told me. At the time I couldn't imagine why she wouldn't want that known, why she wouldn't enroll. Now I think that she was probably frightened. If hers was an Indian adoption, if the thing that scattered her siblings and changed her life was because of her Native status, it isn't that surprising that she would want to avoid it even though she'd married a Native man. Humans are complicated.

In and amongst all of these official facts that are lacking I should say that I have no idea about simple things regarding my grandmother either. I don't know what her natural hair color was, for example. I've seen it be a few different colors, most often red, which judging by her skin color was probably not natural. She was very careful about how she looked and how she presented herself. She was very careful about many things. I heard from her mouth a couple of different stories about her degree. Yes, she graduated from college. Either she majored in home economics or she had an English degree. She did end up as a journalist for a very small local newspaper called the Tri-State Tribune… telling stories. She was gentle with people in the stories, very, very gentle. She would soften any horrors they'd committed saying that they had to live in the area and so did we and so did their children. She was as happy with everyone else's convenient fibs as she was with her own, and she kept the secrets of others in the interest of community. When I was sixteen this seemed terrible, I'm a little less upset by it now.

Dad has always been Edward Elliott Shuck though he grew up thinking that his middle name was Alan.

Eventually grandma found and was found by a few of her siblings. She was either the youngest and her mother died in childbirth having her, or she had a younger brother and her mother died in childbirth having him… or that's a story she told to make herself feel better about the adoption. I just don't know. My father got to meet his uncle Jack and we both got to meet his aunt Elizabeth. There is one other sister we are certain of, her daughter came out from Ohio to visit with us some years back and we were both so stunned that neither of us remembers the name and we are turning the house over now to find the information so that we can include her in what looks like a very long term project to come. Uncle Jack got angry at my grandmother when she brought up the Sauk and Fox connection, seriously angry. He told her not to dig into it because it wasn't true. He said that it looked as if their father had been enrolled because he'd been out drinking with friends when they were making those lists and was talked into being included. Great grandpa is listed with a very high blood quantum. This is why, although I don't know the whole truth, I think that grandma was Sauk and Fox. Well, that and the fact that I've spoken to elders who have said, "Yes, I knew that family" and then let me sit with them at events. It's interesting that there are things you can prove without knowing if they're true and things that you can't prove that you are pretty sure are true. I think that my uncle Jack possibly had a few issues himself. We still don't know how many siblings there really were and when gran told the story the numbers varied.

There are a couple of historical notes that seem relevant here. In the early 1920s many members of tribal nations were not also automatically citizens of the United States, they were still yanking Native kids from their homes and putting them into boarding schools against the wishes of both parents and children. In Oklahoma at that time there were problems with people adopting Native children to get access to allotment land. Sometimes the children would suspiciously vanish after these adoptions, sometimes they wouldn't. I know that it seems odd to consider the lack of 'evidence' and paperwork when it comes to this story, but that lack is anything but unusual under the circumstances. Native children at this time were very often prisoners of war, either warehoused in those boarding schools or used by adoptive parents. The Indian adoptions were a stealth act of genocide. It is to be expected that some of the stories are only coming out years and years after the fact.

I'm not trying to manufacture or find a Native identity. I have a Native identity from my grandfather that is documentable and unassailable and believe me, people have tried to assail it. I'm not interested in finding family for medical reasons, for childbearing reasons or because the family I do have lack story. We're three generations out from the crisis, I'm not having further children and we have more than a manageable amount of story as it stands. I am, at this point, only really interested in my grandmother's history for my father's sake, and maybe also for all of the potential cousins who are out there. Because there are so many strange expectations around Native people, folks are very quick to invalidate any suggestion of a Native heritage. They frequently react as if a person has claimed to be part mermaid or elf. Literature and movies haven't helped, mascots, coins and commercials haven't helped. The notion that over 500 different cultures are meant to look and behave alike and that all are 'extinct' has emphatically not helped. It doesn't help that frequently any supportive paperwork is difficult to lay hands on even if a family hasn't had an adoption in the mix. Add to all of that that some people's desire to identify only to collect tribal money or make themselves more exotic and it becomes a full-blown minefield. I'm not claiming a Native identity, I'm claiming my Native identity. That would be the one that got my ancestors force marched from Georgia to Oklahoma and had their lands seized... twice. That would be the identity that got my grandfather sub-standard health care at a notoriously bad hospital, probably got my great grandmother killed by ineptitude in the 80s at the same hospital and oh... maybe got my grandmother yanked from her father in the 20s. That's the identity that I claim, not some Dances with Wolves, Big Chief Wampum, fake Halloween war-bonnet identity, but the real one with an educated grandma who did crossword puzzles in pen, fell in love with my handsome career army grandpa and his crazy family and was a champion Avon sales rep. While I've been writing this I've started to consider grandma's reticence to stick to a story as a complicated hide and seek game. We've had one look through the playing field and I haven't found her yet but you know... I did inherit something from her, I am viciously competitive and I will find her. Who knows, maybe I'll like the grandma I find better than the one I thought that I knew growing up.

Kim Shuck is an award winning poet and visual artist. Most days find her forging butterflies or some plant or other in glass beads. Her third book <u>Clouds Running In</u> was published by Taurean Horn Press in 2014.

11

Split Feathers

STARLA BILYEU (Eastern Band Cherokee Indian)

I am Eastern Band Cherokee Indian and this is a brief synopsis of my story.

While I dearly love my adoptive family (I was a daddy's girl), I never seemed to fit in with my peers. Fortunately, my parents did the right thing and from birth, I always knew I was adopted and Cherokee. Though, I had always thought I was part of the Cherokee Nation here in Oklahoma, I never knew the EBCI existed.

About 20 years ago, I chose to attain my tribal membership card. It was difficult: the social worker at the hospital told me that I did not want to find out anything about my birth mother. I told her I did not want to find her, just whether or not I could acquire a CDIB card. Of course after her comment, I thought it might have been a horrid situation when she gave me up for adoption.

Several years later, around 1995, as a mother, I wanted to know that I tried all avenues to attain my children's birthright and medical history… I again sought out to try to acquire membership with my tribe. Once again, I met with the social worker at the hospital I was adopted through. This was a new, younger social worker, in a totally different location. She helped me. A couple of days later, she phoned me to let me know that she found no record of my birthmother with the Cherokee Nation; so she called the EBCI in North Carolina since that was where she was from.

It was determined that my mother was 13/16ths EBCI and so I am 13/32nds. I was to then to acquire my birth certificate to complete the process to acquire my card. My parents and I went to Lawton, Oklahoma to meet with a judge to open my birth records to get my birth certificate to mail to the tribe. He asked me, "What if she does not want you to find her?" Again, I told him, like the hospital social worker, I did not want to find her, just my birthright.

He granted us access to the birth certificate but ordered my records to remain closed.

I did not want to disrupt her life, nor mine, so I was not ready to find her yet, but did indeed acquire my CDIB card and membership with the EBCI nation…as did my two children. Several months later, I received my first per capita check, I had no idea what it was, but was delighted. The EBCI nation initiated minor funds for both of my children at that time as well.

Three years ago (2011) in September, I determined that I did indeed want to find my birth mother. I returned to the hospital social worker, and she had me write a letter to my birth mother. I did so. Approximately 6 days later, I received a phone call that she had contacted my mother and she would be calling me. Martha called and after a few verbal exchanges, she had me talk to the eldest half sibling, my brother, Joey. We discussed how they had always known about me and wanted to find me. I told them of my struggles with my feelings. We discussed children and our lives.

The following December, my husband and I drove to Cherokee, North Carolina to meet my birth mother and my half siblings. While growing up, my father's family lived in Oregon, we rarely saw them but when we did, we just loved each other and were indeed family. Meeting my birth family was much the same feeling. We all enjoyed one another's company and were just family.

Martha experienced relief. She had always wondered about me. Her husband, my half-siblings father, Joe had told them that if they ever found me, to "welcome me with open arms." This is exactly what has happened. I am part of their family as they are part of mine. We keep in touch and my husband and I just returned from our second visit to NC with my daughter and three granddaughters.

My daughter has not understood my need to find my birth family. She would become agitated with my strong need. After she met them, she too felt the family caring and bond that exists.

Since our first phone call, I have started an American Indian Studies degree option at the community college I was working at in 2011. I am now working on a PhD in higher education/community college with a focus on tribal colleges and taking Native American Studies courses as well. Currently, I am the Indian Education Coordinator for a medium size school district here in Oklahoma with 700+ Native American students I oversee through the Title VII Indian Education program.

My focus is on career and college choices after HS graduation and presenting cultural and historical educational opportunities to my students and their families. I am able to intervene with families when there are concerns for the children. As well, I am able to facilitate with parents that did not realize or know how to begin or complete the education needed to better provide for their families. Navigation through the "system" is difficult for those of us who have an understanding of the system, but for those who have no idea about it, it is daunting to say the least.

My adoption was indeed part of the removal and relocation that our government was imposing on Native peoples across the United States. I do feel the anger and frustration of not being raised with my culture and people. While I firmly believe that my adoption was an atrocity to myself and my people, I feel that I am able to combat and address these issues because of the adoption. Chances are great that I would not be affecting our people and our children if I had not been adopted. Then again, I would not and could not do what I do to facilitate the education and occupational choices of Indigenous people if I were not an EBCI.

My need to affect change is strong and while I am not able to positively impact my people, I can have a positive impact on other split feathers, whether due to the system, or their own choice, for in actuality, they too are split feathers.

Starla Bilyeu, Eastern Band Cherokee Indian, MS Educational Administration, is working on PhD in Higher Education and Native American Studies at OU, focusing on Native American student persistence, retention and preparation for college and on tribal colleges.

12

Welcomed

MARY CHARLES (St. MARTIN) (Koyukon Athabascan)

Mary Charles

In the fall I had a vivid dream. I was crouching down in a wheat field. A Native man was standing at my left side. I was nervous and tried to impress him, so I blew my breath into the palms of my hands. In my palms I held my voice. I then tossed my voice into the sky. My voice made the call of a red-tailed hawk. He wasn't impressed with my distraction techniques. He pointed and said, "Look into the brush." There in the camouflage of the brush laid a fox curled up. The man said, "He's always been there, you just didn't know." The fox jumped up and ran. We chased the fox into a clearing where the fox entered a horse paddock. The horse paddock enclosed a bear. The bear began to attack the fox and they fought violently. The man put up a bow and arrow to help the bear kill the fox. I was scared and put my hand in front of the arrow which was about to be set off. I said, "Wait, are we supposed to do this? Are we supposed to mess with nature?" That is where the dream ended. That is when the alarm went off.

I am an adoptee. I don't ever remember being told that I was adopted or told that adoption made me different. But since my memory began, I longed for home and I instinctively knew I was different. Although my most successful search efforts came after the dream, I have searched my entire life. I secretly searched throughout territories across the United States. I feel my personal and spiritual association is Native American, but had no Native Americans around me to liken myself with.  Since I can remember, I loved the earth and the animals on it but lived in a world where self-gain and superficial materialism was the human goal for status and respect. I was provided a set of parents and siblings. We lived in a big house and had nice cars, but I never felt like I was home. Inside my deepest soul was longing and searching for the candle in the window that burned for me.

The loss of feeling connected as a child compelled me to behave in tempestuous ways. I ran away, attempted suicide, did almost every drug and became an alcoholic early on. I left the big house forever one week before I turned 16. I moved in with my boyfriend who was 20 years old at the time. There was no peaceful home there either and quite frankly more unstable and even more violent. At 17, I found a job serving food in a dormitory full of college boys and was able to provide monetarily for myself. There were many prospects at the dorm and I befriended the first boy who had dreams of getting out of the midwest as well. Three years later, I was on the road to Los Angeles looking for another home.

Fast flying through the next 25 years, I buried the emptiness with busyness. I would make success and downfalls. I earned my GED and went to community college. Weekends of binge drinking continued when I wasn't keeping my mind busy with other things. I married a man who provided a handsome home, nice cars and gave me five children. The imagery of my house as seen from the city street contrasted the scenery on the inside of the walls. The marriage fell apart; I drank again and sobered up again. I am pure mid-life now.

My life circle is closer to completing the round than it is from the beginning of formation. I ask myself again, "Who am I?" There are so many questions still unanswered. The forbidden questions I dared asked as a child were met with unsympathetic responses, rigid tones and nervous tapping fingers. Answers I did get were, "We were told your birth father was one quarter Aleutian Indian; you don't want to open doors you cannot close; your adoption records are sealed and that is the law. We follow the law." But an enduring cry for home persisted.

After the dream, I was inspired to research DNA tests available on the market to test for ancestry/ethnicity. I've been waiting too long to know if I was just a tan looking white chick, or if I really had Native American ancestry. The tests also offered a promise of meeting a cousin or distant relative. I literally had no concept of a cousin or distant relative related to me through DNA. That part of the test meant nothing to me and didn't have any impact on my submitting my sample to the labs. I sent off for my test in October. It took one week to receive the test and about six more weeks for results. When the results came in, I did not expect all the answers I got nor could predict where I am today.

I was shocked and elated. Almost like finding out you're pregnant. The results read 51% European and 48% Native American. The ethnicity didn't fit what I was told. The most thunder-striking result was a man with whom I shared 25% DNA. My heart skipped a beat and I was shaking. The test said he was my nephew. A 99.9% European nephew but I knew in my heart he was my half-brother. We were too close in age at exactly one year apart in birthdays. Upon reading his profile, he was born in the state next to where I was born. He also had the name of his birth mother, our birthmother. I concluded she was white.

The clue of my birth father being part Alaskan Native and the clear-cut divide between my half-brothers European lineage and mine made for definitive answers to my ancestry when compared to all the cousins. The many cousins I now had which included photos, names and where they lived. One of my first impressions from the photos was "Wow, do I look like that?" They were all Athabascan Indian coming from villages along the Yukon, Koyukuk and Tanana rivers in AK. I had not one Aleutian Indian cousin.

For the next three plus months I became detective. I searched the internet for my birthmother every day and for hours. This entailed taking in all clues and following all paths to the dead end. I emailed all Native cousins and tried building trees backward to forward. I was looking for a relation of theirs who may have traveled to the lower 48 in the 60s. Searching consumed me. I encountered old emotions. Feeling of fear and not finding the correct path. Fear of never knowing the truth. Fear of rejection. I didn't fall on old ways of coping this time and tackled the emotions sober and grateful. This time around I found answers.

After three months of daily searching I located my birthmother. I found her on a web-based public tree which also had a second cousin listed from my DNA profile. I scrolled through the photos and there she was. For the first time ever, I saw the woman who carried me into this life. I can't say we look alike, but I knew instinctively it was her. I noticed she left a message with her married name and location. I then located her on the social media. I sent her two messages and one to her sister asking for help. Help in answering the questions I have. The answers she solely held to my beginning of this journey. It took her a month before she responded to tell me she will write me a hand-written letter and send it via the US Postal service.

The week I was expecting snail mail from my birthmother I had prayer requests on the social media and with personal friends that my birth mother would honestly, to the best of her ability, provide me the name of my birth father and circumstances regarding my birth.

During this same week a 3rd cousin from my birth father's side took personal interest in my search. She posted my photo and prayer request to her social media page for her/our cousins to see if I looked like anyone in the family. I waited.

My letter came on a Friday evening and in it was the name of my birth father. The name wasn't what I pictured a Native man's name to be and thought maybe my birth mother didn't remember correctly or spelled it wrong. I searched the internet Friday evening and found no leads. Saturday I put in a few searches in between my household chores. I went to church Saturday at 5pm; but before I went, I posted my father's name to my cousin's social media post. An hour and a half later, when church was out, I read the responses. In that hour and a half, with altruistic heartfelt acceptance I was welcomed into my father's family with tears of joy, phone calls from Alaska and stories about my father.

He walked on in 1992 when his boat ran into a sinkhole on the Yukon River while hunting. Every word spoken about my father was that he was so nice and had a goofy sense of humor. My family sees my dad in me through the photos I have shared with them. My Koyukon Athabascan family is huge. Some still live in a village with no running water, some are transplanted to Fairbanks and Anchorage, and some to the lower 48. My father traveled to the Midwest in the 60s joining the Job Corps in Chicago where he met and had a brief relationship with my mother. He returned home to his Native family and Alaska in 1975. I

Henry Demoski, my birthfather

believe the Native man in my dream was my father. He was always there but the fox tricked us. My family tells me my grandmother was from the bear clan. I believe they are calling me home.

My story has new beginnings now. I leave my mother to her privacy and she has her family that does not know about me. I wish to honor her desire and protect the emotional well-being of my half-siblings. My father has two more daughters that are known about and I will be praying for their safe return home. I hope to soon visit the villages and the river where my father lived and died and to attend a summer potlatch to meet my elders and cousins where we will share stories and carry on the oral tradition. I will in turn share the stories with my children so they can share with the children yet to come. I will share my personal story of being called home.

My last dream I share for those who understand and who may be searching still. My eyes laid even with the ocean resting on the surface of the water. I couldn't see activity under the water, but I knew it was there and my body felt warm and safe. All around the surface of the water, huge whale tails would come up out of the water and splash down. The water splashes collected and rose up toward the sky and came together to form into one giant eagle. He was facing me with his wings spread out over the complete horizon. He looked at the calm water and nodded a signal for the whales to make more waves. The waves began again. Many waves covering the surface. Inside the rippling rolling part of each wave, and what I thought was a white cap, was another eagle resting with his wings tucked. As each wave made a complete cycle to gather back into the ocean, a white eagle flew up out of the resting wave. The whales continued splashing all around with more eagles waiting on the water and thousands of eagles flying around inside of the wingspan of the giant eagle. That was my most recent dream in colors of ivory, gold and blue.

13

Josie/She's There In My Bones

C SUZANNE ZAHRT MURPHY (Cherokee)

JOSIE
    She was heavy, and her body labored to walk. She wore black heavy shoes and dark
    brown stockings, and always, printed dresses.
    She had a wide mouth and a seeing stare. They told me I had her eyes.
    She sang like an angel and kept the party going in her youth.
    They say it's hardest to write about what is close, like a secret.
    In secrets there is shame. In secrets there is suffering. In secrets there is sickness.
    Her secret was being Indian. Her shame she learned when she was thrown away.
    Her sickness came from betrayal, ignorance and hate, heaped upon her in those bleak
    punishing rooms, where she was taken.
    Josephine, my Cherokee great grandmother was not a ticket to an identity.
    She was part of me, before I could know it.
    In our veins: The stomping, rattling of dancer's feet, the singing of the headman and the
    chorus, revering Spirit's gifts.
    From this she was taken. From this, she was put asunder.
    I had only stories,
    revealed over time from a third person (her grand daughter, my mother) into the ears of the fourth, mine.
    They were the stories of one who suffered, who stubbornly survived.
    Josie came from a full-blooded Cherokee mother, a Scot father;
    from the sounds of bagpipes and *Selu*, the corn, swishing in the wind.
    From the sound of mourning and the sounds of *Ganodu,* life.

She was thrown away when her mother died,
flung from a good way by sorrow and grief, into
a convent, separated from kin who were scattered, too.
When she emerged, she was suspicious and wily.
She made moonshine and lured her husbands with it.
She stuffed the krinkled money into her mattress.
She sang her silky tunes into dark downturned hours.
She muttered to her granddaughter about dark basements and dead babies,
spitting out a cauldron of foreign words.
But when her granddaughter asked what she said,
Josie, remembering the downward arm, the angry slap, said only,
Never mind.

Once Josie took her granddaughter to school, and let her out of the car on the road side.
Her granddaughter was struck, spun, fell down.
Josie said not a word as the driver rushed over, said are you all right?
Josie drove away in silence.
Her granddaughter was all right, but she remembered.
Once Josie said to me, her great granddaughter:
You'll never be as pretty as your mother, you know.
As if she wanted to wound, before being wounded.
Yet she grew good medicine,
She slathered goose grease on her granddaughter's chest when sickness made her cough.
   birthed babies and prayed for them in a good way.
How can we love and hate someone all at once?
How can we stop the shame?
At thirteen, angry over something trivial, I refused to say goodbye.
As I kept my face buried in the pillow, she walked out the door, disappointed.
I never saw her again.
She died saying she'd been poisoned.
The truth is, she was, poisoned by those horrible days of loss and punishment.
What happens before comes down to us. What happened to her, to them, comes back to us.
Of course, I am thinking a lot about the journey, the one we all must make.
I don't want to pass on the shame. Forgive me great grandmother,
For not saying goodbye.

Hey ya na hey hey ya he ya he no.
Carl Jung said that when we dream of marriage, we are nearing an end.
Don't worry, I haven't dreamed it yet.
But when the groom of after- life carries me over the threshold to all that is,
I hope I have it ready, that I will have time to utter it, to sing those few notes
I remember.
I want to believe that Josie's existence and yours and mine will somehow
Join together in one unending whole thing: summerfallwinterspring,
the bagpipes, the corn, the beauty of our gifts, even of our darkness.
A thing that hums like a song, our final home.
(2013)
~~~~~~~~~~~~~~~~~~~

She's There In My Bones
I remember hearing that Austrailian Aboriginees knew where to go because they had the songs.
If they sang them the way they were taught they would find
Water,
A place to rest.
How to live.
Sometimes, when I want to know how to live,
I tap my chest like a drum,
Listening for our
guiding verses.
If I bow my head, and turn inward, I can hear, those sacred moonlight dances giving homage to *uwoduhi*, to **the Beauty.**
If I listen, I hear the shake of the turtle shells on dancing feet,
And the crickets singing after them.
I plant corn in my garden each year to honor them.
When I hear the tassels rustling in the breeze I remember the old ones
Who stomped beneath the moon in reverence for life.
I hear the head dancer calling, and the men responding.
I hear the women behind them, stomping their feet, raising their arms.
Last year the yellow corn nuggets, more precious than gold, gave themselves to me.
When I eat them I hear the old ones singing.

Before she died, I told my mother about them, about the corn, about the dances.
I told her
How our people tried to do everything to save the land,
how they tried to live with the encroachers,
how they were torn from the table at supper,
and forced to walk in bitter cold,
how so many died, how the ones who made it
were punished
for being Indian.
My skin is white, and stretched from living.
My face is round like my German father's,
my body is pear shaped like my great grandmother Josie, the wily survivor.
My eyes are deep and brown and some say, sad.
If you look maybe you won't see her,
The Cherokee,
But she's there in my bones
There
In my heart.
(c) 6/28/13

14

It's a Wild World

SAMANTHA FRANKLIN

Earlier today I found myself standing in front of a huge wall of flowers, picking out just the right ones for my family's graves. So many in my family have passed on. My adoptive family was older when they "got" me, so I have lost many aunts and uncles who hold special places in my heart. My beloved Mother by adoption passed away Thanksgiving Day after a short illness. I am still in shock and miss her so much. Through all the ups and downs of adoption and reunion and the emotional turmoil for both of us, her love never faltered. She taught me trust.

Red roses for Nanny and her twin sister, Aunt Kay… Lilies for Aunt Hazel and Uncle Dean. Then there are years of memories—placing flowers on graves of great grandparents I never met, and feeling no connection whatsoever….but that's another story. It provided a "tradition" and "familiarity" for my childhood "roots."

Well into reunion, I now have the added work of grieving for biological relatives who I had the great blessing of growing close to before their passing—my GREAT-GRANDMA Grace, who was the one lady in my blood family actually shorter than me! She passed away at the age of 93, and left me a beautiful painting that now graces my bedroom wall. Her family (the Derricksons) were one of the first settlers near Oolagah, OK and were childhood friends with Will Rogers!

My maternal grandmother, Carolyn, who was a ballroom dancer well into her senior years. The year before she passed away, my husband and I spent New Year's Eve with her dancing to big band sounds—what a treasure.

Then there are my paternal grandparents who I grew the closest to… sitting at the dining room table hearing heart-warming stories of their childhoods, growing up in rural Oklahoma, WWII stories of my grandfather's plane making a crash landing with narrow escape, and their travels all over the world, including a trip to Europe on the Concord. Nothing can adequately describe the feelings of completeness and strength these precious years have given me—in reunion with my family.

As I was contemplating which flowers for each person, I suddenly realized that a special song was playing over the sound system of the store, and it seemed as if it was right over my head. "Cats in the Cradle" by Harry Chapin has always reminded me of my mother Norma Carol. I think it is because of that reminiscent 70s sound that, for some reason, resonates deep in my soul and brings peace to my mind. My connection to her.

It amazed me when her sister told me that one of Norma's favorite songs (during the 60s) was "It's a Wild World" —when I hear the lyrics of these songs, it seems as if my Mother is singing her love and advice to me from far away. It certainly IS a wild world, and it does take more than a smile...that I have learned.

So...standing there amongst the flowers, hearing the soothing melody ring in my ears, I carefully reached out and pulled out a big bouquet of sunflowers...for my Mother. The Mother who had no options at a tender, young age in the late 1960s, but to lose me. And I her. Twice.

All of a sudden it seemed as if all strength left my body and I went weak. So empty. So helpless....standing with sunflowers gracing my eyes, but feeling so lost inside. She is gone and I miss her so much. I want to touch her and hear her voice, and feel her arms around me—just once. It would be so amazing.

My Mother passed away—while searching for me. She thought she was searching for a son, because the hospital personnel and attorney gave her false information during the whole surrender...and since she wasn't given the opportunity to even see me, she had no way of knowing that I was a daughter. I felt her voice singing to me in the store today...

"...When you coming home, son? I don't know when...but we'll get together then...you know we'll have a good time then."

Tears...

Samantha Franklin lives in Tulsa, OK with her husband, Brian, and son, Andrew. She is thankful to be reunited with her first family for over 20 years. Her first Mother passed away before she was able to meet her, but Samantha

Samantha and Brian

was told that her first Mother's family shared Native American heritage. Growing up in Oklahoma, this has been a wonderful journey of discovery.

15

When Love Cannot Conquer

A 60s Scoop Adoptee's Journey from Reserve to Mainstream Society Back to the Reserve

KAREN KAMINAWAISH M.A., M.S. (Anishinawbe)

Part I: Life Before Reunification

Introduction

When meeting someone for the first time and they ask, "Where are you from?" i hesitate because their inquiry cannot be answered with a short answer; but it opens the door to a very long interesting story. i ask the person if they can sit a spell while i tell about my jour-

This is dedicated to all the adoptees that are still searching for their families or has already found their way home. Where ever you are at in your journey i wish you well and the best as our Creator gently leads and guides you.

ney. Afterwards the person just sits there in awe, and tells me that my story needs to be written, so this anthology is the beginnings of my journey in print.

A journey about myself, being taken as a toddler and adopted into a loving Mennonite family, searching for an identity that is my own, finding my people and finally moving back to live in my reserve, which now i call home. My journey is of many faces and many places i have lived and traveled making the life that i live. My journey is filled with feelings of loneliness that grew to be a protective armor. The feelings of never fitting in, never feeling "a part of," always on the outside looking in; until i was fortunate to "find my family" and that hole inside has been partially filled. My journey is wrought with a myriad of varying emotions: happy and sad, filled with laughing and crying, a watchful eye for acceptance or rejection…an adoptee's journey…mine.

Adoption:

In the course of my life i have been given different names given by birth, adoption and marriage. But the various names have never affected that i am me, having beliefs and opinions, happiness and sadness as life is lived. Born as Lillian, the half-sister to twelve siblings, whom all shared the same dad, i was the baby, but fathered by another man. By the time of my adoption, i had experienced several different placements so i was never able to adequately bond with anyone. Bonding is crucial for human development to occur, but because the bonding did not happen, this has impacted negatively throughout my life as i find it difficult to form healthy relationships. The fear of rejection is a daily occurrence, while the feeling of acceptance has been somewhat fleeting.

There are numerous stories that were told to me regarding my apprehension at the age of two. One story unfolds as: i was living with the Bottle family, and a government car pulled up one day and the lady asked, "Where is Lillian Kaminawaish?" and the Bottle family was forced to give me to her.

Another story was that i was given to the Bottle family and Mrs. Bottle, who was elderly, had gotten sick. A white woman came to Mrs. Bottle and said she would take the baby (me) for a few days until Mrs. Bottle got to feeling better; but she never returned with me. i was gone, vanished seemingly forever. For a very long time, i detested all white women, for they were all symbolic of the white woman that stole me. As a result, there were years of counseling from my teen-age years to the time i met my biological family and this counseling continues on…to me counseling is a needed and helpful venue to help me make sense of everything that has happened in my life.

Another story (which i believe) is that my big sister, Josie, worked hard to keep us all together as a family and worked long hours to put food on the table. She was walking home on her lunch hour to feed me and change my diaper.

Then one day, the government car came and took me. There must have been some clue that the CAS was inquiring about me. I learned recently from Temius Nate, who told me how my brother Patrick kept saying, "They are not going to get my baby sister." My family and i never set eyes upon each other until 1990.

Despite the various apprehension stories, the part that remains consistent is about my older brother Frank who was away working in the mine when i was apprehended. When he returned from work, he was told of my apprehension. Immediately he set forth to Sioux Lookout to the Children's Aid Society's (CAS) orphanage. He told me that i was not to have been adopted and that he went to get me at the orphanage and he was told i was already gone...adopted out. Had i known this, perhaps my teenage years would have not been as turbulent as they were; for i was constantly looking for love and acceptance, and a sense of belonging. My whole life i grew up believing there was something wrong with me because no one wanted me...how wrong i was.

The story i was told from my adopted parent about my adoption had a different twist to it. Because my parents did not wish for my sister, Connie to be raised alone, they opted to adopt a Native American child and therefore, an adoption procedure was begun with Children's Aid Society in Canada. Why my parents choose to adopt internationally, i do not know...perhaps the international adoption was easier back then. But all said and done, my parents drove to Sioux Lookout, Ontario to pick me up. At this time i was at a foster home, and my Mom told me that the foster mom treated the dog better than i; this knowledge contributed to me having a low self-esteem and self-worth.

My parents took me to the United States via Sault Sainte Marie to their home in Elkhart, Indiana to become "a daughter of their own." Unfortunately, this all took place when i was two-years-old and i had already several placements that were disrupted; thus breaking any attachments or bonds that are crucial in a child's formative years. Because of these disruptions in my early life, later in life i had a very difficult time with bonding with my adopted Mom, thus creating tension in my teenage years. The inability to form solid relationships continues to plague me to this day.

As a part of my graduate work requirements, i studied the importance of the Attachment Theory using my sister's and my adoptions to substantiate the theory on the imperativeness of bonding. My professor was astonished that two children raised in the same family with equal amounts of affection and resources available could have such polarizations in their life's trajectories, as a result of the bonding experience, or in my case the lack of.

My Adopted Family:

My adoptive parents were from a strong conservative Mennonite stock, religiously attending church whenever the church doors were opened. We were there usually forty-five minutes early because being on-time was a virtue and they instilled in us, "Do not make someone wait for you, but you be ready and wait on them." My parents were a typical Mennonite couple with Dad, the head of the household and Mom the backbone of our family. Both were hard-working and committed to providing the necessities of life in a warm and caring atmosphere. My Dad was a factory worker and my Mom did odd jobs to help out financially and many times our home was a placement for a foster child. Daddy inherited some acreage of land which a few acres were sold over the years, down by the highway, away from where we lived on the edge of the woods back a long lane.

My parents married and had two sons of their own, Ellsworth and Wayne. My Korean sister, Connie was two months when she was adopted through Holt Adoption Agency. My two brothers were already married and on their own when my parents decided to adopt another girl…me…so my sister would not be raised alone. Because i knew this, i always felt that i was my sister's play toy. An amusement to be taken out and played with and then put back on the shelf when my sister decided she was done playing with me. Perhaps this is why today i feel that i have a responsibility to make people laugh and often do. It has been said, "Where karen is, there is laughter."

Our home life was filled with good biblical teachings and unconditionally love; although at the time i found the teachings to be boring and the love stifling. Because my Dad worked in town and had to be at work by six, we all rose at four and ate breakfast together, strengthening the familial bond after family worship. My sister and i could then go back to bed and sleep for an hour. We were required to run the vacuum throughout the house and do the morning dishes, before we left for school. Because our parents worked hard and saved what money they could, we always went on a two- or three-week summer vacation, sometimes traveling to relatives afar, seeing different sites or sometimes camping.

Our place was the place where there were many happy reunions filled with plenty of laughter and food because we had a large expanse of yard and plenty of shade. We even had room to play softball and hide-and-seek and it was not unusual for the whole family to get out and play softball. Our home seemed to always have friends and family visiting from all over or Mennonite people passing through as we were listed in the *"Mennonite Your Way"* directory.

On the downside, i never felt that i fit in, always the peg in a round hole. No, it was not because of my phenotype. It was something from within, something i could not explain. My Mom longed for a mother-daughter relationship with me, and it was something she never got from me. Part of the crucial bonding that is a necessity for a child never happened between me and my adopted family and that is why i titled my journey "When Love Cannot Conquer" because all the love that was shown and given to me, for some unknown reason i could not acknowledge and return. i need to say "part of the crucial bonding" because there were definitely good times while growing up.

While growing up, a part of being Anishinawbe i believe was innate as i constantly needed to be outside with the elements, alone. i enjoyed spending time in the woods, ice skating, bicycling, tennis, but always alone with my thoughts. i counted the years, then the months till i turned eighteen, till i could leave home. i was rebellious and ran away from home twice; once going to New Orleans. i believe i was trying my wings out, but in a negative way. i did not wish to conform to the Mennonite way nor to a loving family…for i knew i was Ojibway; although i did not know what an Ojibway was. Hindsight reveals that i was searching for a sense of belonging…a world where i could "just be".

My Biological Family:

My Mom was the late Sarah Kaminawaish and my Dad is Solomon Williams from North Caribou Lake. i was the youngest of thirteen children and a half-sister. i do not remember anything about life as a toddler, but do have one residual effect, which i will share. While growing up and even today if i am ever given some catastrophic news i immediately cross myself. Growing up, i never knew why or where i learned this religious gesture, The Sign of the Cross. Today i know that my Kaminawaish family was at the time devout Catholics and i was taught to cross myself at an early age.

My Dad Solomon had four children, with myself being the oldest and one sister and two brothers. To this day i would like to meet my siblings. i am close to my cousin-brothers Charlie and Billy and enjoy spending time with them and their families. i am extremely close to my two of my nephews Clayton, Billy's son and he wrote on Facebook, "You are the best Auntie God has given me Karen Kaminawaish and that's why I love you Auntie for it being my Auntie number 1", while Charlie's son, Mike wrote, "Auntie, next time u come here I will bake u a birthday cake."

The First Connection:

My first connection happened when i was thirteen. A Mennonite couple, Clair and Clara Schnupp had opened mission schools for the First Nations across the north. Their program is called the Northern Youth Program, which in parts still exists today. Family friends Levi and Anna Otto asked my parents if i could travel back to Ontario to help out for two weeks in one of the mission schools, Sterling Lake. My parents allowed me to go. i did ask my parents if i asked Clair to help me find my family and if my family (biological) wanted me back, could i go? To this day, i often think of the openness and love my adopted parents had for me, even if their decision at the time may have hurt them…for they said yes.

Unfortunately, finding my biological family was not to be at that time and i call it a "God-thing," why i did not locate them at that time. It was coincidental that while on that trip, we stayed in Pickle Lake at the hotel with a kitchen on the bottom and rooms on top. While the Otto's and i were dining, an inebriated Native man entered and talked to me. i was terrified…for i had never been around alcohol nor drinking of any kind. i ran back to the kitchen and told the cook to "get a knife." i do not know what i would have done if the cook would have given me a knife! i do know now, if i would had inquired about my Kaminawaish family i would have found them, right there in Pickle Lake for i was born there. It just was not the time for my reunification.

Although, in 1999 i finally got to meet face-to-face with my biological family. My daughter Octivia Micaela had asked about her maternal grandparents and so i called Children's Aid Society in Winnipeg and they informed me that the agency in Sioux Lookout was no longer there, but instead Tikinagan Child and Family Services. So i called and the receptionist asked me if i wished to find my family; of course i said, "Yes" and she commenced to do a phone intake. Since i knew my name Lillian Kaminawaish, it was easy for her to know immediately where i was from: Osnaburgh House, which was later changed to Mishkeegogamang. Perhaps i was Dorothy in the Land of Oz incarnate…perhaps.

Two weeks later she called me back and she said she found my family. i was all giddy and wanting to know their names and their phone numbers. i was told that i must wait for them to call me…the anguish of waiting was excruciating. Finally about five days later i received a phone call asking if i was Lillian Kaminawaish and i said, "Yes…no…yes i used to be." It was one of my big brothers, the late Chief Roy Kaminawaish. i was FOUND…that day started a whole new life for me…many questions begun to be answered and i WANTED TO GO HOME.

Two weeks later, i was on the Greyhound going north. My big sister, Josie and her daughters, Rachael and Waylona picked me up at the border and took me into the interior of Ontario. My sister told me that my Dad was still alive. i was awe-struck as i had never gave much thought about my Dad; it was always my Mom whom i yearned for and wondered about down through the years.

i stayed with Frank, my brother, and got to meet my Aunt Penona. Upon meeting her, i knew how i would look when i get older for i am her "mini." My Dad was in the hospital in Winnipeg and he was called and then he and my Uncle Isiah left the hospital without the consent of the doctor and came to meet me. When i first seen my Dad i was nervous, but happy. As the car pulled up, i seen the top of a mop of unruly hair in the back seat and this little man get out. He was MY DAD!!! All of 5"2 with curly hair, just like me.

Several days later, i traveled back to North Caribou Lake First Nation, (It's also called Waegomow Lake or Round Lake) to meet my Dad's people there. My Dad's people have been really accepting and caring throughout the years. My cousin Rhoda, her Mom Jenny, and her son James and sister Barb and her daughter Taylor are close to my heart as i often stay at their house and it is "my couch, my bed" when i visit. i spend a lot of time with James, as i showed him *Angry Birds*. Today James calls me Kokum, which means Grandma. My other cousin Marlene, i love dearly and her family and mother-in-law Geordina. Marlene's raises her grandson Sundance and he and Checotah are close. There are many who are dear to my heart: Melody, Theron and Raven, who are Martha's children, James B. who serves the same loving God as i, all the Chikanes, the Williams', the Johnups. i must not forget to mention, my friend Nathan Johnup with whom i have been fortunate to develop a long, friendly friendship.

In the summers of 2009-10 i came back to the reserve for summer employment. Sociologically, it was rewarding as i became aware of how various social problems were affecting my people and how resources were not available as readily to the on-reserve population. Additionally, i became cognizant of the length of time to obtain certain resources and how distance affected First Nation populations. For example: if a female felt a lump in her breast, she could not just pick up the phone and call for an appointment and in one-two days be seen; but rather she would have to call Niika Transportation for a ride to the clinic, be seen by a nurse who called the doctor, the doctor advised for the patient to be seen in Sioux Lookout, the nurse calling Meno Ya Win Hospital to make a mammogram appointment which would be the following week or next. Then the patient goes back home via Niika and waits for the appointment day. If the appointment is at 9 a.m. the patient must travel the day before, sleep at the hostel and then go to the appointment the next day. If the patient is from a fly-in reserve, this only prolongs the time of appointment and flight connections must be made.

This concludes Part I: Life Before Reunification; although it does not conclude the feelings that are part of my being. My life before returning home, i cannot change anything about it, but i can change how i think about my life's trajectory and i can turn this experience into a positive and be of assistance to other adoptees that are still searching for their bloodlines and a home that continues to be an illusion, seemingly just beyond their grasp.

Part II: Life After Reunification
Introduction

After much preponderance, i have decided to not paint the picture prettier than what it really is. Because this book and the authors' work is about the honesty, the pain is interspersed with happiness, with the realness of the effects on the adoptees of the 60s Scoop. Of course, i shall omit actual names, but shall pen the situation as is and not "clean-up" the ugliness. i owe this to my fellow adoptees of what i am about to pen; the pain, the reality of "going back" to one's roots and being accepted and other times the acceptance is withdrawn. i have learned that acceptance is conditional as long as one does not question or ask for accountability.

However, through the difficult times, there are so many rewards in my life returning to my reserve, a place that i call home now. Good people who their doors are open to stop in and have a cup of coffee, to receive birthday party invites, to give a ride too, to share living our Anishnawbe life.

Going Back:

While growing up i spent many hours on a childhood swing, imagining who my parents were and the time that i would return home, to the place of my roots. My imagination was filled with a "peaches and cream" homecoming, not knowing then the reality and cruelty of human nature.

In 1999 i made my first visit to "exploring my roots" and went back to the States to continue my education journey. At this time in my life, i was earning my education as an Associate degree and advanced to earning two Master's in Sociology. Studying came as an opportunity to shine and do well. It gave me a purpose, it gave me a peace that i was achieving, it gave me positive recognition…and it gave me a quality of life that my son and i enjoy.

But upon returning to live at my reserve, at first my education was seen as helpful, but that has changed to where now my education seems to thwart how certain people interact with me as they seem to "hold it against me" and i now question why there seems to be a thread of jealousy that seems to prevail and have entered into the equation from all levels including the leadership.

One frontline worker refuses to recognize there are many types of knowledge and that she has bush knowledge, just as important as my textbook knowledge. Bush knowledge is about how to survive and live off the land. A reserve in the far north needs people to be either bush knowledgeable or textbook knowledgeable and each can complement the other; each can lend support to the other. Many times this person has locked horns with me because this inability to respect my level of textbook knowledge and one time she said she "pitied me" for being taken and not knowing my traditions and language. i do not wish to be "pitied" but only ask to be understood or an explanation when i do not understand.

The Chief assisted me with monies to return, we were given a trailer that we call home, and a job of Case Manager, which i thoroughly enjoy. Our home is warm and comfy with always a pot of "good coffee" brewing and Native artwork displayed, both Southwestern and Ojibway. My job is one where i wear many hats, donning one hat for this job and another hat for another job. Part of the day consists of being at the computer planning or writing proposals for reserve activities. Another part is going into the community helping out by listening to someone's dilemma and assisting them to the best of my ability, or sitting in a case conference.

The segment that i truly enjoy is being part of the Restorative Justice in the courts. Currently, i oversee the Diversion Program with the help of Vernon, ensuring that Justice Circles and community hours are completed in time for the client's next court date. Just recently, i was told by a band councilor that he would begin the process of having me removed from being the court worker due to my more lenient attitude towards marijuana smoking. i am quite sure i will be called in soon to sit in front of the Chief and Council. i believe that there are other problems with staff and the band council that are more pertinent such as frontline workers physically accosting each other and other band members with or without weapons, problems dealing with addiction, bootlegging, and other ensuing problems that are more serious than a lenient attitude regarding marijuana.

For me not knowing the Anishnawbe language presents a multi-faceted problem. i know it is my duty to learn the language and learning would eliminate a lot and i am willing to learn. It hurts when i walk into a room and the people who are present are talking and laughing in English, but suddenly switch to Ojibway and no interpretation is rendered. Or i am present and everyone is talking in English, but one or two comments are spoken in Ojibway and everyone laughs. Although, i am cognizant in each of these situations i am not the one being laughed at, but it hurts not sharing in the knowing the "inside joke" or the punch line. i have begun to ask for interpretation, but it feels awkward to keep asking and asking again in the same setting.

Not knowing our traditions, our customs follow the same as the language, but here i can watch and copy. i have begun to go to my big sister Josie and ask. Our traditions and customs are interesting and the "why" behind them are needed to fully understanding them.

Good Times:

My biggest enjoyment is being "Candy Gurl" and given candy to the children with a teaching and they must say "please and thank you" and they must not put the candy wrapper on the ground. Some of the teachings are: Just saying no to drugs and alcohol that it's OK not to drink and drug, healthy touches and respect or "despect" as Jershawn says it.

One teaching is so memorable: there were three little boys Trinton, Shawn and Danny sitting on "Candy Gurl's" steps listening to a teaching about chivalry. The boys and i practiced saying the hard word and i explained what chivalry was. They gave examples of chivalry. i then asked, "now what is that big word again, what are we talking about?" Shawn answered without hesitance, "Jiggers." Of course, then they were given their piece of candy!

It is so heartwarming to hear all the neighborhood children come running when i get home from work saying, "Candy Gurl, you are home, oh Candy Gurl i am happy to see you...oh Candy Gurl..!!!!" One time there were hearts written all over in the dust on my truck with hearts saying, "I love you Candy Girl" and "u r cool"...these are just several of many interactions with the children on my reserve that make life here so enriching.

It feels good that my place is seen as a safe haven or a place to go for a good cup of coffee or to sit and just talk. People know they can tell me things and i do not tell. In the evenings, i never know who is knocking on my door and why. But the door is always open and i am willing to listen. Or sometimes a person is in need of the police and they know i do not drink or take pills or "smoke up" and they know they can get help when they come to my door.

One funny story is about Sara Lee, a young lady came to talk and we sat at my kitchen table as she begun to share what was troubling her. There was a two-liter of root beer sitting there and as she begun to share i got out two small glasses similar to shot glasses, although i call them juice glasses. In the course of the evening we pushed that "jug" back and forth filling up our glasses. And as the night wore on, the "jug" became emptied. We had a good laugh as we pushed it back and forth and she said, "At least we are not getting louder and louder!"

Another favorite is when the electricity goes off for a day or more. We see the community helping each other, eating and cooking for one another with no electronics interrupting. It's a time to really socialize; of course, the young people do not think so!

i would have to answer to my colleagues Ronald, Tom and Kenny if i did not mention them. Each morning we meet over coffee and have the reserve's problems worked out. But honestly, these three men have taught me a lot by sharing their stories, their wisdom with me.

Today i am blessed to be able to assist the Thunder Family Ministries: Lott & Millie, Alicia and of course, Roy! Several times a year, i travel to help out where needed and of course, there are always plenty of laughs, whether it's a revival or gospel jamboree.

Sports are an all-time favorite of the reserve people and mine as well. Although i do not play, i contribute by sponsoring a team. Sometimes it's a half sponsorship and other times, it's a full sponsorship. When i first came back, i heard about the various tournaments and so i volunteered to sponsor. Many people were amazed and questioned why i would do such a thing. But i told them i have always sponsored a team. In Oklahoma it is a norm to sponsor or co-sponsor a team. i chose Mish Thunder because of my friendship with Destani, Maxine and Gina.

One full sponsorship is my Mish Thunder Ladies Broomball team. i deeply love and care for my Mish Thunder ladies and travel with them at one of the tournaments that i sponsor. They have gifted me with two team jerseys, a team jacket and one of the best Christmas presents i have ever received; a plush fleece queen-sized blanket that has a Medicine Wheel on it. Since i was given it, it has been on my bed and i often think of my gurlies and their appreciation is in the blanket and their love transferred through the warmth and coziness of the blanket. i must add this, GO MISH THUNDER!

When i moved back i put a teaching that was given to me to use and that is to stick with the ladies, get to know them and so i have. In AA i was taught to stick with the ladies because "the men will grab your a#@, while the women will save your a#@", which is so true! Having done that i have made some good friends, such as Maxine who i can tell anything too and it's not broadcasted; Elizabeth, Vivian, Diane, and Lena who we share many laughs over coffee or tea. My funny friend Moana who calls me "her crazy old lady friend."

i am close to my two nieces, Lisa and Linda, and nephew, Mike and his children, since i have moved back to my reserve, Mishkeegogamang First Nation. Lisa and her family's place is always is the place where my son, Checotah wants to go if i am required to be off the reserve or he just wants to be on the main part of the reserve to visit. He feels love and acceptance from each of Lisa's children; especially Meequin who is in constant mortal combat (!) with

Checotah. We will never know which one will be the demise of the other! Each spring Mike's son Kege hunts with his toy gun and gets me a goose.

Just recently, my big sister Josie had her birthday and i went over there to wish her birthday wishes. When i was leaving, she hugged me and i whispered, "I love you" and she whispered them back to me, "I love you." What a birthday present to me, since my birthday was two days before hers.

One event that happened to me that shows my family has my back was when i had fallen on an ice patch in Pickle Lake outside of the building where court is held and busted my knee and could not get up. People came to help, but it hurt too badly and i told them to get the OPP officers (Ontario Provincial Police). i was hurting, but laughing as i felt ridiculous being on the ground in Pickle Lake. The OPP officers were so gracious as they took off their coats to make me a blanket to lie on, a blanket of coats to keep warm, another jacket rolled up to make a pillow and a toque given by one of the officers as we waited for the ambulance. i was just lying there waiting for them to begin to take their shirts off!!! Here came my nephew Glen, my nieces Racheal and Waylona, to find out what they could do. Waylona drove my truck to the clinic at Osnaburgh and later drove me home. i was so thankful to have the help of "my family".

One of the biggest honors in my whole life was when i was asked to be kokum/grandma to lil Shekinnah. It is exciting to be part of a little one's life and getting to know her. i started to visit, but always take a nappie with her because it seems she really quiets my spirit and i want to go to sleep. And so i hold her and talk with her as we both take a nappie.

Purposely, i saved my family members relationships to make a transition into the Part III: The Effects of My Adoption.

Part III: The Effects of My Adoption
Introduction

The effects of my adoption have been long-standing and sometimes overwhelming. On one hand, i believe my adoption was something good that happened to me for my adopted parents instilled in me many good ethics and morals with a strong biblical belief. On the other hand, so much was "taken" from me that have left me spiritually, mentally, emotionally crippled; although through therapy i have worked through some of the traumatization that continues to plague various parts of my life. Although, i have touched on some of these areas in my story, i shall pen the impacts and their effects. i may leave out some effects, lest i forget as my time frame is getting to be a factor for this document. The intensity and duration of the effect may not be adequately presented as the pain and hurt is too unbearable as i must "take care of karen" first and foremost.

Adoption agencies do not explain the negativity that may occur throughout the adoption, especially if the adopted child is adopted at an older age. This is often due to the lack of bonding between the essential caregiver and the infant. The absence of bonding in my experience has affected me in many areas of my life. Not only is it difficult to personally bond with my own children, but i have difficulty developing a healthy relationship with the opposite sex. i am sure it has to do with being abruptly "taken" from my biological family at an early age, then being in foster care to finally being placed with my adopted parents. Today i fear close connections because i do not know if and when these connections will be forced apart. The fear of rejection is with me at all times. Acceptance is somewhat fleeting even today.

Bonding with my adopted Mom was disheartening for her. Because of this, she would often cry because she wanted to have her unconditionally love reciprocated and in ways i could not fill. Having mother-daughter talks was what she wished for, but something inside of me prevented me to offering her these talks with me or telling her that i loved her.

i know my adopted parents and family gave immensely of their love and caring and i just could not reciprocate and today i feel bad that i could not. To this day, after years of therapy i still do not understand why i could not. This is why i titled my journey "When Love Cannot Conquer" because my adopted family gave their love unconditionally to me, but it was not welcomed by me. It seems as if i had constructed a mental fence around myself to protect me from an unknown danger.

Although, i acted out in unbecoming ways to possibly seek attention…today i still do not fully understand my teenage years' actions. i am very sorry for any undue embarrassment i might have caused my family, specifically, my sister Connie.

One significant problem i have deals with alcoholism. For many years, i drank to kill the pain of being "not wanted," being different, and then i drank because i had to physically to avoid the shakes.

i believe i drank alcoholically from the beginning. When i consumed alcohol i could forget "something was wrong with me" since no one wanted me for i believed i was flawed. i could be like everyone else while alcohol was in my body. Afterwhile, i lived to drink and then i drank to live and vice versa.

Today is totally different as i live a life of sobriety for over nine years now. AA has taught me how to face life and i know i never have to be alone with whatever i am facing. i can pick up the phone and call someone and share what is happening or share in meetings. Today i have a life worth living and i can be a respectable person of society, i can be a Mom and Grandma/Kokum, i can be a loving and funny friend, a "Candy Gurl" and i can laugh belly laughs and i can look in the mirror and love that person looking back at me. Today i am free…i can feel all the pain even when it's so very hurtful…i still do not have to reach for alcohol to numb the pain…my life is worth living without alcohol.

Language was touched on briefly before and it continues to be all-encompassing living my life here on my reserve. My language was brutally taken from me the day i got apprehended, along with my reserve's traditions and customs. i have to work at getting them back daily by asking questions, listening to Elders and others who know. But there exists the hurt of not knowing what the inside joke is and but more so, the pain of people changing into Ojibway from English when I come into a room.

These three subjects: language, traditions and customs of our culture continue to be obstructions in my daily life and i believe they are part of the foundation of a Mishkeegogamang First Nation band member. The hurt caused by not having these three are immense; the pain of "never really fitting in" is part of my daily life. Part of me is angry because of these three so rudely "taken" from me as a toddler and never have been replaced. i know i am angry at the Canadian government who must have thought it as "in being in my best interests to take me" to cause such an obliteration from my family, my language, my traditions and customs.

Having come back to the reserve to live has definitely been trying. But for the most part, i have been making happy memories with the general population. However, it seems to be the part of the leadership that i have been having great difficulty with. From accusations about unknown situations, to being told i was not First Nation because i was not strong enough to move my office and it's furnishings to the next building by myself. Then through the grapevine i was told that i was "overstaying my welcome" and that really hurt. i was so traumatized that i had an emotional breakdown and was required by a doctor to take some stress leave which to this day i am fighting to get paid for the time required off. i became so disheartened that i came close to "turning my back on God" if this is the actions of Christians, but did not because of my own personal walk with God and the place He took me from to where i am today: spiritually, emotionally and mentally. Additionally, recently i was told i was being removed from being the court worker due to my lenient attitude on marijuana smoking. It seems like something is always brewing concerning me. i simply abhor the chaos and do my best not to instigate nor "add to" to keep a situation brewing.

One commodity of being adopted is the fact of the skill of being able to move with ease in and out of both worlds: mainstream society and Native society. Some people call these people "Split Feathers." For me, i think nothing of slipping in and out of both worlds; to me this is second nature.

All in all, returning home is not at all what i expected. It is very painful to be shown such negativity from those in leadership and other frontline workers. But the good times definitely outweigh the bad. i constantly analyze my part in a situation and keep my side of the sidewalk clean. There are days when i think i have had enough, but then a small child brings joy to my heart and i still stay, despite the hurt and pain i experience.

Lastly, and most importantly is my gratitude to my God, *the God of my own understanding* for walking with me and sometimes carrying me throughout my journey…through the good, bad, lonely, funny, and sad times. Today i know i am never alone, unless i chose to be. Today i walk hand-in-hand with HIM and know HE sustains me. i am nothing without HIM and my personal motto is: "Serving HIM means serving OTHERS."

To all my Relations…Meegwich!!!

16

Michelle's Spirit Can Now Rest

PATRICK QUINTON YEAKEY (Sugpiaq)

Signing adoption papers

My name is Patrick Quinton Yeakey. I was born on September 11, 1983, in La Mesa, California. I was adopted at the age of three by Patricia Louise Yeakey and John Edwards Yeakey. My birth mother, Michelle Vee Berkman, also known as Michelle Vee Williams, was no longer able to care for me. In or around 2004-2005, my mother asked me if I'd be interested in getting ahold of my half brother. She gave me a number to call and so I did. After calling for several days, I finally got a hold of someone. When I asked to speak to my brother, Francis Elsesser, the woman that answered the phone seemed confused. When she asked who I was, I told her that I was Francis's half brother. Again, she seemed confused and told me that she was Francis's mother. I was shocked to be speaking to my biological mother on the phone and I'm sure there are no words to describe what Michelle must have been feeling. I was very lucky to get to meet both my half brother and my birth mother. Unfortunately, Michelle passed away shortly after our meeting in 2006.

Growing up as a child I told everyone that I was Eskimo. When I got a little older and did some research based on what Michelle told my parents, I discovered some things that suggested I was Aleut. I was pleased by this knowledge and the fact that I got to meet my biological mother. However, there was something she said to me that seemed to resonate. She insisted that she had tried for many years to get her own adoption records unsealed because that would have provided proof of our family lineage and our connection to Alaska and our tribe.

In the summer of 2012, I met a woman by the name of Karen Vigneault. I was drawn to her because of her tribal tattoos and awesome handwoven basket hat. I introduced myself and told her I was Aleutian. She told me she was Iipay from Santa Ysabel and that she was an active member with in her community. I explained my situation to Karen and she said she might be able to help me out. Karen is the Regional Librarian at Kaplan College here in San Diego. I gave her all of my adoption information and Michelle's name. At first, we weren't able to do much but the timing was right. Karen introduced me to a gentleman by the name of Thomas Elliot Lidot who is a member at Central Council Tlingit Haida Indians Alaska. He was working on a project to help adopted Aleutians get their adoption records unsealed. I was able to get Michelle's death certificate, fill out the paperwork Tom provided, and petition to get Michelle's adoption records  unsealed. My petition was granted and I was able to get the adoption records which provided Michelle's natural birth mother's name. Michelle's natural birth parent is listed as being Anita (Williams) Gaines also known as Anita Lou Gaines, nee Nieminen, born May 10, 1935, in Kodiak, Alaska.

I gave this information to my friend Karen and at first, we were confused because there were no Lou's listed up there and Nieminen is Finnish. Karen did more digging and discovered a typo. Anita's last name was misspelled as Lou instead of Loe. Once she came upon this, everything just fell into place. My grandmother's name was Anita Loe Nieminen. This information allowed us to track Anita back to her parents, Ingwald J. Loe (father) and Irene or Erina Y. Yurioff (mother). And this allowed us to find Irene's parents Kuzma John Yurioff (father) and Froklar Zourioff (mother).

Irene Y. Yurioff was my great-grandmother and was born on Afognak Island. My great, great-grandmother, Froklar Zourioff or Yurioff was also born on Afognak Island. My grandmother, Anita Loe must have been born on Afognak Island. She was not born until about 1936. In a 1930 Census of Afognak, Anita is obviously not listed because she was not born yet. However, she is listed as living in Kodiak Village in a 1940 Census. On the contrary, her father, Ingwald J. Loe passed away January 1936 on Afognak Island, which indicates Anita was conceived and born on Afognak Island.

After Ingwald passed away, Irene remarried to a Finnish man by the name of John Nieminen. He immigrated into New York from Canada and within a year, he was working in Washington as a fisherman. Rumor has it that the fisherman would talk of the beautiful women from Afognak. I am assuming this is how John and Irene had come to marry. All of Anita's brothers and sisters had moved out of the household except for her little sister Mariie who recently passed away in Afognak and was a well-known and respected elder. The sisters were raised by their mother and stepfather.

When Anita was old enough, she married to a military man named Roy Williard Williams and relocated to Virginia. She became pregnant with my mother Michelle out of wedlock and moved to San Diego. This is where she met her second husband (also in the military) by the last name of Gaines. For unknown reasons she gave Michelle up for adoption to a very nice, older couple, the Berkmans. The Berkmans passed away when Michelle was 13 and unfortunately, she got lost in the foster-care system. I can only imagine the terrible things she must have seen and experienced that caused her to want to live on the streets. She chose a very hard life of drugs, alcohol and prostitution. In her later years, she cleaned up from the drugs but could not abate her drinking. She passed away from cirrhosis and lower lobar pneumonia.

With all of this information, I was able to contact the Village of Afognak and apply for my tribal card! I came in contact with a second great cousin named Taletha Gertz that helped me though the process. I am thrilled to proclaim my success and was more thrilled when my tribal card came in the mail. Since then, I have been able to contact many of my relatives. I can now proudly say I am Sugpiaq, also known as Alutiiq. "Sugpiaq"is an ancestral term for ourselves, meaning "real people." "Alutiiq"is our derivation of the Russian name for us of "Aleut," which they used to label most Alaska Native people they contacted; younger generations are moving away from using this term to distinguish ourselves from our neighbors...

Since registering with my tribe I discovered that the Village of Afognak has a successful corporation. I attempted to become a shareholder but came to find that shares had to be gifted. Michelle swore that we had money and land in Alaska and I believed her. I know in my heart, Michelle loved me and wanted the best life for me and that's why she had to give me up for adoption. That must have been one of the hardest things to do, especially after losing my sister, less than one year old, to SIDS. I also knew that she wanted us to have a right to the families shares. I just had no way to prove anything until now. Following my success with registering with my tribe last summer, I explored our peoples history, culture, language, and recovery from Russian colonization. To my surprise, not only did our people have one successful corporation, but two! The other corporation is called Koniag Corporation. I read that you could petition to become a member of the corporation but not a share holder. So, I pursued the opportunity of becoming a member. I wanted to do this for Michelle. I called the shareholders department of Koniag and talked with a very nice lady by the name of LaToya Lukin. She told me that I had to send my original documents in order to move forward. I was very hesitant to do so for obvious reasons. Since then, I had become very busy with school (I am a full-time nursing student at SDSU) and lost contact with LaToya. In April 2014, LaToya sent me a Facebook message letting me know that she left the office for another job with her native corporation. She told me to contact a women by the name of Jaqueline Madsen and to tell her I will be sending her those document because Anita Bell, my grandmother, had a 100 shares with Koniag! They have been trying to find an heir for ten years and I am the only living heir. So, I mailed my documents and am awaiting good news. I know this would have made Michelle very happy. I succeeded! With the help of some AMAZING people, I finally discovered my origins and feel like Michelle's spirit can now rest.

This whole experience has been quite the journey and I want to thank all the people that helped me achieve my goal. Thank you for letting me share my story.

17

On the Red Road

THAYLA BARRETT (Cherokee)

I was born Baby Ellis on August 5, 1964. Thayla Jean Mallette was the name given to me by my adoptive parents Floyd and Betty Mallette. I was nine days old when I was placed in their home in Buena Park, California. I grew up with two siblings James and Scott who were also adopted.

My father Floyd worked for North American Rockwell International and I was so proud of him and his career. He was a planner for Rockwell which included the design of the Space Shuttle transport systems. Floyd and I had a great father-daughter relationship, and I was daddy's little girl. My mother Betty was a stay-at-home mom and she did her motherly duty of taking care of the kids. She was very strict, not like my dad who was very lenient. Like I said, I was daddy's little girl. I think my mother may have had a jealousy complex. Yes, she loved me but it was different with her. The discipline was very harsh when it came to her. She'd pull me by the hair and drag me from room to room picking up what was mine. I remember her throwing things at us when we had done something wrong. One thing that I thought was strange was since the age of 10, she'd dye my hair blonde and keep it cut very short. As I grew up it seemed like I was out of place. Yes, my mother did things with me, like shopping for clothes, going out to lunch, but it just seemed different in my mind. Our family was not the family type, I would say, and the only time we got together was for weddings and funerals. That was not my idea of family. My father's side of the family was always loving and genuinely happy to see me. My mother's side, not so much, and I always felt unwanted by them.

We attended a funeral for a family member when I was 9 or 10, and all I remember from that day was my Uncle Billy telling me, "You know you're Red, not blood, so you're not a part of this family." I was young and didn't really know what to think so I just kept on like I normally did, not thinking too much about it. This went on through my childhood.

My mother took us to visit my Uncle Darryl and I was so excited to visit because he said a swimming pool, and I thought I could go swimming with my cousins. I thought wrong. When we arrived at his house, his kids were just getting out of the pool. I asked if I could go swimming and he flat out told me no. I asked my mother if I could just dangle my legs in the pool to cool off and she said yes. So I did. My uncle came out and saw me. He began to tell me he'd just put acid in the pool and that my legs were going to be eaten away. "And you can't swim in my pool anyway." The nightmare I had, as a child, was dreaming that the skin on my legs were peeling off and I could see the bones in my legs. This was so traumatic for me.

A lot of my mother's side was very mean to me. Growing up only got worse. I pretty much stayed away from them and only went to events if my mother made me go.

The cousins were not much better, either. I couldn't play with their toys or do anything with them. Even if I tried, they would walk away from me. So it wasn't a great childhood.

As I grew up I was becoming my own person. In 1982, I gave birth to my beautiful son Joshua. I was 18 at the time. He was my pride and joy and he would never snub me like the family did.

At this time, I remember a cousin Roland was trying to get me to be his girlfriend. He tried so hard. I was not happy about this. He tried for a long time and said, "we could be kissing cousins." I flat out told him no, told him to stay away from me and leave me alone. I was absolutely horrified by this. It made me sick to my stomach. I went on like nothing happened. I never told my mother or father about this, I kept it to myself.

Then my mother passed away in December 1990. I was really hurt from all this, although our relationship was strained. The day of her funeral, my Uncle Jimmy and Aunt Tilly were standing at my mother's casket. My aunt was crying and putting a crucifix in the casket with her. I looked at my aunt and said, "Hello," and she gave me a very harsh look. She said nothing, not even consoling me, or any of my family for that matter. After the funeral, they didn't even show up for the get-together we had at my father's house. I thought they were all evil and didn't want anything to do with them from then on.

My mother was gone and I felt I had no reason to continue any relationship with them at all, considering how I was treated by them. Nine years later, my father passed. This was the loss that I never wanted to happen. My father and I were so close and he was the only one I felt really close to, so I was heartbroken.

A few months after, I got a call from my cousin Pam and she asked me for money to help pay her bills. I knew this wasn't for bills; it was for drugs or something, so I told her no. My father would give her money without my aunt knowing. I wasn't going to get involved with that. The next day she called, saying there was something she needed to talk to me about. I hesitated but went to see her anyway. It was not a nice visit. She began by saying, "You know how you felt growing up and you always said you didn't feel like you belonged in this family?" I said, "Yes."

She said, "Do you know that you are adopted and you're really not a part of this family? But we love you like you are, and I want you to know that. We were never supposed to tell you. It was a secret." Then she said she was sorry that she didn't say anything to me sooner. "We were told never to say anything to you or your brothers."

That explained everything. Now I knew why I was treated so badly.

Pam felt bad and said, "I'm sorry you don't have any family but you can use our family tree if you need to."

Like that made it all better? I could feel the anger building up inside of me. All the memories of how they had treated me were coming back with a vengeance. And let's not forget my kissing cousin Roland! They ALL KNEW I was adopted the whole time. The fact that I was Indian made it worse. They had made it very clear to me I was not wanted.

My anger was raging like a fire through dry brush, and I told her. Although I was not going to mean like they had been to me.

Then Pam asked how I felt. How did she think I felt? I told her and everyone else in the room, "You can keep your wonderful family. I'm going to find my own, my real family, my blood family."

From that day on I started my search for my biological family. If they were out there somewhere, I would find them. In 2000, I searched for about three years and found nothing on the internet. I checked into all kinds of website for adoptees, and still nothing. I stopped for three or four years and kept trying to think of what I could do to get some answers. By 2004 I started again and I wasn't going to give up. Maybe there was a little anger pushing me, so that when I did find them, I could rub it in the family's faces.

I was determined to find my birth family but in 2007, I stopped again for about a year. In 2008, I searched with the help of search angels. To my surprise I was given a list of women who had given birth to a female child on August 5, 1964. One of these women was in fact my birthmother. I went through the phone books and tried directory assistance hoping I could find her but this wasn't working out. In 2010, I found a wonderful woman named Cher and she told me she could help me find my birth family. I was ecstatic to hear this! I made a donation to her for her help and time. For me it was very much worth it. Two days later I got an email from Cher, asking me to phone her. I did and was set back that she had found my grandfather. She gave me all the information and she also gave me my niece's phone number. I didn't know what to do at this point. I pondered should I call or not. Would they accept me or not?

I waited a couple of days and called my grandfather. I was fearful and trembling. The phone rang a few times and then a woman answered. I asked if I could speak to George Jeffrey. The woman asked who I was and what I wanted. I told her my name and that I was given up for adoption by Betty Jeffrey after my birth and that I was looking for my birthmother. The phone went quiet and I started hearing little sniffles and then full-out crying. "I am your mother," she said behind all the tears.

Oh my God! I found her. I was so excited and terrified at the same time. My birth mother started in with 20 questions: where do you live, what do you do, do you have brothers and sisters, when can I see you? And she said, "I have been looking for you for so long."

That night I went to see her and it was amazing. We talked about everything. She spoke of my father Travis, everyone called him Skeeter and that he was very loving and caring to everyone. She told me he was a real cowboy in rodeos and rode bulls and broncos. That is what he loved. She told me when they were together, while she was pregnant with me, at that time money wasn't good. "Your dad just got fired from the ranch they were working on. We decided that it wasn't enough money to care for you like it needed to be… Your father used to rub my belly and say 'this is my baby.' He would talk to you."

I was given up right after birth and my mother and father never saw me.

We continued to talk the whole night. We realized that the whole time we were 10 to 20 minutes from each other my entire life. I even went to school with my brothers and sisters. I am accepted. And I am loved. This was a new beginning for me.

The next thing on my list was my father's side of the family. I had been given my niece's phone number and I called the next day only to get her answering machine. I left her a message. Creator was on my side as Lola was in the process of moving and had left her answering machine there to catch any calls. Lola my niece called me back and asked me all sorts of questions. She was very protective of her mother Diane. I told her my story and asked her to give my information to her mother, who is my sister. I waited for what seemed like forever and finally about a week later, I got a phone call from my sister Diane. She asked for information about our father to see if I was on the up-and-up. She finally let her guard down and we began to speak about our family. She was so caring and accepting, I couldn't believe this. What a great feeling to have all these new family members that didn't even know me, but they accepted me by only the conversation. This was real family.

I went to Las Vegas to visit her on a whim. She was wonderful and so loving, I felt like I belonged. This was going to be an exciting new adventure. The thought of me with real blood relations was incredible but I didn't know just how incredible it really was going to be.

We sat down and Diane began to tell me about my family, who I was and who I should have been with at birth. The first thing she said was, "Do you know that you are special? You are from a long line of medicine women. You have special gifts which make you so different than others."

I told her how growing up I was always interested in animals, trees, birds and how I felt they could speak to me. I was defiantly different from all the other children I had met growing up. I told her I was never accepted by my family or friends because I was in tune with the world around me. I was called names and shunned by them because of the way I was. I was bullied and beat up for being different.

Diane said, "You are special. Little sister, you are home now from your long journey. You no longer need the white man's world to be happy. You are with us now and you have a lot to learn and a lot I need to teach you."

My sister told me about our father Travis Milton Ellis, that he was Cherokee and how our grandparents were full Cherokee.

"You are from a long line of special people who have been around for centuries. Your ancestors were with you this whole time and you didn't know it. You will learn who you are and who you were born to be," she told me.

I found even more information about my family: I am Cherokee, half-blood from the Red Paint and Long Hair Clans. I am the third-great-granddaughter of Chief John Bold Hunter Bowles or Chief Duwali. He was murdered in the Battle of Neches on July 16, 1839 with his long-time friend Sam Houston, who became the first president of Texas. Before his death, he was named Chief of the Cherokee People, after the death of Chief Dragging Canoe in 1792. This was in Running Water, Tennessee, at Muscle Shoals. I am so very proud to be his great-great-granddaughter.

As times goes on, in 2014, I've found the rest of my father's family. They are accepting of me. We keep in contact by way of the internet. My sister Diane and I keep in contact always. I still have a lot to learn.

I have found a group of Cherokee where I live now in Riverside, CA. They are the Cherokee Chapter Inland Empire. I am accepted. I am loved. I am Cherokee. I am learning my language, my nation's ways. And I am involved with my Native sisters and in the process of getting my original birth certificate so that I may enroll in my nation.

It has been a long bumpy road for me but now I excel. I am now in a world where I am accepted to live my life on the Red Road like I should have been years ago. I am so blessed the Creator stepped into my life to get me where I need to be. This Lost Child or Split Feather is now home with her people. My Split Feather is mending every day. My journey has ended. I am no longer ridiculed for who I am or how I am. I am no longer lost. I am home.

I am Thayla Cherokee and so very proud of it. I want others to know that no matter how long it takes, you will return home to the Red Road.

It was a long 14 years of frustration and tears, some happy, some sad, but I am whole again and a new page of my life has begun.

Dohiya, love and blessings.

18

I am Cynthia with Two Birth Certificates

CYNTHIA LAMMERS (Lakota)

Cynthia (1970)

My adoptive name is Cynthia. I was born in Pine Ridge, South Dakota on February 10, 1966. I was taken from my mother Amy Standing Soldier, a member of the Rosebud Sioux Tribe, when I was nine months old and put up for adoption at the Nebraska Children's Home in Omaha. I don't know much about my father. I have the name George Scott and notes my mother wrote that he was a landscaper/tree cutter. I was placed with a loving middle class Caucasian family who lived in Nebraska and I don't recall being told I was adopted. However, as I looked at my family as I grew up, I was clearly different. I had black hair, dark brown eyes and skin. I had two older siblings also adopted, but they had light-colored hair, skin and eyes, just like our parents. I enjoyed summer family vacations. I loved camping and fishing with my family on the weekends, spending time on my grandparent's farm and doing the usual things a kid does growing up. I felt there was something missing in my life as I grew up, but I wasn't able to figure out what that was.

As I was preparing to graduate from high school, I was interested in going to college to be a veterinarian. I loved animals and I had many pets of my own, not to mention I was forever bringing home hurt or stray animals that I would nurse back to health or find them a home, if I didn't keep them myself. After my parents and I visited a college in Kansas, we began discussing the cost of tuition, etc.... My parents told me they had heard that because I was a Native American, that there could possibly be assistance for me to go to college that I would need to get enrolled in my tribe. My parents also mentioned that if I wanted to know more about my biological family they would help me and support me, however, I was not interested in doing so at that time. So we wrote the Children's home in 1983 to inquire about how I could get enrolled in my tribe and that was when I began to receive different stories about my mother and the stories kept changing over the next 20+ years. I was told I was born on the Pine Ridge Reservation, then later the Rosebud Reservation. I was told my mother was an alcoholic and she could not take care of me so that is why I was taken from her that I was better off without her. There were many stories, many lies. I felt resistance from my parents, even though they said they would support me in finding out about my biological family history. I felt very confused and hurt, so I stopped asking questions.

I began trying to get enrolled in my tribe again the summer of 2003 when I lived in Santa Fe, New Mexico. I received a letter from my case worker at the Children's Home that started something like this, "Are you sitting down? I have been working with two men who would also like to get enrolled in their tribe and noticed on your birth certificates that you have the same Mother. You have two older brothers in Indiana!" She also mentioned that she told my older brothers about me and that they wanted to get to know me. I asked my caseworker if I was her daughter, how would she tell her to proceed with contacting her newly found older brothers? She told me to be cautious. So I told her that they could write me a letter and send it to her and she could forward their letters on to me. I never received any letters from my brothers.

She enclosed a notarized copy of a South Dakota birth certificate and mentioned she was not supposed to do that. Now suddenly I had two birth certificates. The one from Nebraska that had my adoptive name, Cynthia and adoptive parents name and a second birth certificate that had a totally different name for me, Sherry Kay Scott and different parents, Amy Standing Soldier-Mother and George Scott-Father, it stated at the time of my birth that there were two siblings. I did the math and figured out my mother was about 20 years old at the time of my birth. I figured there was a good possibility that I had younger siblings as well. Where were they? How would I ever find them?

I returned to Nebraska in 2011 to help with my adoptive mother who had many health problems and lived with my friend's family, the father also had health problems. I wanted to start my search again. I contacted my case worker, she told me I had to write a letter to my birth mother, explaining why I wanted to know her. Why did the Children's home or the State of Nebraska need to know why I wanted to know my mother, or were they going to give the letter to her? More hoops, but I went ahead and wrote the letter and sent it in. Then I had to do some legal paperwork for the State of Nebraska and pay $15 to have it processed. A few weeks later I received a phone call from my case worker, telling me to come to Omaha on a certain date, that I was not to come alone, to have a friend or family member come with me. My best friend Susan Grove went with me to Omaha. We had no idea where or why we were going and what was about to happen? Was I finally going to meet my birth mother? We arrived at the address that I was given at the time they told us to be there. We were at a College Campus, in a classroom, filled with about 50-60 people, sitting at round tables with 6-8 people at each table. We ate lunch. Then a Native American man started the meeting with a prayer. Then several different Native men and woman got up to speak, each one telling a story about their lives. The strange thing was, almost every story was almost the same about how they grew up and who they grew up with. Native people growing up in white families. We were all adopted. We all had alcoholic mothers who couldn't take care of us. We all felt lost at some point in our lives and maybe some of us still did. We all had questions about who we really were. What was our Indian Culture or Heritage about, we didn't know. Were we all related? Probably not, I thought to myself. Then suddenly, it hit me, I turned and looked at my caseworker from the Children's Home. She had tears running down her face. I said to her, "You have been lying to me all these years, haven't you?" She began to cry. I began to cry. Once I got myself back together, I told her it probably wasn't her fault, that she was just doing her job. She'd been telling me what she was told to tell me.

I was given hand-outs to take home and read. One hand-out was "The Split Feather Study." This summarized case studies of how Native American children were affected by being raised in a culture other than their own. I had another handout that told me about how our government took Native American Children from their mothers, mothers who may or may not have done anything wrong to have their children taken from them. The government wanted to "Americanize" us. How could this be, I asked myself. I was in shock. Did my adoptive parents know this? Had they been lying to me all these years too? I was crushed, not sure who to believe, who I could trust.

I took the paperwork to my parents, the only parents I knew and deeply loved. The only parents who put up with me and all my foolish behaviors and sometimes self-destructive behaviors. My mother responded by telling me this could not be true, that my mother was an alcoholic who couldn't take care of me. They wanted to give me a better life, and not to believe this. I told her I understood that they wanted to do a good thing and give me a better life. A better life and more opportunities that I would have never had growing up on a reservation. I loved them for doing that for me. My mother refused to discuss or believe anything I was told or given to read that day. We did not talk about it again. Every once in a while I would find more articles about this on the internet and I would send it to her and my older sister. One day my sister called me and asked me why I was doing this to our parents. Why did I want to hurt them? I told her I didn't, that I wanted to share with them what I was being told or finding out about what happened to me. I felt now more than ever that I needed to find my biological mother. If this was true, maybe she wanted to know me. It wasn't fair to her, me being taken from her as a baby, maybe she didn't do anything wrong, maybe there was no legitimate reason to take me from her. It wasn't fair.

Later I found an article on the internet about author Trace DeMeyer and her book "ONE SMALL SACRIFICE." Her story is similar to mine as well. I emailed Trace and she sent me a copy of her new book, "TWO WORLDS: LOST CHILDREN OF THE INDIAN ADOPTION PROJECTS" and from that day on, she became a supportive friend. Answering questions I had, then she gave me the name of a genealogist, Sandy White Hawk, who she thought might be able to help me find my biological mother. I tried to contact her, but didn't have any luck in speaking with her.

A couple of months later I received a letter in the mail from my caseworker. It had a picture of my mother with a poem next to it. It was my birthmother's, Amy Standing-Soldier-Busch's obituary. The first picture I had of my mother and she had passed away. I looked at the date of the obituary and it was dated October 13, 2001. I was furious and hurt. All these years, all these hoops the Children's Home and the State of Nebraska made me go through, only to send me this. My hopes and dreams of ever getting to meet my biological mother was crushed, and my search was over. The many questions I wanted to know, now I would probably never get the answers. It wasn't fair. How could they make me do all they had me do just to send me this?

I called my adoptive mother, telling her the news of Amy's death, crying so hard I could hardly speak. Her response wasn't what I expected or what I wanted to hear. I responded to her by saying mean things I didn't mean and hung up on her. I never got to speak to her again, she passed away the next year. Now I have to live with myself and the mean things I never got to apologize for saying and tell her how much I truly loved her. I couldn't bring myself to attend her funeral. Now totally estranged from the only family I knew, I had to move. I had to get away from all the pain and rejection I was feeling. I moved over 800 miles away from the only family I knew and my friends. I went to work in a city where I didn't know anyone.

After nearly a year of diving into my new job, trying not to think about my life, I began to become depressed. Not able to continue to work anymore, unable to run from my feelings, I contacted Trace again by email. I updated her on my desperate situation, telling her I wasn't sure how I could continue. Unemployed, nearly broke, facing the fact I may soon be homeless and I had no family to turn too, I was truly alone, ready to give up. Trace didn't realize I hadn't contacted the genealogist she had previously referred to me and that I had not located my biological mother. She suggested finding my siblings and maybe this could help me in many ways. I agreed, not knowing what else to do. She gave my information to reach Karen Vigneault, a genealogist she was now working with, who was able to provide me with vital information that I needed. I also found a group on Yahoo called "Soaring Angels," a group that was dedicated to helping adoptees find their families. An angel from that group, Candy Eigenbrod, emailed me information. Part of the information that I received from everyone within 24 hours included the name Jessica. Jessica was the daughter of my oldest brother, she had been trying to locate all the sibling's for her father.

It was time. The time had finally come that everything came together in just over 24 hours. I had the names of my siblings. I had five brothers! Two older brothers, John and Jeff Moss, who were adopted, and lived in Indiana and 2 younger brothers, Johnny and David Blankenship, who were put in foster care in Nebraska and the youngest brother, Earl Soden. I will never have the privilege to meet him and I have little information about him. He committed suicide at the approximate age of 22 years old.

As of June, 2014, I have had the pleasure to meet Johnny Blankenship and talk with David Blankenship. I am in contact with my niece, John Moss's daughter, J. Kathryn Casey often. I look forward to meeting everyone and I would like to make Amy Standing Soldiers-Busch, our mother's wish come true...have all of her children together. I would also like to find my biological father, George Scott. I would also like more information about our youngest brother, Earl Soden.

19

Wolf Clan

JESSE STONEFIELD (Cherokee)

Jesse

I was adopted shortly after birth. My mother, Tracy Stonefield, was only 19-years-old when I was born and my father, Chris Ward, had bailed on her as soon as he found out she was pregnant. In fact, she lied and told him she was going to get an abortion, so he went to his grave back in August of 2009 never knowing I even existed. My biological mom's family is Irish and Scottish and my biological dad's family is Irish, Scottish, mixed Native American, English, African American, and Dutch.

However, I never knew really anything about my heritage until my earl 'teens. Although my adoptive parents were open about the fact that I was adopted, I feel like they always wanted me to identify with their respective ethnic backgrounds. When pressed about what I actually was, my adoptive mom went so far as to say I "looked Czech" (whatever that means) when I was little. Not knowing my real ethnicity—beyond Caucasian—was something I struggled with a lot growing up.

It wasn't until middle school that I found out what I was on the Stonefield side. I was working on a kinship project for one of my classes and I insisted to my adoptive mom that I wanted to figure out what my biological heritage was. Obliging me, she called up Tracy's mom and made me wait outside the room with the door closed until she came out to report back to me about what she learned. It turned out that Stonefield was a made-up name my ancestors took after fleeing Ireland to Scotland.

"Stonefield" was the place in Argyll, Scotland where they settled and they took that name to avoid persecution at the hands of the traditionally Irish-hating Scots. *Braveheart*, despite its historical inaccuracies, has always been one of my all-time favorite movies, so now I had something to be proud of. However, Chris Ward remained a mystery.

Despite the resentment I held in my heart toward my biological father for abandoning my mom and me, I still had an interest in learning about his family. As a teenager I committed hours of my time after school to researching the Wards. I had very little to go on, but I was able to find out that they came from all over the British Isles and most significantly of all to me, they were also Cherokee, among other tribes. I was stoked. Not only did I fit in a little better—at least ethnically—with my mostly Latino friends, but I wasn't "just another white guy" anymore. At the same time, though, it kind of threw me off in terms of how I related to my primarily white adoptive family. As an angst-ridden adolescent I had in a lot of ways estranged myself from them and I feel that this revelation made me drift away even more. Then something happened when I was 17 that changed my life permanently.

I was hanging out with my friend Joey and I happened to mention that I was part Native American. Jokingly, he told me that one of his buddies at high school was also Native American and looked just like me. He introduced me to Eddie Dang and after less than five minutes of talking we discovered that we're cousins. The funny thing is, Eddie had auditioned to be the drummer for a metal band I was in back in high school. I remember walking into the burger joint that my band hung out at and seeing this guy sitting there talking with my bandmates. There was something about this guy I couldn't put my finger on and we just kind of glared at each other—clearly, he felt the same way about me.

Anyway, Eddie introduced me to the rest of the family. I learned that I'm Wolf Clan Cherokee and that ours was a historically prominent family within the Cherokee Nation. The Wards, the Vanns, and the Ross's were renowned chiefs and warriors. Principal Chief John Ross led the Cherokee Nation through the innumerable trials and tribulations of the horrific genocidal Trail of Tears. Eddie's grandfather told me a story of how in the early years of the 20th century, one of our family members, Rufus Rowe, drove the first getaway car (at a time when horses and even people, for that matter, could easily outrun cars) for infamous Cherokee bank robber Henry Starr. These little anecdotes don't even begin to scratch the surface, believe me, but the rest of those many stories are for another time.

The close bond I've developed over the years with my long-lost cousin, coupled with our incredible ancestry, has made me proud to be who I am. Having grown and matured since my teenage years, I've managed to square my adoption with myself in a lot of ways. My relationship with my adoptive parents has improved and even though I don't speak with my biological mom (or rather, she won't speak to me), I love her very much. After I found out that my biological dad died, I eventually got in touch with his half-sister and her husband and we've developed a great relationship. Although I do have mixed feelings about him, I no longer hate Chris Ward—a fair amount of that hate having been impressed on me by Tracy's bitterness toward him, anyway.

Yes, I'm adopted. Yes, I'm Native American, but, as cheesy as it sounds, most of all I'm just me.

20

Lost Bird Jefferson

KAREN ANN (Wounded Cougar) JEFFERSON (Choctaw)

I have written my story as well as I can remember it. Writing is a small part of the healing process for me. But I also write this story for my children, their children, and their children. I believe it is very important to know who we truly are, and where we came from.

When I was around five years old, my adoptive parents told me I was Cherokee Indian and Irish mixed blood, and that I was adopted. I have since discovered that I have more Choctaw Indian blood than anything. This was a very pleasant and exciting discovery for me.

But my adoptive parents were not Choctaw, Cherokee, nor any other Indian Nation and were not able to tell me anything at all about my Indian heritage or Culture. I have spent most of the past forty years learning of Indian Cultures in general. I will never learn it all. There is too much to learn, to know, and to understand. In this sense, I have been robbed of my life by the United States Government, Department of Welfare Social Services, who took me from my Indian mother and placed me in a white home to be adopted.

This process is called "assimilation," an attempt to "kill the Indian, save the man." What they apparently do not realize is that being Indian has very little to do with the outside. Being Indian is very much on the inside. It is in our hearts, our minds, and our spirits. Being Indian is who we are, no matter if we physically live in a tipi, a wood house, or a mansion. I heard an elder Cherokee man put it this way, "Our Spirits don't speak English." Most non-Indians won't have a clue of what that means. We Indians understand it completely.

When the U.S. Government was relocating our People, the Oklahoma Choctaws and Cherokees, from their homes, my family ended up in the Sacramento, California area. They were also removing Indian children from their homes and placing them into white homes to be adopted. This is not only an attempt at assimilation; it is a form of genocide. When a child grows up around only non-Indians, they are very likely to marry and breed with non-Indians. It's an effective way to end the different Indian Nations.

I am first and foremost Indian. I am Choctaw. I am Cherokee. My other blood is not important to me as a person. I am very proud of my Indian heritage. My great-grandfather on my mother's side was a full-blood Choctaw. He lived from 1836 to 1898. In the American Civil War, he fought on the side of the Confederates. His Regiment was the 1 Choctaw and Chickasaw Mounted Rifles, CSA. His rank was a Private.

His father was Hon-a-tubee, and his mother was Hata-hynah. There is a town called Hontubby in Oklahoma that carries his name. Many of my relatives are buried there.

On my maternal grandmother's side, I have some ancestors who were Cherokee Chiefs. One of them was Little Carpenter, or Okoonakullakulla, a Peace Chief of the Cherokees. Little Carpenter was born in 1699 and died in 1797. He was of the Wolf Clan.

Another Maternal Ancestor was the great War Chief of the Cherokee, activist and spokesman, Tsiyu Gansini, or Dragging Canoe of the Paint Clan. He was born in 1730 in Tennessee and died in Lookout Town in Chattanooga, Tennessee in 1792.

Today I walk the Red Road and I am very proud of my Indian Heritage. It is my hope that my children, their children, and their children will also be proud. This is their story, too.

Indian Country, Kansas, 2013

How does one write about a lifetime of being separated from their People, about a lost identity, about not having all the necessary pieces of one's own life? Mere words are not enough, but I will do my best.

I was born on November 2, 1950 in Sacramento, California. My birth mother was a 17 year old Choctaw/Cherokee girl named Charlotte Louise Jefferson. The United States Government had relocated her family from their home in Clayton, Oklahoma to California by the time I arrived. The Social Services of the Welfare Department also convinced my mother to put me up for adoption, which she did.

I have no good thoughts about this. My identity, my family, my culture, and my heritage were stolen from me because of being adopted into a non-Indian home. I have lived a lifetime of feeling like a fish out of water, of not truly belonging anywhere, of not fitting in. Many people claim that our Indian-ness is not in our DNA memory. I completely disagree with that opinion. My DNA is definitely Indian!

The couple who adopted me was a young Air Force Major, Donn and his wife, Evelyne. Donn was born and raised in the Shreveport, Louisiana area of the "Old South." Evelyne was a first-generation Danish immigrant from Eldora, Iowa. Evelyne stood just under five feet tall and was a pretty woman. She also had Grand Maul Epilepsy. Donn was a career military man, retiring from the Air Force as a Lt. Colonel.

I was alternately spoiled and abused as a child, which was extremely confusing. I never knew what to expect. But I thought that every household was like that. I thought it was normal. The abuse was very bad. I suffered mental, physical, and sexual abuse, often extreme. I can still vividly remember being called a "heathen," "wild" and a "savage."

I didn't know what those words meant, but by the way they were said, I knew they weren't good. This alone causes me to wonder why they adopted me. It is now too late to ask Donn, who has Alzheimer's disease. I think it's something I will never know.

On the other hand, I was spoiled at times. In fact, when I was around five or six years old, I wanted a big brother. So, Donn and Evelyne took me to an orphanage and told me to "pick one out," which is what I did. The boy's name was Richard. The reason I chose him was because he was unlike anyone I had seen before. Richard had pale blue eyes, and hair so blonde it was nearly white. We took Richard home for a "trial run," and he became the newest member of the family.

Turns out Richard didn't want a little sister hanging around, so I was left alone with Evelyne while Donn was at work. Those times were usually bad when she was drinking. Evelyne drank a lot, often. She and I would get into physical fights, and then I would get a severe beating when Donn got home and saw the destruction. But Donn wanted me to "take care" of Evelyne when he was gone. Our roles were reversed to a degree. Well, more than a degree, hence the sexual abuse. How I hated my childhood!

Then came that horrible day! I came home one afternoon from playing in the woods behind our house and it scared me because Donn was home. It was too early for him to be home, plus there was a big black car in our driveway. And to top it off, the police were there. Donn came outside and I could see he had been crying. He would not let me go inside. Then he told me that Evelyne had died. I am still not clear as to her cause of death. Some say she strangled on her tongue during a seizure. Others say it was a combination of her phenobarbital medication and alcohol.

Earlier that day Evelyne and I had another of our fights and I screamed at her, "I hope you die, you bitch!" Then I took my dog and ran into the safety of the woods. It was because of this that I honestly believed I had killed Evelyne by wishing her dead. I was ten years old and it was a childish thing. Children don't know any better.

Donn kept Richard with him in Virginia, which is where we lived at that time. He sent me to stay with his parents in Shreveport, Louisiana while he sold our house. Around two weeks after I arrived, Donn's mother and I were alone together in her house when she took a loaded gun into the bathroom and shot herself in the head. That was when I began sleep-walking. It was also then that I began to seriously believe there was something very wrong with me. People were starting to drop like flies everywhere I went.

I next went to live with Donn's sister, Nelwyn and her family, out in the country in Louisiana. Her husband, Fred, was a farmer. They had a girl named Lydia, who was Richard's age. Their son John was my age. It was okay there until John tried to get into my pants. I didn't like that one bit! But I was too afraid to say anything. Being considered a "savage" and a "natural born liar" will do that to a child. It will cause deep and permanent harm. Harm that does not heal.

As I said, our home was full of extremes. Such extremes can result in severe emotional and mental problems in any child. In my case, I developed a dissociative disorder which manifests in MPD, or Multiple Personality Disorder. I also have PTSD (Post Traumatic Stress Disorder), plus Bi-Polar disorder and Panic Attacks.

I was very shy and fearful of people. Many times I hid behind Evelyne's full skirts, especially around strangers. But my precious animal friends were always there for me. They never let me down, abused me, or called me names. They never told me I was ugly when I cried. Instead, they licked the tears from my face. They never treated me with anything but pure love and acceptance.

Donn and Evelyne used to have parties when I was a child. The adults would be drinking alcohol, of course. I remember going around the room "sipping" their drinks, which they thought was cute. I will never forget the feeling of euphoria from the alcohol. Suddenly everything was okay. In fact, that feeling was so good that I wanted to keep feeling that way! I believe that is when I became alcoholic.

After Evelyne died and was buried, Donn chose a hardship retirement from the Air Force and bought a modest house in the small town of Benton, Louisiana. It was the summer of 1961 and I was soon to enter the fifth grade of school. Donn had hired several housekeepers, but none stayed long due to my anger issues. Then he hired an older woman named Mrs. McAuliffe who was to remain our live-in housekeeper. She and I had our share of run-ins, but she was able to deal with my anger. I liked her, and we remained in contact after she left us.

Then, when I was around twelve or thirteen, Donn met a woman named Margaret Nell. Donn approached me one day and asked me how I would feel about his getting married again. I was a very sick child. I can remember thinking that Evelyne was going to come back from the dead to live with us again. Of course I said "yes!" It never occurred to me that Donn was speaking of Margaret Nell! When they were married and she moved in to our house I was very angry and jealous. I blamed Margaret Nell for preventing Evelyne's return. I did not like this new woman one bit nor did I want her there, and I let her and everyone else know it. In fact, I attacked her one day. I threw her to the ground, got on top of her, and beat her with my fists in a rage. Then I ran away on my bicycle and stayed gone for several hours. But I knew I had to go back home and face the music. I was severely beaten for my actions.

I was beaten quite often. Donn had quite a temper himself. His weapons of choice were his leather belt or a willow tree switch. I can remember having to wear long skirts to school in order to hide the cuts and welts on my body. This was when mini-skirts were popular, and dressing differently than my classmates was very embarrassing to me.

It was about that time that I began drinking alcohol in earnest. Donn kept a well-stocked bar in the house. I would take alcohol out of the bottle and replace it with tap water. I don't know if Donn realized what I was doing, but he never said anything about his weak liquor.

I also started sneaking out at night. I would wait until everyone was asleep, then I would slip out my bedroom window. I would usually meet with other school friends who were also out drinking. Then I would sneak back in through the window, fall into bed, and pass out. No wonder it was so hard to get me up in the mornings for school!

However, I loved school. Being in school got me away from home all day. I was a loner, but quite often some of my classmates would come to me and share their problems with me during recess. I had no wisdom to give, but I was a good listener and gave them my full attention. Being there for them also helped me feel better about myself.

I was in the Pep Squad, which I enjoyed. It was fun riding to out of town games on the school bus. And I made some of the hoops our football team ran through. I also attempted playing violin, clarinet, and piano. I enjoyed being in Debate, and I love playing Chess. I've been a member of Mensa for over twenty-five years. I am a very artistic and creative person; I love the gifts the Creator has blessed me with. He has been so very good to me!

In 1969 I wore my cap and gown and graduated on the Honor Roll. I'm sure people thought my tears were of joy, but they were of sorrow. I truly did not want high school to end. So, I immediately went to summer semester of college at Louisiana Tech in Ruston, Louisiana. Even though I was enrolled as an Art Major, my true major was Party 101, and did I party! I hardly ever went to classes. Instead, I partied myself right out of college.

Enlisting in the Navy seemed to be the next logical step. But a trip out to the West Coast was first. I went to visit Evelyne's sister, Dine, out in La Mirada, California. She and I worked together in her hat factory during the week days. Then we'd go back to her house and drink. Every day. I began using Aunt Dine's car, staying gone long hours, and running wild. My vacation in California didn't last long.

It was then that I enlisted in the Navy WAVES. I really liked being in the service. I had only a couple of days until graduation when I started feeling very sick. In fact, I thought I had the flu. I went to the doctor on base who informed me my "flu" would last another seven and a half months. I was pregnant. It had to have happened right before I entered basic training.

The Navy issued me an honorable medical discharge and sent me back to Louisiana. Donn and Margaret Nell met my plane at the airport and got me a motel room instead of taking me back to their house. Then they started talking about abortion. Well, there was no way I was going to kill my baby, so when they left, I left too.

A couple of weeks later I caught a ride up to Boulder, Colorado. Those Rocky Mountains spoke to my very spirit. And Boulder was full of rock and roll, drugs, peace, love, and Hippies. I was in my element! I found a commune to live in and wait for the birth of my child.

On a beautiful August night in 1970 I caught a ride to an outdoor concert up in the mountains out of Boulder. I had been sitting on the ground and when I stood up I heard someone behind me say, "Look at all the blood!" I wondered who they were talking about until I looked down at myself. I was covered in blood!

I managed to find a ride into town and my friend Laurie stayed with me for the next 24 hours I was in labor. Then she took me to the hospital. Laurie was allowed to sit with me in the Labor Room for a couple of hours. When she left I was alone in the Labor Room. Even though I yelled for someone to come and help, no one did. I gave birth to my son, Johnathan Michael, all by myself. He was born alive. I heard him cry, a strong cry.

A nurse hurried in and took my baby away. I never saw him again. They gave me a shot of something and I was about to fall asleep when a lady came in with papers for me to sign. I was told it was a death certificate, but today I believe it was adoption papers. I was moved to an area far away from the maternity ward, and to this day I do not know what happened to my son. John, if you ever read this, please know that I never stopped thinking of you or loving you!

My story is full of gaps due to two major factors: 1) My dissociative disorder, and 2) The massive amounts of alcohol and drugs I was using. Being high was the only way I knew to stop the mental and emotional pain. Drugs and alcohol were an effective way to do that. The side effects, however, were horrible, including several suicide attempts.

Eventually I went to Amarillo, Texas and found a new running buddy. Debbie and I were the same age and we had a lot of fun together. We got into some trouble together, too. In fact, I ended up going to a women's prison. I plead guilty to "possession with intent". My sentence was one year inside, but I was released early on good behavior. I next went back to Shreveport where I met a cute long-haired guy at a party one night. Larry was a Rock-N-Roll drummer, and a good one. It was pretty much the old "love at first sight" for us, and we were together from that night for the next six years. When we met, I was twenty-four, and Larry was sixteen.

In our second year together I saw a commercial on television about something called "Alcoholics Anonymous." I had never heard of A.A. before, but the commercial said it could help. I called the telephone number on the screen. Two women arrived at our motel room, spoke with me a short while, then took me to my first A.A. meeting. I was fairly drunk when I went, and I don't remember much of the meeting. But I do remember how angry Larry was when I got back!

I attended A.A. off and on for several years. I had also started going to Narcotics Anonymous meetings and seeing a substance-abuse counselor. David was very patient, loving, and encouraging. It was David who helped me see that I could not give recovery an honest shot while I was still living with and around drugs and alcohol. I had to make some hard choices.

When I told Larry I was giving him up for recovery he cried and I cried. It felt as if my heart was being ripped out of my chest, it hurt so badly! But I didn't want to die from addiction, which is what I had come very close to doing several times.

On the 8th of August in 1983 I was sharing an apartment in Shreveport with my long-time friend and running buddy, Helen. We had been partying together for about two weeks, drinking the same things, and using the same kinds of drugs. One morning Helen woke up not feeling well, so I left for a while so she could sleep and try to feel better. I went to a park to hang out with some friends and get high. Later, as I was walking past our place on my way to a convenience store, her boyfriend saw me and yelled "Come here! Now!" He was very agitated and upset. And then he said the words I will never forget, "Helen just died!" I asked him to repeat that because I was sure I hadn't heard him right. But he said the same thing again.

Helen didn't look sick at all. She looked normal to me, but she was dead. Her liver had stopped working and it killed her. Of course, this was a direct result of all the drugs and alcohol we had been using. Helen was only 28 years old when she died.

I did not know what to do. I felt totally lost and alone without my best friend. I know I went to her funeral, in a borrowed dress, but I don't remember most of that entire August. My drinking friends made sure I never ran out of booze.

Then in late 1984 I was still deep into drinking and drugging when an old biker friend started coming over to visit. Butch was one year clean and sober, and was intent on seeing me that way too. I finally agreed to go to an N.A. meeting with him on the night of 2 January, 1985. I don't remember much of that night, but I do remember a guy named Matt telling me they were glad to see me and to come back. Not many people had ever told me that, and it really made an impression on me. I kept going back.

In fact, I did not use any drugs or alcohol for the next eight years after that. I went into a five day detox center and stayed for nine days because I was in such bad shape.

When I got out, I went to around 280 meetings during the next three months, and then at least one a day for several years.

Eventually I met a man named Jon. Jon was a very angry and abusive person, as I was to discover too late. He was so nice to me before I married him, but that all changed immediately after our wedding. In fact, on our wedding night he told me "I hate you!" and proved it. I honestly don't know why I stayed with him for those eight horrible years. I was drunk, high, or both for some of that time, but I was clean during most of that nightmare, and am still clean and sober today.

During the final chapter of our marriage, we lived in "Indian Country." In fact, I still live in that small Kansas town, not far from Wichita. The "Mid America All Indian Center" in Wichita is where I sell most of the bead Medicine Bags I make. I go to Powwows when I can, and I really enjoy being around other Indians. It is good for my Spirit.

I have a photocopy of some of the legal paperwork from my adoption. It gives my birth mother's name, her place of birth, and the fact that I have a brother named Jerry who is one year older than me. It reveals almost nothing of my natural father except a few facts. Apparently he was 24 years old, stood 6 feet 11 inches, had brown eyes, black hair, and was dark of complexion.

I searched for many years, looking for my mother and other family members. Then in July of 2013, one of my Facebook friends, Wayne, began posting items of interest to me. His posts concerned the "Lost Birds" and his own experiences. Through Wayne, I contacted a woman named Trace DeMeyer who suggested a "Yahoo!" group called "Soaring Angels". I eagerly joined that group and posted the information I had available to me. Less than a week later, one of the members replied with some information for me that she had found on a website called Ancestry.com. My heart was racing and I could barely breathe! This was the answer to my life-long search at last! Not just my hands, but my entire body was trembling as I got online and went to Ancestry.com. I opened an account there, punched in a search for Charlotte Louise Jefferson, and there she was! There was even a picture of my mother when she was around fifteen years old! I was so excited and happy I began to cry! In fact, so many feelings washed over me at once that for several days I didn't know exactly what it was I was feeling. Joy, hope, love, excitement, anger, fear… so many thoughts and feelings hit me all at once. I cried many tears for many days.

The person who had posted the picture of my mother was the daughter of my brother, Jerry. She and I sent a couple of messages to each other, but I got the definite impression that she was not pleased to hear from me. In fact, she told me that Charlotte was not a good mother and that I should consider myself lucky to have been adopted! I have not responded to her since then.

Unfortunately, I discovered that my mother crossed-over in 1991 and my brother passed in 2006. Both of their graves are in the Memorial Cemetery in

Charlotte Louise Jefferson

Heavener, Oklahoma, and it is my hope to be able to go visit them before I leave this planet. I will probably not be able to afford a burial plot in Heavener, but it is my desire to be cremated and my ashes sprinkled over my mother's grave. In this way, we will be together at last. We should never have been separated in the first place. The United States Government, in my opinion, hates and fears all American Indians, and wants to end our Race. They should be required to be held accountable for all the harm, damage, and destruction they have done against all Indian Nations. But, as Jesus said when He hung on His cross, "Father, forgive them, for they know not what they do". Yes, I do my best to forgive, but I will never forget! I do not want my children, their children, or their children to forget, either.

I pray that all "Lost Birds" are successful in their search to find out who they are and where they came from. This is a Human Right that should never be denied to anyone, ever. So, all of you "Lost Birds," keep looking and do not give up! To encourage you, remember this message from a great Indian Chief and Holy Man:

Sitting Bull stated shortly before his death that if a man loses something and goes back to look carefully for it, he will find it.

I finally found mine, may you also find yours!

21

Baby V

TRACE A DEMEYER (co-editor)

From left: Claire Chung, 3L, Supreme Court Advocacy Clinic, Yale Law School; Joel West Williams, Staff Attorney, Native American Rights Fund; Jacqueline Pata, Executive Director, National Congress of American Indians. Introducing them is Sparky Abraham, 3L, Yale Law School (moderator). The lecture hall was filled to capacity with law students. (Photo by Trace A DeMeyer)

Baby Veronica case discussed at Yale

On Feb. 21, 2014 at Yale Law School in Connecticut, an expert panel (above) said that the adoptive couple, Matt and Melanie Capobianco, won this legal case in the media **first** which paved the way to their winning permanent custody of Veronica Brown in rulings handed down by the Supreme Court and the South Carolina Supreme Court. Despite 17 total amicus briefs, written support by 393 tribes, 600 groups interested in this case including some adoption agencies, and 19 State's Attorneys Generals in support of Dusten Brown keeping his own daughter, the Supreme Court did not and **does not** rule in favor of Indians. American Indians don't win in public opinion polls either.

Tribes are actually discouraged from taking cases to the Supreme Court: Out of nine Indian Law cases, only one won in the Roberts/Alito-controlled Supreme Court.

Asked whether the Indian Child Welfare Act should be amended or made stronger—Jackie Pata said no. Pata admitted that NCAI and NARF waited too long to respond in the media to the Baby Veronica media circus, though they tried to rally support for Dusten and met in weekly committees to discuss the case and did try their own media coverage. (Too little, too late.) Pata said by the time the Dr. Phil show happened with the Capobiancos, Dusten Brown had a gag order placed on him and he was not able to respond or play the same media game as the Capobiancos did.

In the Q&A, a man in the audience asked Cherokee citizen and attorney Joel West Williams of NARF, "If the Capobiancos could sue the Cherokee Nation for one million dollars, then why can't the Cherokee Nation sue the Nightlight Adoption Agency for their errors in notifying the Cherokee Nation (with Dusten's name misspelled and the wrong birthdate)?" These details were not insignificant and actually started the nightmare for Dusten Brown and the Cherokee Nation along with the adoption agency's failure to abide by ICWA which is federal law. Williams said he could not comment on any pending lawsuits.

As I have written on my blog American Indian Adoptees, the Department of Justice needs to interview Christy Maldonado and investigate the Nightlight Adoption Agency for moving and selling children like Veronica across state lines which is in violation of the Interstate Compact.

The way the Capobianco's PR campaign was run by Jessica Munday and Trio Solutions who played this case in the media, capitalizing on Social Media with the Save Veronica Facebook page, filling mainstream newspaper opinion pieces with sympathy for the infertile Capobiancos in their late 30s, to demonizing Dusten Brown for text messages to his ex-fiance, then confusing the public and essentially attacking anyone who supported Dusten Brown retaining custody of his own daughter, this case was doomed from the beginning.

Dangerous Times

There is a clear and present danger that this will happen again—I say this because the American public (and Supreme Court) is clearly anti-Indian until a white couple wishes to purchase a newborn baby and the only ones available are from Indian reservations. To be safe, NCAI, NICWA and NARF are obviously trying to educate on the Indian Child Welfare Act of 1978 since the Baby Veronica case created such a nationwide stir.

Sitting in the hallowed halls of Yale Law School, there weren't any surprises for me unless you count how these panelists didn't use the time to discuss the genocide that actually occurred prior the passing of the Indian Child Welfare Act of 1978 and the child abductions by social workers and missionaries—nor did they mention human trafficking and the Nightlight Adoption Agency dealings with Maldonado, the birthmother. They did mention Indian boarding schools.

So, I was truly upset. From what I heard, it appears American Indians are eons behind in civil rights and we can't seem to win a case in the Supreme Court. I'd heard that warning years prior but this time at Yale was a bit more in my face. This case was about adoption by non-Indians, something I lived myself.

We had Justice Alito writing an opinion that Veronica is 1.2% Indian. NARF attorney Joel West Williams asked the Yale audience, "Who in America is 1/16 or 3/256th anything?" Yet we have a judge issuing his opinion by measuring an Indian for their Indian-ness which equates to measuring a child's blood? That is still happening? What century is this?

- JUSTICE ALITO delivered the opinion of the Court:

This case is about a little girl (Baby Girl) who is classified as an Indian because she is 1.2% (3/256) Cherokee. Because Baby Girl is classified in this way, the South Carolina Supreme Court held that certain provisions of the federal Indian Child Welfare Act of 1978 required her to be taken, at the age of 27 months, from the only parents she had ever known and handed over to her biological father, who had attempted to relinquish his [**736] parental rights and who had no prior contact with the child. The provisions of the federal statute [*2557] at issue here do not demand this result.

- Jun 25 2013: Judgment REVERSED and case REMANDED. Alito, J., delivered the opinion of the Court, in which Roberts, C. J., and Kennedy, Thomas, and Breyer, JJ., joined. Thomas, J., and Breyer, J., filed concurring opinions. Scalia, J., filed a dissenting opinion. Sotomayor, J., filed a dissenting opinion, in which Ginsburg and Kagan, JJ., joined, and in which Scalia, J., joined in part. Read more at the Scotus blog here [1]

Dusten Brown never had a chance. He went to Iraq knowing the Capobiancos had his daughter but he had to serve a year and a JAG lawyer took his case. The puzzle remains why Maldonado mysteriously breaks up with him and severs all communication. Was she punishing her high school sweetheart Dusten by abandoning his baby or was she manipulated by the adoption agency to take their money?

Then it hit me—keeping America ignorant of Indians, culture, actual history—this all works to take Indian children. Judgment is easy. Third World poverty (which we didn't create) somehow equates to abuse of children. Add their general ignorance of sovereignty and culture, what it means to be Cherokee or Lakota or Navajo or any tribe—and it means you can't win public opinion polls or cases before the Supreme Court?

Ignorance about Indians? Exactly!

It's been going on since colonial contact. Please, let's not call them settlers anymore but invaders. America has always been the Great Divider, building its fences, writing its laws, counting on classism and racism to divide us.

America wins every time when it perpetuates this ignorance of Indians. Do Indians do a good job of educating others about culture, or what's important to us? Not really. We're way behind in any civil rights movement. We've had movies romanticizing us over 100 years and it's hard to kill those "savage" "redskin" stereotypes drilled into all our heads!

What do Americans know about Indians? Nothing. Practically zilch.

America's "taking care" of Indians only works to create HATE among Americans who view us as privileged in some way that they are not. Like why do we even have a law that keeps nice white people from adopting Indian babies? Trust me, ICWA is under attack.

I do know that Indians are way ahead in surviving every broken treaty and then fighting each other over small scraps of power. Some tribes even subscribe to "blood quantum" as if they need to purge their citizen rolls of those who may be too white or too black.

We have Supreme Court Justices using the blood quantum argument and you see that is not entirely their fault (they all went to law school but didn't even have a course on Indian Law at those Ivy League schools) but it tells me—do not go anywhere near them. They are not even aware of their ignorance.

Dusten Brown didn't have a chance, not in that court.

What the panel did say was each and every tribe needs to create and have their own child protection network. I agree since it's pretty evident that you can't trust any non-Indian social worker to go to the reservation and use their mother-father "family unit" example. Only Indians can decide who the right people are to care for its children. That person might be an auntie, grandmother or another relative, depending on who in the tribal family is willing and able.

And the panel said we need more American Indian lawyers who become judges—because the way it is now—Indians can't win.

I attended white schools like most everyone else—really nothing I learned was true or real about Indian culture or history. I learned more sitting at the kitchen table of my friend Ellowyn who is Oglala Lakota, who gave me an education about Indians not written about anywhere. Then there was my one adoptive aunt (a first-born American) who calls me a liar when I told her there were Indian Boarding Schools, and this was right after I visited Haskell in Kansas.

No, Americans are not learning about Indians or the truth of our history.

For many years Vine Deloria and others did try very hard to educate others (with their brilliant books) on the white man's level, even earning degrees in white man's colleges like Yale and Harvard, but it all comes down to this: whites don't really care.

And if we really think about it, this is a very dangerous situation to be in.

FOR MORE INFORMATION:

Kristen Carpenter and Lorie Graham have posted a very compelling and powerful paper about the Supreme Court's decision in Adoptive Couple v. Baby Girl. It is required reading for anyone interested in the case, and is destined to be the definitive paper on the international human rights aspects of the case.

The article is titled Human Rights to Culture, Family, and Self-Determination: The Case of Adoptive Couple v. Baby Girl. Here is the abstract:

The well-being of indigenous children is a subject of major concern for indigenous peoples and human rights advocates alike. In 2013, the U.S. Supreme Court decided in Adoptive Couple v. Baby Girl that the Indian Child Welfare Act did not prevent the adoption of a Cherokee child by a non-Indian couple. This occurred over the objections of her Cherokee biological father, extended family, and Tribal Nation. After the decision, Baby Girl's father and the adoptive couple contested the matter in a number of proceedings, none of which considered the child's best interests as an Indian child. The tribally-appointed attorney for Baby Girl, as well as the National Indian Child Welfare Association and National Congress for American Indians, began examining additional venues for advocacy. Believing that the human rights of Baby Girl, much like those of other similarly situated indigenous children, were being violated in contravention of the United Nations Declaration on Indigenous Peoples Rights, and other instruments of international law, they asked us to bring the matter to the attention of the United Nations Special Rapporteur for Indigenous Peoples Rights ("UNSR"). We prepared a "statement of information" to alert the UNSR of the human rights violations occurring in the case. With the permission of the attorneys and organizations involved, this chapter introduces the Baby Girl case, contextualizes the claims in international human rights law, and then reproduces the statement of information, and portions of the UNSR's subsequent public statement. It concludes with an update on the Baby Girl case and broader discussion about the potential for using international law and legal forums to protect the human rights of indigenous children. [2]

[1] http://www.scotusblog.com/case-files/cases/adoptive-couple-v-baby-girl/

[2] http://papers.ssrn.com/sol3/papers.cfm?abstract_id=2401886

22

The Holocaust Self

LEVI EAGLE FEATHER (Lakota/Dakota)

Levi in Germany

My name is Levi. I am a 56-year-old American Indian man. I was born in 1957 on the Rosebud Sioux Indian reservation in Rosebud South Dakota. I am of Lakota and Dakota heritage: Lakota on my father's side and Lakota/Dakota on my mother's side.

I want to share my thoughts about adoption in western society and how I think it affects us American Indian people. And I explain a bit about how it affected my life and what it is I have been doing about it. To be blunt and upfront, I see adoption in America as being just another part of a large industrial complex that is western society. I base this on the fact that, first and foremost, it is an entity which is controlled and operated within and by a capitalist system where nothing moves without the involvement of money. As it pertains to us American Indians though, I think it is used as a weapon against us, both presently and historically. And as it is used and how it works, it is a weapon of genocide! I also think that its ability to stay active is because its true intent and purpose stays hidden behind an impenetrable ignorance and false, yet unassailable, sense of self-righteousness and entitlement that blinds the majority of hearts and minds in American society!

People in general, but American Indians specifically, need to become aware of this and understand it. Especially for those of you, who like me have gone through the adoption process. We have too many unmet needs, which are tied to the existence of adoption and the adoption process that it is foolhardy not to notice. Realistically though, I don't think an understanding like this is going to be gaining much traction or will be a topic for dinner time conversations anytime soon. Too many panties get bunched up over thoughts like this! It doesn't mean there isn't any truth to it or that I shouldn't try. It never hurts to try. Because if we try, maybe someday our non-American Indian brothers and sisters might begin to see our light, too. Whether they ever come to the table in an open and honest way though, without a neatly pre-approved capitalist agenda leading the way, remains to be seen. I'm not holding my breath! For now though I'm content to work this out with just you guys. Maybe if it turns out to be useful we can start getting our panties out of a bunch over it.

What the heck it's worth a try, isn't it?

For most of the developed world, at least those that politically and socially consider themselves developed, genocide is a crime. Here is what they consider that crime to entail:

> "...the deliberate and systematic destruction, in whole or in part, of an ethnic, racial, religious, or national group" ...... "a legal definition is found in the 1948 United Nations Convention on the Prevention and Punishment of the Crime of Genocide (CPPCG). Article 2 of this convention defines genocide as "any of the following acts committed with intent to destroy, in whole or in part, a national, ethnical, racial or religious group, as such: killing members of the group; causing serious bodily or mental harm to members of the group; deliberately inflicting on the group conditions of life, calculated to bring about its physical destruction in whole or in part; imposing measures intended to prevent births within the group; [and] forcibly transferring children of the group to another group."[1]

The many wars with our people, the boarding school programs, the relocation programs and the American Indian adoption programs all fit within this UN description of genocide.

The president of a group "Genocide Watch," Gregory Stanton, developed a paper called "The 8 Stages of Genocide." Stanton wrote it as a briefing paper in 1996 to be presented to the U.S. State Department shortly after genocide had occurred in Rwanda. You might even remember that situation yourself. Maybe you heard about it on the news or read about it in the paper. It was a very tragic and hard time for a lot of Rwandan people during the summer of 1994 and got quite a bit of attention around the world. In his paper "The 8 stages of Genocide," Stanton said that:

> "Genocide is a process that develops in eight stages that are predictable but not inexorable. At each stage, preventive measures can stop it. The process is not linear. Logically, later stages must be preceded by earlier stages. But all stages continue to operate throughout the process."

The eight stages are:

1. Classification: "All cultures have categories to distinguish people into "us and them" by ethnicity, race, religion, or nationality….."

2. Symbolization: "We give names or other symbols to the classifications….."

3. Dehumanization: "One group denies the humanity of the other group. Members of it are equated with animals, vermin, insects or diseases. Dehumanization overcomes the normal human revulsion against murder. At this stage, hate propaganda in print and on hate radio is used to vilify the victim group. In combating this dehumanization, incitement to genocide should not be confused with protected speech. Genocidal societies lack constitutional protection for countervailing speech, and should be treated differently than democracies. Local and international leaders should condemn the use of hate speech and make it culturally unacceptable. Leaders who incite genocide should be banned from international travel and have their foreign finances frozen. Hate radio stations should be shut down, and hate propaganda banned. Hate crimes and atrocities should be promptly punished."

4. Organization: "Genocide is always organized, usually by the state, often using militias to provide deniability of state responsibility….. Sometimes organization is …. or decentralized….. Special army units or militias are often trained and armed. Plans are made for genocidal killings….."

5. Polarization: "Extremists drive the groups apart. Hate groups broadcast polarizing propaganda. Laws may forbid intermarriage or social interaction. Extremist terrorism targets moderates, intimidating and silencing the center. Moderates from the perpetrators' own group are most able to stop genocide, so are the first to be arrested and killed...."

6. Preparation: Victims are identified and separated out because of their ethnic or religious identity. Death lists are drawn up. Members of victim groups are forced to wear identifying symbols. Their property is expropriated. They are often segregated into ghettos, deported into concentration camps, or confined to a famine-struck region and starved.

7. Extermination: "begins, and quickly becomes the mass killing legally called "genocide." It is "extermination" to the killers because they do not believe their victims to be fully human. When it is sponsored by the state, the armed forces often work with militias to do the killing. Sometimes the genocide results in revenge killings by groups against each other, creating the downward whirlpool-like cycle of bilateral genocide....."

8. Denial: "is the eighth stage that always follows a genocide. It is among the surest indicators of further genocidal massacres. The perpetrators of genocide dig up the mass graves, burn the bodies, try to cover up the evidence and intimidate the witnesses. They deny that they committed any crimes, and often blame what happened on the victims. ...." [2]

There is ample "documented evidence" throughout the official and unofficial recordings of American history which show that genocide as this definition describes it, was and is practiced against us American Indians. And it always started from the top down, too, which normally is the case. For many, and here I refer to Americans in general, it is nearly inconceivable that this could be true. Maybe as a thing of the past but certainly not in today's modern times. How could it be? Well, it's been around a long time, that's why! Normalize it, make it sound like the right thing to do. By changing the narrative, genocide becomes a necessity of conquest, one of the main goals.

Documents recording world history, western history in particular, are full of its accounts. If we are to take anything Gregory Stanton said seriously in his briefing paper to the State Department. Even if the State Dept. chose not to act on it. Is that the whole glorious recorded history of western society's expansion itself, for all intents and purposes, is a very likely sounding first-hand account of genocide in action!

Simply because Americans in general have a very limited knowledge of their own roots and what happened historically to deliver them into westernization. This does not make it impossible, nor implausible, that we might, very well, all be survivors of genocide. Hell, I've heard it said many, many times that violence begets violence. If genocide were a sport, I would be inclined to think that historically maybe it has always been a very ultra-violent sport reserved only for the uber-rich and famous.

If there is any truth to this at all, then institutionalized western religions could very well be considered willing partners as its tools of propaganda. Think about that one for a minute and let it soak in. Like I said, genocide continues to stay active, because its true purpose and intent stays hidden behind an impenetrable ignorance and false, yet unassailable, sense of self-righteousness and entitlement that blinds the majority of hearts and minds in American society!

Dirk Moses, in the conclusion of his critique of Stanton's paper, "Why the Discipline of 'Genocide Studies' Has Difficulty In Explaining How Genocide Ends?" explains it this way:

> "In view of this rather poor record of ending genocide, the question needs to be asked why the "genocide studies" paradigm cannot predict and prevent genocides with any accuracy and reliability. The paradigm of "genocide studies," as currently constituted in North America in particular, has both strengths and limitations. While the moral fervor and public activism is admirable and salutary, the paradigm appears blind to its own implication in imperial projects that are themselves as much part of the problem as they are part of the solution. The US government called Darfur a genocide to appease domestic lobbies, and because the statement cost it nothing. Darfur will end when it suits the great powers that have a stake in the region." [3]

Anyway, notwithstanding the core of this problem: that starts with moneyed interests and filters down through the political and legal system of American governance and then gets passed down to its mainstream. Western adoption has cruelly cut a particularly wide swathe through many American Indian families and has left a lot of damage in its wake.

In my family on my father's side, out of two brothers and three sisters, seven of us kids were taken and adopted out. Beside my baby sister and me, five of our cousins were taken. Only two kids were left to our family at the time we were taken! Those were my oldest sister Alva and Pee Wee, a daughter of one of my aunties. This happened to us in the early 1960s when I was four and my baby sister was two. That's a lot of American Indian lives that got twisted all at once and that's just from my dad's side of my family.

My own baby sister was raised as an only child, by an older white couple, in a small reservation border town across the state line in Nebraska. I was raised with two of my younger cousins, a boy, Conrad and a girl, Madonna. We were sent to a white family in a white community in north-central Nebraska where we grew up with three other non-Indian adopted kids on a ranch/farm. The rest of my cousins were adopted by a Mexican family and were moved to Omaha, Nebraska. We are all members of the EagleFeather *Tiwahe* (family) originally from the Ring Thunder community on the Rosebud rez.

I eventually reunited with my mom and other members of her family in the late 1970s and my baby sister a little later in the early 1980s. But it has only been recently that I have been able to hook up again with another one of my cousins who was sent to the Mexican family. She is the oldest sibling of her family and Conrad's biological sister. Her name is Lynn. I don't know a lot of particulars yet, as to what happened throughout Lynn's life. From what I have gathered, so far, I can already see that they fared no better than me or my two cousins who grew up with me. In some ways, for them as young girls, I would say that they fared much worse.

I left my situation at age 15, by simply running and making a go of it on my own! Though this turned out to be a good thing for me, I'm not so sure it was for my little cousins I left behind. In talking with Madonna some thirty years later she shared with me her feelings of abandonment. Though it was heart-wrenching to fully hear her out at the time, I am glad I did. I understood and we both ended up crying out our sorrow and pain. First with curses and then with real tears. There was nothing else we could do! Conrad, my cousin/brother still suffers from back in the day, too. He has not been able to rid himself or overcome the cruelties that happened to us in our youth. I still love them both very much!

Our being taken away from our families by the adoption process, while bad enough in its own right, is just the tip of a very large iceberg of bad that's been happening to our people for a very long time.

Considering our relatives on the Dakota side of my mom's family, it began sometime around 1805 with the signing of their first treaty. Down through the years from that time on, there have been many military campaigns, governmental acts and programs aimed at destroying my Dakota relatives as well as my own Oyate (Nation), the Sicangu Lakota of Rosebud. So for us the Nakota, Dakota and Lakota people of America, this has been happening for at least the last 200 years. Even though the term genocide is relatively new to a lot of us and is not used lightly, we have a very good understanding of the reality of it. How could we not? We have first-hand experience! This does not deter us, however. We find ways to survive the bad and soldier on putting up with those sometimes inconceivable incongruities that exist as a part of our lives. Never doubting that the Creator has put us here on our mother to fulfill a purpose. For what purpose exactly? I'm not always sure, but then I remember that that is why we have one another. So that we can remind each other!

The many numerous military campaigns directed against us numbered in the thousands. These campaigns killed and wounded many thousands of our people while many more were captured and taken from us. And this was taking place all throughout the many years that the US government was making Treaties with us.

> "According to federal records between 1866 and 1890, the United States Army engaged in 1,040 combat actions against American Indian opponents. In that time, the army experienced some 2,000 casualties and killed over 4,000 American Indians, wounded close to 1,300, and captured over 10,000 more." [4]

That quote will put this in a bit broader view for those who might not know the particulars of American Indian life during this period of time. This documented example of military incursions into our land, Lakota land, began one year after the Civil war ended and was being carried out before during and after the second Fort Laramie Treaty was negotiated in 1868. It concluded right after the Wounded Knee Massacre on Dec. 29th 1890, the same year that Idaho and Wyoming were granted statehood and the same year Ohio State University played its first football game. Prior to this time, 25 treaties had already been negotiated and violated by the federal government or agents under their supervision. Treaties that were specifically negotiated either with ourselves, the Lakota or with our relatives the Dakota and Nakota Oyate's. There were other battles and massacres of our people, too, before 1866, as well as a mass hanging that occurred in Minnesota on December 26, 1862. Thirty-eight of my ancestors on the Dakota side of my family were executed on that day. The largest hanging execution to ever happen in the history of the United States. It happened under the leadership of Abraham Lincoln, the day after Christmas during the second year of the Civil War.

The overt planned military campaigns ended at Wounded Knee, but the war didn't! Exterminating us was still on the agenda. There wasn't any way of escaping what was coming either! The boarding school programs, the relocation programs and the adoption programs would continue into and through the 1900s. This agenda that the military had started and faithfully carried out during the 1800s continued. Adopting out members of my family in the 1960s was just an incremental part of the overarching effort against us. And regardless of the many American efforts to dehumanize and blame us. Trying to make it appear we were responsible for what was happening. This wasn't just happening to a bunch of drunken shiftless and worthless Indians or savages. It was happening to people we know and love, cherish and respect. Grandmothers, Grandfathers, it happened to me and my family! This bad unhappy part of our lives, all the bad things that had been happening to us over the past several generations. Well it left some pretty big wounds across the soul of our tiwahe (family), our tiyospiye (community), and the Oyate's (nations) of our Lakota people.

All of our wounding has causation! As with most cause-and-effect scenario's where wounding is involved, there are characteristics associated with each wound that identifies it and helps to determine the severity and effect that it has on the well-being of the wounded. An effective diagnosis leads to a better understanding of not only the wound itself but to appropriate and effective remedies and possibly quicker healing. I have a friend, Jerry Fjerkenstad, who over the years has helped me on several occasions with various projects for youth and adult males that I worked on while living in the American Indian community of St. Paul, Minnesota. Jerry is a psychologist who works within the Minnesota Department of Corrections as a clinical supervisor and therapist. He works there specifically with sex offenders. Jerry's influence on me besides that of being a very good friend, and helping me out when he had the opportunity, was to open my eyes to the concept of "The Holocaust Self."

The "Holocaust Self" for us, as American Indians, can best be understood I think, as an often invisible and unnamed condition—the condition our heart or soul is left in after the kinds of attacks that we have undergone. Jerry has outlined nine basic traits or characteristics that help us identify, make visible, and name this condition which I think lies at the bottom of a lot of identity issues and personal problems that seem to plague a lot of our people.

The Holocaust Self is comprised of the following characteristics:

1: A sense of imprisonment —something is locked up/in, can't get out. When you try to express your needs and wants they come out muted, compromised or even silent. A sense of freedom and full expression is experienced rarely and then only under extraordinary conditions of "safety."

2: An underlying and constant sense of anger and rage, but so controlled and "canned" that it is experienced primarily as depression and angst. This is also called "emotional constipation" or "the need to hate" and it comes from many, many years of "eating shit" —swallowing negative emotions that should have been expressed. People sometimes keep a distance from individuals with this problem, they find it hard to trust them as it feels like their carrying a bomb inside. Also, the anger and rage referred to here is usually way beyond the reach of standard forgiveness. Systematic abuse is usually not forgivable.

3: A constant sense of hunger —An appetite that has addiction-type elements. A sense of eating for two people, craving sweets, obsessing about whatever soothes or momentarily eliminates that urgent hungriness—sex, food, drugs, alcohol—you name it. All satisfaction is fleeting but you keep searching.

4: A sense of impotence —an inability to do what matters—experienced as procrastination, putting things off, weariness and blankness. There is a constant, internal pressure to act and a helplessness/hopelessness accompanying that urge. You know what you need to do but you just can't get in gear. It also feels like the bottom could fall out at anytime.

5: Sneakiness and sliminess —One doesn't want to be seen, doesn't want the hunger or rage or uneasiness to be witnessed. It's experienced as being false, putting on a front, hiding things, even things that people know about. You know how low you had to crawl in order to survive and you can't forgive yourself for it. You also can't tell people because you believe they'd never forgive or understand. To other people it comes across as opportunism.

6: An unimaginably deep sense of integral shame about ones own being —You hate your own guts. You wake up in the morning and the first thing that crosses your mind is that you wish you were dead, invisible, didn't exist. It's not the same as being suicidal—it's more of an ongoing beating yourself up, a condemned sign around your neck. You are utterly unable to value yourself or anything about you.

7: No sense of community — internal or external —at least when in the holocaust self. It becomes virtually impossible to reach out, even to those you know care and would respond. You might wait weeks to call your best friend and let them know how bad things are. There's an ongoing sense of avoidance. On the surface you may continue to remain friendly but on the level where it matters most you are utterly isolated.

8: Automatic lying —people with a holocaust self learn to lie automatically—it's a survival mechanism. You continue to lie even when it looks ridiculous. The truth has become an enemy —something that could get you hurt or killed. You learn not to see, not to hear, not to react—to lie with every part of your body. (See the film **Shindlers List** where the Commandant is randomly shooting Jews and the other Jews pretend nothing is happening even if someone falls dead next to them.)

9: A profound sense of inner deadness —similar to many child abusers who watch objectively and with horror as their own hands go around a child's neck or slam it against a wall. The mind is totally alert but impotent to intervene. You can end up *feeling violently jealous of the aliveness you see in others, including small children, mostly because they remind you of how dead you feel and you hate being reminded of that. This deadness also prevents you from acting appropriately to intervene in situations until things get way out of hand: you're unable to engage or exhibit compassion or outrage when it is needed"* [5]

People are not always affected the same or share the same characteristics in any particular order or to the same degree even. With that said, however, I think that we all share a majority of these characteristics at some time or other throughout our lives, in many different ways and to varying degrees of intensity. I think it would be more of a rarity and rather an abnormal occurrence for us, as a whole, if we did not have them than in the fact that we do.

Anyway from my perspective, I agree with Jerry's thinking that:

"When the "Holocaust Self" is not recognized you can look normal, continue to function, until your "bottom falls out." You're damaged on a deeper level but don't know it—it doesn't show on the surface. But, under stress, when you're drunk or stoned enough, when something goes terribly wrong, when you start to doubt or hate yourself, you can't forgive yourself for something mean or stupid you did, the Holocaust Self kicks in and all your good stuff is instantly gone and your worst comes out. Or, you just don't give a damn all of a sudden and you let your life "go to hell." Progress in any area of your life can be wiped out in a second when you sink into the black hole of the Holocaust Self.

....Think of a human being as resembling an eight-cylinder car. A person can sustain damage to 1 or 2 or even three cylinders and still run. The car will knock, smoke, be embarrassing to drive—but it will get you there. If damage goes beyond that, a car will crack it's block, freeze up, usually require a full overhaul in order to function again. In a human being, the core or imaginal center will go off-line, shut down. A person will feel empty inside—dead. In that state they are likely to engage in any behavior that will give momentary relief, pleasure or take off pressure. Consequences are irrelevant at the moment. They just want to feel better or feel nothing—NOW!!"

[1] http://en.wikipedia.org/wiki/Genocide

[2] http://www.genocidewatch.org/aboutgenocide/8stagesofgenocide.html

[3] http://howgenocidesend.ssrc.org/Moses/

[4] This quote is from a reference that Susan Harness wrote and sent to me that she had used in a presentation she did. According to federal records between 1866 and 1890 the United States Army engaged in 1,040 combat actions against American Indian opponents. In that time, the army experienced some 2,000 casualties and killed over 4,000 American Indians, wounded close to 1,300, and captured over 10,000 more. *Indian Removal and Response, Americans at War*, John P. Resch. Vol. 2: 1816-1900. Detroit: Macmillan Reference USA, 2005. p85-89

[5] Jerry sent me his presentation: Treating Destroyed People's—The Missing Pieces Curriculum, Jerry Fjerkenstad, MA, LP and Bobby Hickman, MSSA Conference, 2009

23

History: Project Papoose

The Editors

ADOPTION AGENCY FOR INDIANS
Miami's Operation Papoose

By BOB WYRICK
Reporter of The Miami News

Florida has cleared the way for a special adoption bureau in Miami to find white parents for homeless Indian children.

The Children's Service Bureau, 931 SW 1st Street, has long specialized in hard-to-place children.

Tomorrow it starts Operation Papoose.

___

These Oranges Have Red Juice

CATANIA, Sicily (AP) — First-time visitors to Sicily are often surprised when they order orange juice and get a glass of something which looks like tomato juice instead.

But it isn't tomato. It's the Sanguinello blood orange Sicilians prefer above all others.

The Sanguinello looks like an ordinary orange on the outside, with only the faintest blush of red. But inside it is extra juicy,

It is hoped the children from nearly every tribe in the U.S. — will encounter less prejudice here than in Western states.

"These are lovely, intelligent children," said Mrs. Margaret Harnett, director of CSB. "I'm sure we'll be able to place them here.

The Indian children will be easier to adopt than white children, Mrs. Harnett pointed out.

"Couples, for example, who might be judged too old for normal adoption, should have better luck getting children from the reservations," she said.

The idea of Indian adoption is still in the honeymoon stage in America. Only 125 adoptions have been made in other states, said Arnold Lyslo, director of the project in New York.

But the need for more adop-

tions is pressing, said Lyslo, mainly because of illegitimacy.

"The number of out-of-wedlock births to Indian women has never been exactly determined," Lyslo said. "But reports from health, education and social workers at the reservations indicate the figure is high."

Frequently, illegitimate children run free (and uncared for) about the reservation, Lyslo said. Help for most of them must be found outside the reservation.

This doesn't hold true with Seminole (Apache and some other tribes. Lyslo pointed out. If a Seminole mother dies her parents take over and raise the children. Every child in the tribe is cared for and the tribe is hostile to the idea of outside adoptions.

There are about 100 unwanted children among the 300,000

The North Dade Unitarian · Universalist
Kindergarten & Nursery
12250 N.W. 2nd AVE.
Pre-School Training In Liberal Religious Atmosphere.

Indians on reservations.

The children come in all sizes, ages and hues although the tendency is to place them with outside families as young as possible. Half the 125 adopted so far were less than six months old.

Adv.

Organist Introduces New Lowrey Organs

Ray Paul, well known local organist, will demonstrate the latest developments in the electronic organ field Friday and Saturday afternoon at Bill Bruce's Organ and Piano Store, 1936 N.E. 163 Street.

Paul will demonstrate thrilling new musical effects now possible for the first time through scientific progress developed by Lowrey Organs.

For those who cannot attend the Fri.-Sat. sessions, an evening demonstration will be

Lyslo Project

"INDIAN CHILDREN WILL BE EASIER TO ADOPT THAN WHITE CHILDREN"
Using adoption to disrupt Indian families, North American Indian children

are placed in orphanages, foster homes or with non-Indian parents. The American government creates the Indian Adoption Project (IAP) run by Arnold Lyslo in New York. These little Indian kids aren't black or Asian but exotic; our race is romanticized by Hollywood, and anxious adoptive parents sign up. Couples who had trouble conceiving a baby, or were too old to adopt, could have one or two Indian kids right away.

Lyslo travels to different states to convince the social workers to line up white parents for the flood of Indian kids being snatched up for adoption. Above is an article that ran in the MIAMI NEWS newspaper about OPERATION PAPOOSE. [June 25, 1964]

In 16 states, 85% of Indian children were removed from their tribal parents. Then 395 parents agree to take part in Lyslo's study and answer questions about their adopted Indian kids every year. The kids themselves were not interviewed.

Lyslo and others claimed Indian children were unwanted, not abducted, (no mention of assimilation or genocide) – so this is the reason these children needed to be adopted. ARENA (Adoption Resource Exchange of North America) continues and expands after the IAP. States create their own programs, like New York's OUR INDIAN PROGRAM. Churches like the Mormons and Catholics run their own programs. Thousands of Indian children are wiped from tribal rolls and disappear into white communities. States seal their records and amend the child's birth certificate.

For over 30 years, Indian kids were lab rats for Lyslo's human experiment, to see how well Indian children adapt being adopted. This war is called assimilation.

By 1976, American Indians go to Congress with these abduction stories and ultimately create the Indian Child Welfare Act.

Further Reading:
Indian Adoption Project
Bilchik, S. (2001, April 24). [Keynote address]. Speech presented at the 19th Annual Protecting our Children Conference, Anchorage, AK.

Child Welfare League of America. (1960, April). Indian Adoption Project. New York: Author.

Demer, L. (2001, May). Native receive apology for 1950s racial adoptions. Pathways Practice Digest, 1-2.

Lyslo, A. (1962, December). Suggested criteria to evaluate families to adopt American Indian children through Indian Adoption Project. New York: Child Welfare League of America.

Lyslo, A. (1964). The Indian Adoption Project: An appeal to catholic agencies to participate. Catholic Charities Review, 48(5), 12-16.

Lyslo, A. (1967, March). 1966 year end summary of the Indian Adoption Project. New York: Child Welfare League of America.

Lyslo, A. (1967). Adoptive placement of Indian children. Catholic Charities Review, 51(2), 23-25.

Lyslo, A. (1968, April). The Indian Adoption Project – 1958 through 1967: Report of its accomplishments, evaluation and recommendations for adoption services to Indian children. New York: Child Welfare League of America.

24

History: The Rainbow Project

The Editors

HOME HUNTERS: $100,000 helps Indian Council seeks families to adopt children

The Pittsburgh Press – Aug 30, 1984

As many as 3000 Native American children in the United States are waiting to be adopted and the Council of Three Rivers wants to increase the pool of families ready to take them. With a $100,000 grant from the Departments of Health and Human services, the Council of Three Rivers American Indian Center plan to begin collecting information about families willing to adopt Native American and other special needs children who are difficult to place in homes.

A home study includes gathering background and financial information about a family and are necessary to qualify parents for adoption.

Most of the council's efforts will go toward conducting home studies of Native American families in Pennsylvania and eligible families would be matched with Native American children throughout the country. The council does not know of any Native American children in Pennsylvania who are waiting to be adopted.

A Native American is usually defined as a person with one-quarter Indian blood, which usually means a grandparent was an Indian. A Native American family has to have at least one Native American parent.

"They aren't a lot of Native American families who have gone through the home study process and are ready to adopt," said Linda Flanigan who will supervise the project at the councils' offices in Dorseyville, Indiana Township. "They may not have the money or they are on long waiting lists."

According to social workers there are as many as 100,000 special needs children in the country. Nearly 600 are in western Pennsylvania. Besides Native Americans, these children include blacks, Hispanics, the handicapped, children over 12 years of age, and sibling groups.

While healthy Caucasian infants are placed quickly, others may wait for years for a family to adopt them. One reason for the delay is lack of home studies. In the next two years, the council hopes to complete home studies on 195 families in Pennsylvania, 105 are Native American, who are interested in adopting the special needs children. It aims to assist adoption agencies in placing 50 Native American children and 75 other special needs children.

In the project called rainbow, the Council will use the grant money to hire three persons, develop the program, and pay the costs of state licensing as an adoption placement agency. The new employees, a social worker and two paraprofessionals will help with the home studies and prepare families for adoption.

As part of the six-week process, the social worker and a parent who has already adopted children will work with about 10 families at a time. The prospective parents will talk about their concerns and experiences with children in weekly counseling sessions. The social worker will also have private meetings with the couple or single parent. When the counseling sessions and private meetings are completed, the social worker will summarize the findings. Adoption agencies will review the summaries and decide which family is suitable for a child in its custody. The family will decide whether it wants to adopt the child and visits will be arranged.

"The groundwork has to be done before families get to the point of going to an agency," Ms. Flanigan said. "If there's a call from a specific agency, we may have the right family, a two-parent family or a single parent who may want a six year old child."

After adoption the Council will provide family or individual counseling and other supportive services to ensure there is no disruption, a word used to describe an adoption that fails.

"Sometimes parents have problems in the transition from being childless to having maybe too many children," Ms. Flanigan said. "From the other side, we help the children adjust. If they have been living in foster homes, they may have anxieties about whether the placement is permanent."

The Council expects to receive it provisional state license as an adoption placement agency in the next month and to start the home studies in October (1984). The Council, which hopes to continue the rainbow project without having to rely on government grants in the future, will charge between $100 and $600 for the studies, depending on family incomes.

Federal statistics show a higher percentage of Native American children in foster homes, group homes and institutions, more than any other minority. Same-race placement is required for Native American children unless a Native

American family cannot be found, according to federal law. And it's preferred for other minorities.

"One reason is to avoid problems that may occur in adolescence. During those years, there's the problem with self-image. If the child is of a different race, he may wonder why he's different from everybody else around him," Ms. Flanigan said. "There is a special difficulty with Native American children because of stereotypes perpetuated in history books and films. You hardly see an Indian without a headband and feather," she said. "The Native American family could counteract the negativeness of the media and instill pride in the child."

Although the emphasis is on doing home studies for Native American families, the project is open to all families, regardless of race. The only restriction is that the families be willing to adapt special needs children because "these kids are out there."

Ms. Flanigan said, "It makes no sense for us to interview families who want healthy white infants when they won't be available."

The project is called rainbow after an Indian ritual in which bands of color are placed on a babies cradle. The rainbow in Indian lore represents goodness and a beginning.

The project was born after the success of the council's Native American Adoption Resource Exchange, a link between tribes and agencies that have Native American children waiting to be adopted and those that have Native American families who want to adopt.

The (ARENA) exchange registered more than 400 families and 200 children across the country in the last two years, and assisted in placing more than 100 Native American children. However, about 200 of the registered families are waiting for home studies.

Source: Pittsburgh Press, August 30, 1984.

PA Indian Council

PART II

Updates TWO WORLDS adoptees

25

Finding Our Meaning

JESSE FASTHORSE FLOYD NEUBERT (Lakota)

Tashea and Jessup

All of us in this book are searching for meaning in our lives. Psychologists say that we accomplish this task through our own personal life narrative: the continuous unfolding inner story that we tell ourselves about our experiences which explains and provides meaning to these experiences. This is why it's so important for each of us to share our stories with one another. In our writing, we also share our meaning and the hope and comfort in finding that meaning. Of course we must all find our own meaning to life individually, but there is a certain strength and purpose in realizing that we were never truly alone in our search for truth and in our striving and suffering as adoptees.

"What we are today comes from our thoughts of yesterday and our present thoughts build our life of tomorrow: our life is the creation of our mind."
—The Buddha

As a Split Feather, I found this to be especially encouraging when I discovered I wasn't alone. My story of being taken from my people and my culture was done through inter-racial adoption. Meeting Trace and learning about how many there of us are out there in the world, I realized that all along my own life story has been connected to a greater narrative that is an intricate part of our tribal people's history and ongoing struggle for survival.

Sharing my story in TWO WORLDS and reading stories by other Split Feathers, I was able to open my mind and reframe my thinking about my own life in a more meaningful context, without all the regret, ignorance and delusions of solitude that kept me spiritually—and now physically—isolated, separated from living my life in a truly genuine way.

After too many years of causing pain and suffering, between silence and violence, I finally accepted only I had the power to change my own thinking and later my life narrative—so I can move from one life of being a victim to a new life of being a victor.

Through changing my thinking about life, I could seek and actually find my own redemption and transcendence—literally from a prison of solitary confinement.

Unfortunately for some of us still, prison can be a poignant metaphor to describe moments in our life when our thoughts about the past—both in its known and unknown details—imprison us daily. That life filled us with piercing loneliness, uncertainty and regret. These thoughts can keep us confined in a sort of psychological prison and spiritual prison cell that we yearn to escape. Feeling trapped or empty prevents us from living our life freely.

From this prison limbo in our mind, it is up to us as individuals to find the truth that will set us free. Even the journey towards truth can be liberating.

Whether the truth of our past is known or unknown, we still need to take responsibility for shaping our narratives and freeing ourselves. (Because severing the most natural bond between a mother and child occurs at a time in a child's life when she/he is unable to communicate her/his emotions and experiences, it's known to be a painful trauma that stays into adulthood.)

As Split Feathers, some of our earliest experiences were marred with pain and sorrow. Or some truths may be entirely unknown to us—which also carries its own pain and sorrow. Either way we have all experienced loss like no other. For some of us, answering our own existential questions about this life, such as "who am I?" and "how and why did my life unfold this way?" may prove to be especially difficult for us. However, every life carries its own share of struggles, failures and adversities that must be overcome in order to find a higher meaning.

We can and we will find redemption and transcendence through our survival of the past, but to truly move forward with personal growth, we must accept this loss forever. If not, our life will be stagnant.

Examining our thoughts, coming to terms with life so far, it's extremely important for us to share our stories with others. Sharing our stories of survival, we are reminded that we are strong not in spite of our adversities but because of them.

With our stories, we offer inspiration and solidarity with each other... Relentlessly pursuing our truth, wanting to understand our past and then accepting it, sharing what we've learned, we create a life of endurance, resiliency and wisdom. For those of us who refused to break, we grew stronger. What we've gained through our perseverance far exceeds whatever we may have lost... By embracing this profound truth, we discover one of life's paramount meanings.

As Dostoyevski said, "There is only one thing that I dread: not to be worthy of my sufferings."

UPDATE:

I am now 29 and have a little less than three years left on my sentence. I'm currently locked down in solitary confinement in a maximum security unit; I may be allowed to go to a lower custody yard sometime this year. With my present focus still toward the future, I continue to work toward my first college degree through Rio Salado College here in Arizona.

As for as my family, two of my sisters had their first baby. Tonika had my niece Amy Isabelle in 2011 and they remain in St. Louis with my two brothers Michael and Stephen and their adoptive family. Tashea just had my niece Stella Jade last year on my birthday, October 24. They live with my sister Anna and our adoptive parents Sandra and Danny in Utah. They are all happy and healthy.

I reconnected with my mother Cheryl in 2012 for the first time in almost ten years. Unfortunately she still has issues with addiction and stability so our relationship has been vexing at times. However I am grateful to have everyone that I do in my life.

I'm especially grateful to everyone who has shared their story of survival in these books and for everyone who made this sharing possible, especially to my third mom Trace. I send each and every one of you my highest regards. Stay Strong brothers and sisters as you find your way. Mitakuye Oyasin!

Jessup in 2009

26

UUTUQTUA, COMING HOME

ANECIA TRETIKOFF O'CARROLL (Alutiiq)

Young Anecia

First, my love and respect to those affected by adoption who are still searching, wondering; adoptees knowing in your bones, breath, and spirit who you are, yet yearning to see, touch, and feel "home", and to the mothers longing to hold her child, whatever their age. Keep hope close; connection may come in unexpected ways.

Half my life ago, I woke from a compelling dream and said for the first time, 'I am going to find my family!' At the same time, my birthmother started having feelings she describes as faith that we would reunite within the year. We did.

For over 25 years, we visited occasionally for a few days at a time. Then at age 50, an opportunity for a job came up that could bring me to live for the first time in the same town as my mom and nearer to my blood's heritage. I have been here in Alaska for two years now. There is so very much to express. I don't know where to begin.

    <u>Heart-fold of Goodbye</u>
    A baby's mother wept

and gave,
still warm from her womb,
her freshest flesh
to those she believed would give the care for which she longed.
She formed the words, "I wish you a rainbow life.
Goodbye."

Rainbow-Life girl, now a woman….

Some subtle words, or situation,
Trigger inside her the final gestation
Of a long waiting
Quiet
Memory from inside
A warm heart-fold.

A rhythm
sends upward a contraction
acutely.

In this birthing,
each mournful sob presses
from it's dark dwelling
this little heartbeat.
into the light.

Let this!, exclaims Healing!

Let this not-so-small thing
overwhelm every great thing and be welcome
to express it's lonely longings for connection;
reconnection!

Rock it like a wee baby,
the wee baby that it is,
and have it's first cries.

Hold close.
Say, Welcome to the world. You are well. You are safe.
Thank you for being.

You are loved.
Do breathe and breathe and breathe.

Uutuqtwa — *Coming Home*

My mother and I stood facing one another as I waited in line to board the tiny airplane that would take me across the tundra and the Egegik River. She tapped her hand on her chest and said, "Listen for the welcoming drums. Listen for the drumming inside. You'll feel your skin tingle." I let go of her hand and walked to the plane, visualizing drummer's faces with smile wrinkles lit, and women dancers with pulsing upturned palms. I remembered saying to the spirit of my grandmother before beginning this trek, 'Grandmother. Grandmother! Wake up! We're going to Egegik!', when a cry burst from somewhere deep in my being—the experience of great joy, and release of aged sadness. I could feel my grandmother ahead of me, waiting, welcoming. I felt a coming home joy.

We've reached Egegik, the homeland of our ancestors. Uutuqtwa, coming home. Uutuqtwa. Coming home for the first time to a people who recognize my heart and invite me into the village circle, accepting me as one who helps make them whole, while I am made whole by joining them.

It is windy; rain mixed with snow and hail. My husband, two young daughters, my uncle, and I receive warmth as Uncle Frank brought us into Nikoli and Virginia's home; they are two of the three remaining village people who speak our traditional language. While looking lovingly upon grandson Adrian playing on the rug, Nick tells of the days he fished, trapped, and hunted with my grandfather. I learn that my grandfather was the last person in the village to have a dogsled team for transportation. I am grateful my husband is here to help remember the details of the stories because my presence is divided between our hosts and my sense of the thawing walls that kept the Alutiiq-me secure in the world away from my heritage; stone turning to ice; ice turning to flowing water.

We walk outside, past the playing children as we look for the grave markers of my ancestors. The Egegik wind comes sharply, telling of the region's vast flatness. I feel every degree of weather, all 27 of them. The children, deep in imaginative play, subconsciously tuck hands up in coat sleeves while others serve imaginary tea with bumbling, numb, red hands. Having lived in Bristol Bay these few days, even in this modern time of gas, propane, and electric heat, I marvel and am proud of my ancestors. How did they cope? Surely they were a strong people who knew the power of laughter, acceptance, ingenuity, cooperation — and warm, furry hides.

This spirit of home nourishes me. Am I different in any obvious way? I feel more grounded, centered, connected. Now, I've been home. What is this feeling? Grandmother? Grandmother smiles, bones oiled; like an old woman can do cartwheels again. Freed secrets unfold. Life recognizes me. I have joy in place of sorrow. I have life in place of silence. I am more fully alive.

I remember the day at McHugh Creek in the Chugach State Park, picnicking and hiking in the sunshine under snow-covered mountains. The air was clear and my feelings warm as I walked with my mother, sister, and niece up a mountain trail. We walked as family, wrapping outer layers around our waists as we warmed, communicating with the rhythm of our pace, delighted to just walk in thought-filled silence, to be with the mother of my birth, in Alaska, the homeland of my mother's grandmothers.

I wondered, 'What is this pride at being with MY mom? What is this feeling of wanting to tell everyone, 'This is my MOM.' I remember lying on her bed and visiting, like sisters I suppose, though now I'm learning this is also like mother and daughter. I bathed in the atmosphere of our reconnection. She has deep brown eyes; when she smiles, her spirit fills in and illuminates every feature of her face.

My focus returns to the present as we locate my grandfather's grave marker. I stand on ground where people once gathered, mourning his passing and wonder about the life he knew and the lives of his grandfathers.

Uutuqtwa; coming home.

<u>Rhythms of My Blood's Home</u>
In the Alaska Native Medical Center
circular lobby,
patients and family and visitors
gathered around the outer and inner circle
where the drummers and dancers
came to share the healing rhythms
of traditional songs.
The floor is a mural;
shades-of-blue waves energetically flow,
a map of Alaska with a golden crescent moon
and a rainbow aurora borealis across the sky.
There is a sun, embraced by two cloud-people
next to a full spectrum rainbow.
Around this floor mural,
two tiers of curved benches flow around,
expanding the circle, and the padded benches

surrounded by a sculptured semi-open-wall of sky,
bear, walrus, sun, mountain, porpoise, howling wolf.
The smell of fresh coffee is in the air.
Carers arrive with people in wheelchairs.
Others click by with walkers.
It's winter, so the clunk of boots is also heard.

Graced above and all around the gathering space
are sculpted geese placed in a clockwise flying pattern,
made by gifted Aleut artist John Hoover.
The wingtips are faces;
the spirits that soar and soar and soar!

A jovial, round-faced woman walks into the circle,
looks around and says with a twinkle,
"Do I know anybody in here?"

A baby girl stops crawling across the Northern Lights,
now fussing, hungry.
Within moments, drawn to her mother,
nourished;
held close and overcome with calm.

Our culture, tradition, spirit, connection
pulses in, on, through the people
and this place;
now with the addition of that
deep-breath,
mother/baby calm.

We are alive together.

A child converses with her mother
in the language of ancestors,
here and now,
and daily.
Their first tongue.
It is a deep joy that she never has to wonder on
missing that.

The language is not being taught in this moment;
it is being lived.

In time, in this space,
everything that the senses, heart,
and soul connect with tells stories
and stories of an accessible community spirit.
Patients, family members, healers, and friends
in the gathering space speak English,
Yupik, Alutiiq, and Inupiaq and other indigenous Alaskan languages
in gentle, lively tones.
The Native languages flow into my ears,
embrace my heart,
call to my soul,
Come.
Come by here!

I am here.

We are here together.

Remembering another time,
that songs provided the hospitality of
welcome,
the Elder dancer extended an invitation
to join in the dance;
a time to merge with
the resounding ancient echo
and the giving-over of today's
arms, heart, and hands.
A time to
experience the rhythm
as the drummers
ignited a song's long-time story.

While this life-pattern is new to me
the ancestors revel in it's familiarity
and I am feeling their joy
wash through my blood
like a thorough healing.

I have entered this place
which is of the Unknown
and for the time-being am 5000 miles
from my husband and daughers.
I'm looking left and right
above below and within and
at this moment, feeling alone
from those who's love I am familiar.

At times, I feel myself a stranger hanging around my blood;
it's pulse dancing a song
the rest of me does not know;
a cheechako in my own body.

How can this be home
when everyone and everything
I know is somewhere else?

I am utterly disoriented and nothing
makes sense;
nothing is ground,
nothing is sky.
Who is friend,
who is foe?
What resonates?

A new bottomless.

Help me friend.
I do not wish to feel alone
experiencing this place of I-don't-know.
this relatives-pulse land.

I come as stranger
yet as One-of.
I don't know this place.
The rhythm is crushing
"Me" as I know myself.
Oh God it is challenging!

I am dispersing and colliding.
And feel all alone.

I am being born.

Grandmother's Spirit

Yesterday; a new beginning — a wondrous day with my birth mom and hundreds and hundreds of Natives at the Southcentral Foundation Gathering and then the high vibration powwow with so much spirit; I don't know how one room can contain the energy of that many smiles and thundering drumbeats!

Afterward I didn't want to go back to my apartment but wanted to walk outdoors so went walking on a snowy trail.

I thought on the spirit of Grandmother, the one that I believed stayed close and came with me when adopted out. I prayed hard wanting to know if she was really truly real… I looked up to see A Messenger Between the Worlds—a huge eagle flying close and looking at me while flying directly above my head, drawing up my breath and spirit and putting tingled goose bumps in every cell in my body. I sang out a loud, long trill, crying a prayer of quyana, thanks. Quyana! Quyana Nana, thank you grandmother!

I keep my camera ready on walks, and this is the picture of the answer to my prayer question.

Eagle (Anecia's photo 2014)

In My Blood's Home

I am a living collage with a billion pieces, some seen, some unseen; some felt, some numb.

These two years in Alaska have brought personal and community experiences with health challenges, countless hours in the Native hospital, in the care of medical doctors and traditional healers; a time of personal growth, education, the experience of support, care, and healing. Also a time of witness to effects of alcohol, intergenerational trauma, depression, death; but mostly overwhelming encounters of heart and soul and blood connection, smiles, hugs, gifts.... Oh—the glorious fish! Berries, agudak, seal oil, muktuk, herring eggs on kelp from the southwest or on spruce from the southeast; dance, regalia, kusbuks... Joyous reconnection with family, welcoming and warm but sometimes distant. We are all adjusting.

Grandmother's spirit expressed in passionate closeby bursts of numerous eagle visits! I feel her here SO PRESENT; so joyful. That this blood is home... I am feeling her elation and she is feeling mine.

There are walks, hikes, climbs, skiing up and skiing down; touching hands, touching hearts. A shared dancing pulse of birthmother, birthdaughter; pulse keeping time by ancestors' ever-present rhythmic drumbeat.

All this.... It is so incredibly large; this immersion, this baptism in blood. The pulsing blood of the living and the pulsing echoes of blood of the ancestors in the Everywhere.

I am loved. I feel so deeply loved. This is so new and I don't know how to be worthy of this love so I begin with exploring the possiblility that I am a real person; that I am not invisible. That I do belong. That I have a voice; an influence. A presence.

Quyana. Quyana for this life. Quyana.

Anecia (2014)

Thirty years ago, a great loving spirit brought powerful feelings and images to Anecia in a dream. The dream was of a beautiful Native woman stepping out from under a wooden shelter in a rich, lush garden and was getting ready to speak to her. In the same moments that this gift of dream came to her, some fifteen hundred miles away, her birth mother was inspired with deep feelings she describes as faith that they would meet within the year. They did.

Every day that she lives her life in her blood's home of Alaska, she is thanking her ancestors for lifting her spirits up and putting small and large treasures on her life's path that enrich, delight, guide, and utterly fill her breath and pulse with joy.

27

Family Gatherings

ALICE DIVER (Mi'kmaq)

Alice Diver

An adoptive cousin once asked me, '*Would you not go back to your people, now?*'

I assumed from the question (it was the day of my dad's funeral) that she was wondering whether I might have been tempted to bid farewell to Ireland and 're-emigrate' back to my birthplace in Eastern Canada.[1] I had to answer truthfully: '*I don't know who or where they are, and I have no way of finding out.*' [2]

I could have added that I had been searching for birth relatives for over two decades by that stage, with little success. With no access to my original surname, I have very little chance of finding any close ancestors or half siblings. I have made peace with this idea, although I live with the thin hope that someone might track *me* down one day. The phrase '*my people*' still makes me uneasy however—apart from making me sound a bit like a biblical leader, by using it I would be laying claim to a status, identity and kinship that I have no right to enjoy or explore.

The law confirms this, as does much of the thinking of polite society. There are significant barriers in place (closed records legislation, adult-centric case law, Facebook etiquette and norms) to prevent people like me from violating the privacy rights of those who have chosen to sever the genetic bond with their offspring. As such, I cannot imagine gate-crashing a family gathering any time soon.[3]   Without that magical piece of paper, the unaltered birth certificate, my only option is to keep hoping that some reunion registry might one day receive a query from a curious half-sibling or cousin, keen to track down the long-lost rumour that is, or was, myself. Even if this were to somehow happen, it would be foolish to hope that a balloon-filled soiree would then be organised to celebrate my return. Recognition of an abandoned relative, whether publicly or privately done, may represent a sharp acknowledgement of loss, long-held deep secrets and perhaps a variety of family failings. As a well-meaning friend remarked to me back in the 1980's (just after I'd started searching): *'I don't think much of your people to be honest. Out of all of them, was there not even one person who could have helped your mother keep you?'* Strong words, but they provided a much-needed sense of perspective, and to some extent prepared me for the eventual outcome. Birth family searches are not always the stuff of sit-coms and afternoon soap operas; in my case, 'reunion' simply meant rejection letters.[4] So the only family gatherings I am ever likely to attend will be those involving my adoptive cousins: blue eyed, fair skinned and generally flame-haired, I am still always struck at how much they all resemble each other and how easily they seem to take this sign of their relatedness for granted. I remember meeting a group of them for the first time at a wedding, as a gawky teenager, with one of them remarking to my adoptive parents: *'Isn't she swarthy? Very sallow-skinned. Where did you get her from? Bet she takes a good tan.'* They have always been kind to me, despite it being fairly obvious that we bore each other no physical resemblance. Few if any of them seem to have been told that I was adopted: not surprising given that my folks seldom mentioned the 'A' word, other than to ask me to leave any searching until after their deaths, and to express regular surprise and some annoyance over my increasing deafness and adolescent temper (*'But we were assured by the agency that there was nothing wrong with you!'*).

In relation to not searching, I half kept my promise to them; quietly working on it but never daring to tell them about it, for fear that it would hurt their feelings. I sometimes wonder what they would have made of the sharp letters of rebuff that I received from my genetic mother, had they known of them; a useful mixture of outrage and hurt on my behalf, I like to think, coupled with just a tiny measure of *'Well, we told you so'* or *'Aye, but you were well warned.'*

I don't regret keeping any of that unhappy episode from them: they probably would, incorrectly, have seen my need to search as a rejection of their parenting rather than accepting it for what it actually was—the start of a lifelong quest for genetic information and cultural identity, and a desire to be something other than 'other.' Had I been able to explain to them exactly why I needed to search, I would have perhaps put it something like this: *'What is the opposite of 'loved one'? No single word can sum this concept up. A few terms do exist that come close to providing some sort of definition: outcast, stranger, outsider, interloper. My search was not a mark of ingratitude, it was a personal gamble taken with the aim of removing myself from a state of namelessness. It had nothing to do with the quality or otherwise of my childhood or the strength of our adoptive family ties and everything to do with my psychological need for genetic ancestry.'*

I will admit even now to experiencing some level of lingering guilt over my continuing search for relatives via DNA-testing.[5] I can live with it however as I have discovered almost a hundred genetic cousins. In the interests of equality I make little distinction between those classed by the system as a suggested '3rd—4th cousin' (*Utter joy!*), 'Remote' (*Ahoy there!*) or 'Distant' (*Who are we to judge what their demeanour might be? Hello there anyway!*). The precious list of names grows almost monthly—there is fresh delight upon logging in weekly to discover that someone, somewhere, has been added as a new genetic match, however far away they might be in terms of our shared chromosomes. If they have posted a photo and/or a family tree, my day is made and any housework will be quite happily forgotten. Frequently such matches will be with cousins who are dark-haired and brown-eyed and who hail—even if only in ancestral terms—from the Eastern areas of Canada. [6] Certain surnames have started to appear again and again, as have various place names, some of which are well known for their indigenous communities and histories. It is like finding long-buried, contraband treasure.[7]

I am careful not to actively stalk anyone: a single, friendly *'hello, no pressure'* email is enough and maybe a quick glance to see if they might be on Facebook, perhaps even seeking a long-lost cousin. [8] (A little light googling is, I reckon, also acceptable, given that fate has left me with so few options). The kindness and compassion of those who have contacted me or responded to my emails has been profound and I am thankful for all of them. A number of 'my matches' (I do love that phrase – they are *my genetic matches* bless them!) have also turned out to be highly competent genealogists and have put much time and effort into discreetly trying to find out where exactly I might 'fit' within their wider family trees. This can be no easy task for them: imagine trying to draft appropriate questions — '*..so did anyone in your family give up a child or perhaps quietly father one in the 1960's?* Or…'*Have a look at this photo of the slightly crazed looking middle aged lady…does she resemble anyone we know? Could she be a long lost half-sister or aunt?*'

I don't expect anyone to claim a close connection any time soon: again, I am so grateful for the friendships and indeed the sense of kinship that has arisen through having had my dna tested, and for the gaining of at least some sense of identity in respect of where my ancestors—and living relatives—generally hail from. Frustratingly, I have also corresponded with a few 'close match' people who, like myself, were adopted in infancy with no means of opening sealed records, overturning vetoes or accessing their original birth certificate. For genetically-relinquished people like us, our family tree-tracing is much more than just a pastime or hobby (take note please, those who design the adverts). It is a quest for some measure of repatriation, if not perhaps also for some form of reparation. The state-sanctioned loss of identity that can occur with closed records must be viewed as a significant rights violation, in terms of equality, identity, culture, nationality, heritage, health and well-being. Reducing these issues to a simple rights-balancing exercise (parental privacy rights v. child 'informational curiosity' interests) or trying to somehow 'resolve' the arguments by granting absolute veto powers to relinquishing parents, ignores completely the needs and rights of adoptees (and of donor children, I must add).

I have accepted that I am unlikely now to live long enough to see the law in Quebec changed to allow me unfettered, veto-free access to that most basic of concepts: an authentic name. I remain hopeful however that my children might someday uncover those aspects of their heritage that are currently denied to them by fate, law and society. It is probably more likely that this will occur through scientific advances rather than via the evolution of more compassionate statutes and policies on accessing genetic ancestry. Until law-makers, judges and parents adjust their focus on parental 'rights' to give a more meaningful interpretation to the concept of the child's best interests as paramount, there will continue to be sections of the population at risk of being origin-deprived. Arguably, a clear re-think of what it means to 'parent' is perhaps needed: doing what is best for a vulnerable child may require genetic parents to forego the genetic anonymity and denial of their connections that is permitted by law in so many regions. Equally, the legal fictions so often underpinning adoption and gamete donation in law and policy must be recognised as the servants of parental interests. If good parenting involves doing what is best *for the child,* then the title borne by the good parent should be an irrelevant concern: parenting can be done just as well through fostering, guardianship or customary adoption models, without the need for the permanent severance of genetic ties required by formal, closed records or veto-victim adoption frameworks. From the perspective of the child, being well parented essentially means being cared for and kept from harm. A lifetime, legalised ban on genetic identity and ancestry must be seen for what it is: an unjustifiable human rights violation.

Forgive me for digressing. As an update to my story in volume 1 of TWO WORLDS: *Lost Children*, I can claim to have met —and wish to thank—many wonderful cousins and to have made some truly great friends: we are genetically connected, somehow, and I feel a little less lost as a result. [9]

On watching Philomena (on the night before Mother's Day, ill-advisedly)

This was not one of my better decisions. Much as I love Judy Dench and Steve Coogan, and with no disrespect to their outstanding portrayals of 'the Irish mammy' and the 'snottery English git' (I have had front row seats to both characters and they play them to perfection) the film has left me reeling and more than a little upset. The humour is much needed; if not for the constantly trickled episodes of light relief, I would have simply wailed throughout, rather than just for the first fifteen minutes. As it was, wine was sent for and the husband produced a box of chocolates. (For a non-adoptee, he 'gets' it...most of the time). The horror of the children's *abduction*—and no other word does the scene justice, with respect to any adoptive parents and to well-meaning, hard-pressed child-protective social workers who might be taking the time to read this—will stay with me for a very long time. The utter cruelty of those who denied a reunion between bereft mother and dying son was as horrific, if not more so, than their initial, enforced separation decades earlier. That he chose for his ashes to be interred at his birth place, within the penitential grounds of the site of such institutionalised injustices, speaks volumes and provides a clear indictment of all who were directly or indirectly involved or quietly complicit in all of the necessary, systemic deceits. As one IMDB discussion board post commented however, on his decision to be interred in Ireland '*pity the adopted [sic] parents.*' Rather misses the point of the film which was to highlight the dark side of a process based upon the lies and losses which enabled non-consensual relinquishment, and the realities underpinning the purchasing of another's child.

Non-central characters express disgust and shock regularly at the trappings of the system: money exchanged hands, lies and secrecy abounded, the need for maternal atonement, stigma and guilt. The story ends however on a happy note, with the title character Philomena quite edified at finding the grave (and having had a cursory but restorative weep) regaling her now-firm-friends reporter with a tale from her latest paperback. You can almost hear the cinema-goers muttering, '*Ah that's grand so*,' as they brush the popcorn from their laps and sup the last drop of a sugary drink. '*Sure it wouldn't happen nowadays, thank God.*' We are meant it seems to be left with the sense that all this was some sort of rare, sealed-off episode, a history-frozen and easily 'dealt with' chapter by those who have been brave enough to 'take on the system' (politely by the mammy, angrily by her championing reporter) and then move on with their lives. The lost son did very well, materially and career-wise, and he was (largely) free to embrace his sexuality *('sure now he wouldn't have done that in 1970's rural Ireland,'* the Irish audience could mutter). His sister, not so much: she is shown as a stressed, distant mother, nowhere near as affluent as her high-flying brother and with no apparent interest in learning about her birth/first mother or her ancestral background. Her revelation that their childhood was perhaps not the happiest is very swiftly just left there: a dangled crumb to those less than blissful adoptees watching who might dare to ever offer a similar comment (and of course risk being labelled ungrateful for having been rescued from 'orphanage' life or from the shame of their illegitimacy).

Useful (and at times entertaining) as this film was, there was much more scope available in terms of raising public awareness and shining light on those institutions that merit public shaming and profound rebuke. From the perspective of many adoptees (and their relinquishing parents) there are still lies, falsified or forever sealed records, vetoes and face-slammed doors. Apologies are essentially meaningless: calls for reform may be highly qualified, taking care to reassure triad parents that their rights to privacy or to parental autonomy will not be affected by any changes to the established systems and norms of secrecy that still surround all things blood-tied. That birth records can just happen to end up lost in a fire, deliberate or nun-started, is far from surprising: ask the disappointed gamete donor children of British Columbia whether they found that plot twist surprising. Perhaps a sequel could reveal something of the lost child's life other than the affluent snapshot glimpses of his childhood: his fear at being placed in a car with strangers, arrival in a foreign land, his bewilderment and loss at no longer seeing the mother he had known throughout infancy (albeit only 'for an hour a day'). The teenage years are probably unlikely to feature much, and if there was ever a moment when he asked his new parents for information about his 'background' (still the best euphemism out there, really) it is fair to say that this is more likely to feature in a documentary than in any ultimately upbeat, heart-warming tale of a mother's search.

Not to detract from the abject horror of Philomena Lee's experiences or loss (I only wish my first mother had shared an ounce of her compassion or curiosity) but film-makers would do well perhaps to look now at the miracle of adoption from the perspective of the relinquished, displaced child, especially those that have been 'orphanised' by law, policy or social customs. The evils of the church are paralleled, perhaps exceeded, by the actions of the child's grandfather—if not the wider family circle—in sending his pregnant daughter away and requiring that mother and child had to be separated. The film's central horror, loss of one's mother (not to mention the father, and the film largely does this, barely acknowledging him beyond letting us know that he was physically desirable and apparently also good at 'the sex') and permanent separation from her, is still a current issue for many 'adoptees' and donor or surrogate children.

To state glibly that adoption is now simply all about effecting a 'permanence' of child protection, does not address or answer this point. Child cruelty still occurs, whether at the hands of genetic parents, foster parents, adopters or 'professionals' tasked with caring for children. As long as films, discussions, legal reforms and social norms on adoption remain adult-central in their focus, it seems likely that the adoptees will stay exactly where they were in this film: on the periphery, a grainy memory, handily resolved. I hesitate to suggest this but had Anthony/Michael (I won't start on the cruel vanity of having to change a child's name — but had the film been instead named in his honour, which one would they have chosen?) not died a decade earlier, it is perhaps unlikely that the film would even have been made. Had he lived to speak to the audience of his childhood or of his adolescent years, or feelings as an adult, it would probably not have been as easy for the film-makers to send him or his mother off happily into the sunset, chatting about her latest read. Here's hoping that someone looks now to film an adoptee's struggle for truth, and — dare I suggest it — that they might not be as easily consoled by a little light reading if their search eventually ends at a headstone.

---

[1] I didn't, although I was, and at times still am very tempted by the thought.

Family and work commitments make this an unlikely possibility, although I remain open to all offers.

[2] The response to this was an unimpressed and perhaps typically Irish '*Well, sure let us know if you are selling the house....here, have an egg and onion sandwich.*'

[3] Actually, I can just about imagine myself doing this, arms waving and perhaps shouting '*Greetings, my people! I am returned unto thee!*' ...but I cannot see it ending terribly well.

[4] Though heartbreakingly cruel in places, I have kept them and class them as treasured possessions.

[5] I have only a limited idea of how dna-testing really works despite the efforts of many, many kind and patient people to explain to me what a haplogroup is, means or does.

[6] I have a number of Acadian and African American cousins who have been particularly kind to me, and am especially grateful to a dear cousin in Costa Rica who was the very first 'match' to email me: he sent me a lovely welcome, his family tree and some amazing photographs of Canadian ancestors. I cried all day, but in a good way.

[7] One long-suffering work colleague admitted to some disappointment over my finding genetic relatives on the basis that (in her own words) '*We were sort of hoping you were of extra-terrestrial origin.*'

[8] I resist the urge to fire off an immediate friend request, in case I frighten them. That said, I am always very happy to receive such requests and to answer any queries from people who think that I might be somehow related to them.

[9] I eventually finished the PhD, having completed the *viva voce* without knifing anyone. It has since been turned into a dreadfully dull law book, which I remain almost unreasonably fond of.

28

Lost and Now Found

GAIL HUGGARD (Rocky Boy Chippewa-Cree)

Gail Huggard

I don't like this hotel room. The air conditioning isn't working and the TV doesn't work. The hotel clerk calls and says another room is available so I'd better move my stuff over there quickly. I'm lugging my suitcase down the breezeway and up and down stairs. Any minute now my cell phone will ring to announce my brother's arrival in the hotel lobby. Please don't call me until I can freshen up a bit, I say to myself. But there is no time....the phone rings and it's Vern. He's here and waiting for me downstairs.

Nervous and sweaty, with my heart beating out of my chest, I try to stay calm as I walk through the lobby's back door where I will meet my big brother for the first time, ever. And there he is, my handsome brother Vern, the brother who was relinquished by our mother and put into a Catholic orphanage at the age of two, the brother who had no clue he had younger brothers and sisters. Our eyes meet and we walk towards each other, joyful tears running down our faces as we hold on to each other, never wanting to let go. It's the first time Vern has met a birth relative and I feel so privileged to be the first, me, his baby sister.

That was three years ago, and after 30 years of "searching for Bernie," as we all referred to the mystery of our lost brother. You see, our Chippewa mother didn't speak much English. My sisters interpreted Vern's name as "Bernie," in the heavily accented voice of our mother. All we knew was that we had a big brother who was given up at age two because mother Lenore divorced her abusive husband and couldn't take care of Bernie. Sister Betty actually showed me a little black and white photo of Bernie at the age he was relinquished—a cute, little, dark-skinned boy standing in the Middle of Nowhere, Montana. Betty knew Lenore's married name back then so the only information we had was his name—Bernie LaValley—born in Montana, who knows how many years ago.

When I first heard of my brother, I had only just met my sisters a few weeks prior. The day Betty pulled the photo of Vern from a box, I knew I had to find him. So for the next 30 years, I wrote letters to every LaValley or Lavallee I could find in Montana phone books that I ordered from the library. Once in a while, somebody would write back—sorry but they could not help me. Another man called me, stating there was a so-and-so LaValley in prison and is that the person I was looking for? I wrote to the Rocky Boy Chippewa-Cree Reservation but they couldn't help me without any other identifying data. Remember, this was way before the Internet existed.

Then four years ago, sister Shari started contacting adoptee search agencies. She decided upon the Lutheran Children and Family Service. She and I pulled together the fee of $200 and she sent a check to a woman who promised to find Bernie, with the little information we had. After a false start by this woman and much disappointment on our part, another woman took over the search. She called Shari with the amazing result—she found him but he was not returning her phone calls. After what felt like an eternity, Vern contacted this woman, who in turn contacted Shari. At the time of the phone call telling him that he had family in Washington State, Vern had just gotten the diagnosis of cancer and was dealing with extensive surgery and radiation treatments. He didn't want to sound weak or sick with the first-time phone call to Shari, so he waited until he was medically and emotionally stable.

Shari kept this a secret and summoned the rest of us to get together for lunch one day. As Shari, Betty, Ron and I were chatting away and enjoying our lunch, Shari's cell phone rang. She didn't say a word but passed the phone to each of us, starting with me. It was our brother Vern calling to speak with his "new" younger brother and sisters for the first time ever! Emotions ran rampant, as one can imagine, with joy, elation, and an overall sense of completeness, for we had found the last missing piece of our puzzle.

The Cousins

Fast forward to last summer, three years after I met Vern. I had been invited to join the Hill-57 Chippewa-Cree Native American site on Facebook by Brenda Snyder. Brenda is of Metis heritage and had been helping me with my initial search for Vern several years ago. She suggested that I ask the members of this site if there were any descendants of the Lasarte and Larance families. A woman had privately messaged Brenda, believing she was a long-lost Lasarte cousin. Brenda gave me the cousin's FB name and I immediately sent her a message. Yes, indeed, she was my cousin Elaine and she had been looking for family for decades, just as I had. She told me I had many many cousins who had been adopted out or had basically been taken out of the family home as children. Elaine had so much to tell me that my head was spinning.

There were 11 children in her family. Her birth parents, like mine, were rather dysfunctional, both parents alcoholic and the mother mentally ill. Welfare got wind of the circumstances and placed all the children in foster homes. The five youngest children were sent to a Catholic orphanage in Helena, Montana. Eventually, all but one was adopted out separately. The youngest girl went back to live with her parents. Quoted by Elaine, "Anybody with a little money could buy one of us as an Indian slave...that's the way it really was for most of us." Elaine further stated that it was like her brothers and sisters just vanished off the face of the earth and she never saw or heard from them again. She did find out later that two of her sisters went to good homes and had good lives. The family was told that the baby sister died in a car accident; in reality, she is alive and well and was the most recently found sister. Out of their 11 original siblings, five have passed away, and one has chosen not to reunite.

Within minutes, Elaine had notified her sisters that they had new cousins and almost instantaneously, Betty, Shari and I were connected to Dree and Theresa, two of the sisters. Elaine explained that two other sisters, Lois and Maggie weren't on Facebook and therefore, we would have to communicate another way with them. Lois contacted me within a few days via email and she and I have been in fairly frequent contact. Maggie doesn't have a computer so all information goes from me to Elaine who calls Maggie with updates. I also was "virtually" introduced to Elaine's daughter, Paula, who lives in Albuquerque. It just so happened that I was traveling to that city in two weeks and actually got to meet Cousin Paula and her husband. This was the first time either one of us actually met a blood relative other than our immediate families.

A few months later, I happened about the Hill-57 site again and much to my delight, two more cousins replied to my request. These cousins are on my maternal grandmother's side of the family, one residing in California and the other living on the "rez" in Montana. She chooses to use her Chippewa name and speaks fluent Chippewa. This cousin, Linda, just informed me that we have a cousin in Reno. The other new cousins said we have a cousin in Tacoma, just two hours from where I live. All of my new cousins are enrolled Chippewa-Cree and insist that my brothers and sisters and I are of the same band.

I quickly learned from my new relatives that no matter how we are related, we are all cousins. I have been welcomed into their lives with open arms and more love and acceptance than I could ever imagine. And it doesn't matter if we are first, second or third cousins, we are family.

29

Eleven Months/Eleven Years

SUZIE/CRICKET SMITH-FEDORKO (Anishinabe)

Suzie/Cricket

It has been almost eleven years to the day that I received that phone call from my half-sister Sarah. It took Sarah a couple of days to locate me using the internet in 2002. I had been searching to locate anyone in my biological family for twenty-two years.

The things that I have learned in the eleven-year adjustment period have been interesting to say the least. Each year seems to bring a calm and more inner peace along with facing the dramas. I consider myself a very strong person most of the time. There have been some distasteful situations that surfaced that leave me bitter. I have always tried to be the person who tries to see the world through others. My relationship with some of my biological half siblings has crumbled. There is nothing I can do about the circumstances that have played out, except remind myself who my biological parents are.

I have to continue to remind myself that I am the first born. Regardless if I was/was not wanted in either biological parent's life, I am not a discard. I have accepted that I may have been an obstacle, but that does not mean that I did not belong. I have to remind myself that my biological birth mother Cathee Dahmen kept me for the first 11 months of my life. I meant the world to her for 11 months. I have been told two conflicting stories about what transpired surrounding my adoption. Some have said that it was my Grandmother's fault for packing me up and sending me away. Some say it was Cathee herself that surrendered me. Regardless what happened, I was still there for 11 months of her choice. I was brought home from the hospital after she gave birth to me.

I was questioned about my identity by two of my biological siblings. Both of whom I'd met several years ago. At the time of those meetings several years ago, there was never any inkling that they doubted that I was indeed the "real Cricket." Apparently those doubts surfaced a couple of years ago.

I had been cyber-stocked by someone who appeared to know Cathee's family very well. This person was posting very hurtful things with accusations that I may not be the "real Cricket." It clearly was someone close to the family because this person posed as my adopted sister, my half-sister, as well as other made-up characters. I had enough of the drama and sought my local police department and had these emails traced. After several months it was discovered that the source was coming from Brooklyn NY, at the home of my half-brother. This was quite a shock that he harbored feeling of distrust. He tried to pass it off as being his new girlfriend's idea. I was now the person who was untrusting, and I still am. I've always come from a family that discusses issues. I think I knew in the back of my mind that it was coming from my biological birthmother's last/only son all along. I hope that our Mother is looking down with absolute disgust and astonishment that one of her own would react in this manner towards me. I can't help but think my birth mother would be disappointed with him.

During this reunion this has been my only disappointment with all the discoveries. I have had to learn to accept that I will never have all the answers about the circumstances of my adoption. I have been told two versions of what has happened. The first version was that my Grandmother—Mary Morrison was responsible for adopting me out. The second version was that Cathee herself surrendered me. I will never know the exact day and hour. I will never know what it did to Cathee as a young Mother. I will never know if it ever bothered Mary Morrison/Grandmother that I was no longer babbling words from my highchair. I will never know how often I was thought of by Cathee/Mary/Tom Conklin/Aunts and Uncles. I will never know the numerous times (if any) that I was thought of?

Acceptance has been a hard pill to swallow. With acceptance comes a blanket of content. I am not sure if I am there yet? At times I have just had to accept the uncertainty. Acceptance has been a good thing and I am a strong person. I have said it many times during this *Reunion—Adoption is not for the Weak.*

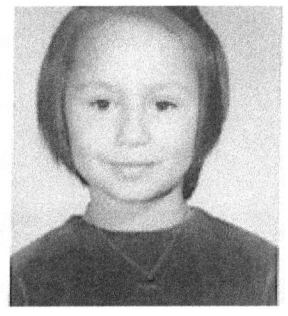

My immediate family has learned to accept all the changes. It was not easy in the beginning. My daughters were answering phone calls from Dahmen relatives who were asking for "Cricket." They did not like that I was referred to as someone else that was *very* strange to them. Time has healed the "Cricket."

Now that my book has been published, I have breathed a sigh of relief. It is in **print**, I am "Cricket." I had to make that finalization for myself. I was validated. I have had mixed reviews from my readers. My sister Sarah said that she enjoyed it. I believed her. I have believed every word she has said to me. This is a Sister's Trust. I find myself protective of the relationship that I have with my sister Sarah. This is as it should have been years ago.

I realize that there are many adoptees's who have had nightmare adoption reunions. I count myself very fortunate that mine was positive. I missed out on meeting both birth parents, but I can feel them watching me. Often at times, I can feel one birth parent more than the other. I hope their spirits crossed paths again after my birth father passed. Their presence is all around me, in my children. This is part of the acceptance. I've allowed myself to imagine positive things as a possibility. I am in a better place today than I was eleven years ago. It has been eleven years since I was found. Many opportunities have become from the reunion. I've met some wonderful people that I would have never met. This is a perk from my grief. Never give up on believing someone may be searching for you!

Suzie Smith Fedorko is the author of Cricket: Secret Child of a Sixties Supermodel.

30

Unringing the Bell: Annulling My Adoption

BEN ANI CHOSA (Lac du Flambeau Anishinabe/Menominee)

Ani in Washington (2001)

I will look forward about as far as I can look backwards, which I warn you isn't very far. When you last heard from me I was incarcerated. I'm still incarcerated.

There is hope. It has to do a lot with what seems to be Indian Country's national pastime: drinking. It would seem that I was born to a couple of hard charging drinkers. And part of the reason that I am the way I am is that my gin-soaked brain makes astoundingly bad decisions. It's all part of Fetal Alcohol Spectrum Disorders. I seem to be exhibiting all the symptoms of this malady, which makes sense given my cultural and family history. My older sister was diagnosed recently with FASD, so it wouldn't be much of a stretch to have some form of it myself.

Ani in Third Grade, 1976

Of course life can't be that easy. I hail from a state (Wisconsin) that prides itself on its beer brewing heritage; its identity is so steeped in alcohol that its professional baseball team is named The Brewers. Not to mention that FASD is relatively new, conceptually/legally in Wisconsin. It's going to be an uphill charge to find out if knowing this about myself could make any difference to me or anyone else, but this Indian ain't got much else to do.

Drinking/FASD plays a part in the other consuming passion of my life: having my adoption annulled. I know that there are plenty of Indians that have walked similar roads: thieved from their tribes, cultures, and families only to later in life return to those things and try to pick up the pieces of their lives. I'm doing that the best I can. Yet for me the bell can't be un-rung. Whatever sop given to my psyche is not going to be good enough. I've lost too much never to be regained unless the dead can be raised and what was done undone.

My goal with annulling the adoption IS FOR THE COURT TO RECOGNIZE THAT IN MY CASE WHAT WAS DONE NOT ONLY TO ME BUT FOR ALL INDIANS WAS WRONG. I know of no other way to get that recognition. Words would be nice but a legal order is forever. Luckily for me the Whites are nothing if not nuts for record keeping. I believe I have enough documentation to be able to prove that what was done to me was in violation of state law. Wish me luck.

I'm still producing artwork when time allows, I'm working in the kitchen at the moment, and I am in the midst of several pro se legal cases which gobble up what little time I have to myself. I'm stingy with my letters and have certainly deprived family and friends of my company, such as it is, but I'm a blessed and lucky man. I'm not alone in this world and for me that is all that matters.

(This man has run out of news.)

Ani's blog can be found at: www.scottckieson.blogspot.com
Ani's artwork can be seen at: www.banishedart.blogspot.com

31

Seven Year Cycles

MESCHELLE LINJEAN (Tsalagi)

Mom, Leona, Meschelle, (front) Genia, Linda

Some say that our lives are lived in seven-year cycles and I'm beginning to have an appreciation for that notion. Between the ages of 35 and 42, my life unraveled, peaking from age 38-41. At age 42, I started the journey toward sewing it back together – hopefully with more even stitching, tighter bonds, and no loose threads this time around. I've been thinking of my entry into middle adulthood as "catharsis unchained." Let me explain…

After having known my birth mom and sisters for over 20 years, I thought I had gotten to a place of complacency about the identity crises I had experienced as a result of being an indigenous child adopted out to a family of the dominant society, then abandoned by my adoptive mother and reared by an abusive Seneca stepmother — but not so much. In my 38th year, fueled by too much alcohol and "benzos" (benzodiazeprines prescribed for anxiety and panic attacks), my unresolved past caught up with me. The pot that had been boiling on the back burner began to spill over. That is the year that I began long, drunken hours on the phone with my birth mom, discussing exploits and escapades in family dysfunction and suicidal ideation — some of it hers, some of it mine. My mom has a lot of pain from her childhood, which really wasn't much of a childhood at all. She was raised in Oaks Indian Mission and rarely got to go home even during the summers because there was no one who would take care of her, my grandma being firmly entrenched in the bottle during those days and our extended family having traditional values severely decimated. When mom did get to be at home, there was abject poverty and violence. There was no nurturing or trust to allow her to develop self-esteem and self-efficacy. She had her childhood betrayed in every way imaginable and her developing spirit stunted. Her brothers couldn't protect her and I'm sure my uncles had their own trauma. Mom and I didn't really discuss her childhood per se. I had learned most of those details from my sisters. Instead, mom and I talked more abstractly about all the pain and the lack of nurturing and kinship values in our family. We talked of problems that were handed down through the generations. We talked of loneliness, lack of empathy, and denial. We never talked of hope or solutions.

Over and over mom and I would go through the history of how no one was there for her when she was pregnant with me, no one would give her a ride to the hospital when she went into labor, how she believed my sisters blamed her and hated her for giving me away… We were caught in a cycle of reliving our pain and perpetually abusing ourselves with it. And we did this for a couple of years. Wanting so much to be a part of my mom's world—to be an insider to her suffering and really know her on the deep level I felt I had been denied as a result of my adoption—I neglected my own responsibilities on the days when we would have our pity parties. Mom cried. I cried—myself getting four sheets to the wind with my own empty bottles in front of me, drowning the pain of reconnection, blunting the discomfort of the unearthing. Probably because of the booze and the pills, I couldn't see that not only was my own life falling apart around me, but that I was beating at it unmercifully with a sledgehammer.

In the midst of our pity parties, I would sometimes ask for information about the identity of my birth father and fail to get a satisfactory answer. She named someone called Mike Stevens, but assured me that they never "finished" the deed that would've resulted in my conception because they were interrupted by her brothers who didn't want her to be with the guy. Something about this story has never rung true for me. One time I created a big brouhaha because I called one of my great aunts to try to get her insider knowledge about the identity of my birth father. Mom found out and the next time I called her she yelled at me and told me that I had stirred up some shit. She called me a drunk and told me I was selfish. Both of those things were true at the time. But because I was hurt and believed she was wrong for withholding vital information from me, I retaliated by telling her I wasn't selfish because I had paid for her to get her car fixed. She set me straight right away by telling me that you're never supposed to bring up the fact that you've done something for someone—that a gift is supposed to be from the heart and it's disrespectful to throw it in someone's face. I was ashamed, but I remember thinking even in my inebriation, "Well, how about that? Maybe all the traditional values in our family weren't lost after all." I was humbled. Mom and I didn't talk for months after that, but I now consider that event to have been a success. Not only did my mom actually correct my behavior as if she was my parent, but we had reached a point where, after 18 years of knowing her, I had gotten comfortable enough with her to show her my anger and my faults. I was no longer treading on eggshells and acting like an acquaintance or a guest. The argument made me feel more like a genuine member of the family—someone who belonged. Mom probably sees it differently, but I think my feelings illustrate something that other adoptees can relate to. I still don't know who my birth father is, and maybe I never will. Somehow, I will have to make peace with that. But not today.

Wanting to be an insider to the rest of my birth family, I would call my sisters to discuss the details of various family dramas as they unfolded: who had beaten up whom, who had created a scene at the hospital, who had stolen what from whom, who had been arrested, etc. I enmeshed with the chaos as much as I could from 1,200 miles away. Since our first meeting in 1990, I had always made a point to embrace the dysfunction within my birth family, wanting to completely dispel any notion that I was "different" or thought I was "better than" them because I had been adopted by a middle class White family, rather than growing up in poverty. I had been prepared to take such flack from my birth family when I met them. I *assumed* they would think I had somehow had it better than they'd had it and that I might be stuck up. For the most part, I didn't experience that kind of attitude from them at all. There was one instance in which my birth mom told the mother of my ex-husband (a full-blood Cherokee), "Meschelle's not like us Indians." That hurt me greatly and I wanted to do everything in my power to prove her wrong. I didn't want to be a "textbook Indian" who only knew things learned from my college anthropology courses (I was an anthropology major before I ever heard Floyd Westerman's "Here Come the Anthros" ... I now understand the need for community-based research). I also didn't have any traditional elders to teach me what was important. So, I lunged headfirst into learning the art of pulling a weekend drunk, riding around on the back roads and showing up at different people's houses—wherever we could keep the drunk going ("Crrrack! (opening a can of beer)...What's that? Indian alarm clock!" was a typical joke). I wasn't going to miss out on anything. I felt like I belonged when I was with the crowd getting thrown out of the bar and managed to have "the laws" take me to jail on a public drunk charge. My insecurities had me working overtime, trying to develop some Indian street cred and fit in. I had some good times, but I'm sure I made an ass of myself on occasion too.

My continual striving for belonging, and perhaps some of the ignorance and assumptions of mainstream America that I had picked up over my lifetime, blinded me to the fact that I actually did NOT escape the family dysfunction that my sisters had grown up with at all. It seems laughable, now that I am out of denial about my own childhood neglect and abuse, that I once had "survivors guilt." For years, I thought I needed to prove myself to my birth family solely because I wasn't raised in poverty and among Cherokees. In reality, my need for approval greatly stemmed from the fact that, like my birth mom, I did not have security as a child and wasn't given the love and nurturing I needed to learn to value myself without the need for reassurance from others.

It was in my 38th year that I began to seek input from others about my upbringing and realize the magnitude of what I had experienced as a child. More significantly, I began to understand the profound repercussions my childhood continued to have on my adult life and my relationships with myself and others. I think the catalyst for this mission was that I was in a relationship with someone with whom I butted heads in a way that forced me to open my eyes and mind to considering that part of the problem could actually be ME—that the way I related to him might be off. I could tell that my methods of arguing and ensuring that I was heard and understood seemed vastly different from his. Although I didn't think of it that way, I spent agonizing amounts of energy trying to control his thoughts about, and reactions to, me. I now realize that trying to control another person is immature, counterproductive, and self-defeating. I think the dawning occurred because, unlike most of my previous significant others, this guy's background was NOT obviously dysfunctional. Instead of fighting with me in the way to which I had become accustomed (yelling back; storming around breaking things; being controlling, manipulative, or aggressive) this guy called my behavior unreasonable. He just did not get it, would not engage with it, and eventually, refused to be around it. Regrettably, this awakening came to me in stops and starts with much backsliding, muddled and hazy through the tranquilized fog of benzos and benders. My discoveries started slowly but I eventually began to seek validation for my growing suspicions.

I first asked my oldest friend, that I had known since kindergarten, if she thought I had been abused. She kind of laughed and said something like, "Well, DUH. Of course you were!" I guess that up until that time in my life, I wasn't sure just how "different" what I had experienced was from the backgrounds of others. I had dismissed the pain and denied the consequences ("Everyone has had something bad happen to them in childhood; sure I had some beatings and yeah, some people took advantage of me sexually, but I turned out okay; it's no big deal"). I had made excuses for my parents ("They grew up during the Depression when times were hard and people had to be tough; they were Baptists who believed in 'spare the rod, spoil the child' and they didn't have good role models"). What is most shaming to admit is that even as I was in denial about the pain and hurt I experienced as a child, I sometimes used my childhood dysfunction to make excuses for my own adult dysfunctional attitudes and behaviors ("I was treated like Cinderella as a child, so if I have to do chores today, then I'm going to drink while I do it to make it more pleasant; I'll buy you your OWN ice cream but I won't let you have a bite of MINE, because that kind of sharing is not natural for me because of how I was raised"). Today, I am still early in the process of creating the balance between loving and nurturing the abused and neglected child within, while relinquishing the selfish survival defense mechanisms I learned along the way (this is referred to as "reparenting"). But it took years to even get to this point. I had more discovery work to do first.

From ages 38 to 39, in a drunken, dazed stupor, I repeatedly contacted the daughter of my long deceased Seneca stepmother—the woman I had come to call my "stepmonster" who had abused me physically, emotionally, and spiritually—to discuss what had been done to me and to find out if anyone was aware of what was happening when I was a child. I was well aware that my stepmother was a boarding school survivor—having been born in 1917 she was sent to Chilocco Indian School in the 1920s and 1930s. But I also had firsthand knowledge of what happens when victims become perpetrators (my stepmother was both and I myself have been both; abuse is the gift that keeps on giving until the trauma is healed and the cycle stops). I wanted my pain, and my wounds, to be known. "Vivian," I slurred, "Your mom used to tell me I was going to Hell because I was a bastard and the sins of the parents are visited upon the child. She was always slapping me upside the head—once for folding my dad's underwear the wrong way—throwing things at me, beating me with belts and willow switches, and telling me that I'd never amount to anything. She called me a sneaky liar and told me that I was ugly and that I stunk. She sabotaged relationships with my friends. She started falsely accusing me of pulling my pants down in front of boys in school when I was only 5-6 years old. I was scared to death of her and didn't have anyone I could trust to help me. This stuff is still bothering me all these years later, so I'm finally deciding to tell someone in your family about it. Maybe if I get it out, I can get passed it." Well, getting it out didn't get me passed it. At least not then. Maybe the boozy whining and crying around about the past was the first step in releasing the pain. Maybe it was necessary for the recovery work I'm doing now. But at the time, it made me more depressed, allowed me to live from the standpoint of a victim (i.e., "My childhood was so bad, I *deserve* to be a little irresponsible and out of control sometimes now!"), and served to alienate my lover and, sometimes, my best friends. Ooooh boy. As much as I thought I was getting to the bottom of my issues, I was mostly just getting to the bottom of a bottle. I still had a long way to go.

By 2010, I was in a sociology Master's program, where I took several courses on the sociology of the family. While I was able to use my intellectual capacity for my schoolwork and professional work, in my home life, I vomited my unwieldy emotions all over my significant other and our relationship was in dire straits. I was too self-absorbed and emotionally impaired by substances to see what was happening, and my priorities in life were still severely out of whack.

In August 2012, I completed my Master's program with a research paper on the experiences and perceptions of American Indians and Alaska Natives who had been transracially adopted. As part of that experience, I was introduced to the Native American Indian Adoptees Facebook group. It was enlightening to finally find, at the age of 42, that I was not alone in my experiences and feelings, or in the unique ways in which my childhood had affected my adulthood.

In November 2012, I attended the Gathering for Our Children and Returning Adoptee Pow Wow in Minneapolis. But as much as I wanted to go, my old insecurities immediately reared their ugly heads— "Is the pow wow only for people from Native communities around the Minneapolis area? Will I be accepted? Will they wonder why I want to be accepted as an Indian when I look so White? Will they think I'm one of those people who claim their great-great-grandmother was a Cherokee princess? Will they think I'm a wannabe?" Sandy

White Hawk, one of the primary organizers and Director of the First Nations Repatriation Institute, gave me her phone number to call when I arrived. She put us adoptees in touch with one another as soon as we got to Minneapolis and made sure that everyone had a ride to the gathering. Thankfully, I was able to meet another adoptee, Jennifer Joy Meyers, for dinner the night before and she drove me to the gathering the next day. We signed in and then went into a room where chairs had been placed in a circle. When Sandy first spoke to the group, she mentioned so many of the fears I had and made them seem normal. I was so relieved to hear that other people had the same apprehensions and questions that I did! Then we all introduced ourselves and talked a little about our backgrounds. Those in attendance included adults who had been adopted out of their tribes as children or had aged out of foster care, currently fostered children, and an elementary school age adoptee and her non-Indian adoptive parents who were there to support her. In addition, Sharyn Whiterabbit, a birth mother who had given up her son for adoption over 30 years ago was there for her own healing. I was slowly put at ease as it became clearer and clearer that I wasn't alone in my feelings any more. Sandy also explained to us what the pow wow and ceremony would entail. When we entered the arena for Grand Entry, the adoptees, formerly fostered, and current foster children came in right behind the veterans carrying the eagle staff and flags. The Wablenica Honor song, created by Jerry Dearly and translated from Lakota into English, was sung as part of our ceremony. In part, the song says, "Orphans/adoptees be strong. Our Indian ways are strong. Listen to them." I was a little self-conscious when the ceremony itself began because we were all in the center of the arena in front of everyone. Then Sandy stood right in front of me and began the pipe ceremony. I had never been a part of a pipe ceremony before, so my first thought, was "Oh no! I can't go first! I don't know what I'm supposed to do!" I knew that tobacco is an offering and that the smoke carries our prayers to the Creator, but I didn't know if there was a particular way I was supposed to hold the pipe or how many times to pull the smoke into my mouth. I got really nervous, but at the same time it was like something was holding me securely. Sandy had told us that we couldn't mess anything up. Once I was able to hold the smoke to my mouth she met my eyes and nodded at me, so I knew that it was time for the pipe to be offered to the adoptee on my left, a Choctaw woman Debra Newman, who came to the gathering with her sister that she had recently found. Next, jingle dress dancers healed us with their medicine dance as they moved around us and touched our shoulders with their eagle feather fans. I stood in the circle, sharing in the ceremony and healing with others who needed the same things I needed. After the ceremony, the pow wow dancers and community members from elders to little children all came in procession and shook our hands and welcomed us back into the circle. I had seen people honored at pow wows before but had never participated in going out and shaking hands with those being honored. The protocol had never been explained to me and I had never felt as if I was part enough of the community to participate in the honoring. Now, here I was on the receiving end. It was such an amazing experience to receive such a gift, and to be honored with other adoptees and recognized as children our ancestors had prayed for. I think that was the most significant part of the ceremony for me—learning that our ancestors had prayed for us to be here and having the community recognize and accept us in that way. That knowledge and acceptance was life changing. It told me that I was wanted and that I have a place in the circle.

    I certainly didn't expect my life to fall apart after that ceremony and gathering, but it seemed that it did. In December 2012, I started reeling from the symptoms of benzo withdrawal (I had actually had my last dose of the medication in July 2012 and had experienced symptoms since then, but it took a while for my body to go into severe shock from the drug's elimination). I developed so many alarming neurological symptoms that I was terrified I had MS or Parkinsons disease, and the symptoms morphed and increased in severity for the next 8 months (I have still not completely healed and some damage, such as new food sensitivities/allergic responses and dystonic reactions might continue indefinitely). I felt like I had been poisoned and my body fluids had been replaced with battery acid. I vibrated all the time as if I was leaning against an electric fence and at times I could barely walk because of balance problems and visual and sensory distortions. I constantly had vertigo and felt like I was undulating on a rocking boat even when I was sitting still. I often felt as if I was experiencing g-force or that the force of gravity had increased a thousand-fold. I also often felt as if rigor mortis was setting in while I was still alive. I developed oro-mandibular dystonia (what feels like episodic lock-jaw and stone-face) and severe chemical and food sensitivities. I was in the ER about 100 times from January to July, convinced that I was about to drop dead. Only about 10 percent of people have such a severe benzo withdrawal experience, but it is very real (more information and help are available at: http://www.benzo.org.uk/manual/bzcha03.htm and http://www.benzobuddies.org/benzodiazepine-information/frequently-asked-questions/). If this had not happened to me personally, I would think someone was exaggerating if they described having these experiences so frequently and for so long. Two neurologists suggested to me that all of my previous traumas had been stored in my neural pathways and the shock to my nervous system from the benzo withdrawal could have been the straw that broke the camel's back—that my body was now reacting to everything (including food and ordinary, everyday smells and sounds) as if it was a threat. Eventually, I was also diagnosed with PTSD. This experience has made me want to conduct a study on the prevalence of prior trauma among those who suffer the most severe and prolonged damage from benzos. At any rate, the stored trauma that I had kept at bay and self-medicated away WAS finding its way out. I was literally bursting at my seams.

After recently speaking with Trace DeMeyer, I was offered another way to look at what was happening to me: the ceremony I had attended in November opened me up to the opportunity for greater healing. I now see the wisdom in her words. I have come to see the "Wiping of the Tears" ceremony as also a "lifting of the veil." It likely opened the door to a release of long buried distress. I will need to participate in the ceremony again to have the tears shed from this newly revealed layer of myself wiped away as well.

After the Gathering for Our Children, a Blackfoot/Apache woman I work with told me that a ceremony with the pipe generally constitutes making a promise of some kind. I had not consciously made any promises during the ceremony. When I reflected on this woman's words, however, I realized that what I could offer is to continue educating people about the Native adoptee experience whenever an opportunity presents itself. Despite my almost constant state of anxiety and physical symptoms stemming from benzo withdrawal, I took this promise to heart and did the best I could with the opportunities that arose in the next several months. I now have to admit that I took on too much when I should have been healing myself physically and emotionally. I made my health a lot worse by undertaking these emotionally taxing activities while trying to cope with the dissolution of my relationship with my significant other and undergoing severe repercussions from benzo withdrawal at the same time.

My first opportunity to continue the work of the Gathering for Our Children ceremony was to speak with my Principal Chief, Bill John Baker, when he came to Washington, DC for a Cherokee Nation community meeting on January 30, 2013. Although I was experiencing substantial visual and sensory distortions that night, I was able to present him with a copy of *Two Worlds: Lost Children of the Indian Adoption Projects*, and a statement and proposal I had written. The statement discussed my personal experiences with reconnecting with my birth family and the Cherokee Nation, and my experiences at the Gathering for Our Children. The proposal was really more of request, asking the Cherokee Nation to consider (perhaps in conjunction with other tribes in northeastern Oklahoma) a program to recognize and heal returning adoptees and formerly fostered tribal citizens, to offer cultural mentorship for those in foster care, to heal birth families, and to educate foster and adoptive families. I offered to assist and collaborate on any efforts considered. I believed the request was timely given that the "Baby Veronica" case would soon be heard before the U.S. Supreme Court. Chief Baker promised he would take the information back to the appropriate division of our tribal government, most likely our Indian Child Welfare department, but perhaps another division. I again spoke briefly with Chief Baker at the Supreme Court on the day of the "Baby Veronica" hearing, but I have not yet had a response about the proposal.

In March 2013, I was able to present the research on Native adoptees that I had conducted for my sociology Master's degree (The Transracial Adoption of Native Children as a Form of Social Inequality) at the annual meeting of the Pacific Sociological Association (PSA) in Reno, NV. I also presented a second paper there, American Indian Grandmas as Custodians and Cultural Conservators and was able to tie in the importance of extended families in tribal life as a protection for our children against being adopted outside their tribes. I received good feedback and could tell that the statements of the adoptees I interviewed (some of their stories are also in this book and the first *Two Worlds*) touched the hearts of those in attendance. I believed those I spoke with at PSA would support Native people, at least in spirit, with the upcoming Supreme Court case on the Indian Child Welfare Act (ICWA). Unfortunately, I was so sick from benzo withdrawal that I thought I might die while I was in Reno. The authorities on this withdrawal syndrome emphasize the importance of avoiding stress while going through it and I couldn't have been under more stress, especially given my phobia of public speaking. When I wasn't presenting, I generally had to lie quietly in my room. I took a lot of Benadryl to help me get through that week. Once I got through my presentations, I was able to have something of a healing respite, thanks to Gina Jackson, a beautiful woman I had met at the Gathering for Our Children who works to educate judges about ICWA. We had lunch and then she took me around to see the wild horses. I am very grateful to her and honored to call her my friend.

I had also met Tara Pretends Eagle Weber at the Gathering for Our Children and she has become a very good friend of mine. She, along with Sandy White Hawk, was instrumental in having the attorneys for Dusten Brown, Cherokee Nation citizen and biological father of "Baby Veronica", interview me for the amicus brief filed in support of Dusten and the Cherokee Nation in the fight for Dusten to maintain custody of his daughter and for ICWA to be upheld in the spirit in which it was intended. The amicus brief included testimonies from Native adoptees who had been adversely affected by being adopted out of their tribes prior to ICWA's enactment. It was an honor for me to be among those who, because they had robbed of their birthrights and had their identities hidden and spirits fractured, were doing what they could to have ICWA upheld so that other Native children need not suffer the same fate. This case was an opportunity for the U.S. to strengthen ICWA and its protections for Native children. It was a special honor for me to contribute to the amicus brief because I am Cherokee by birth and a Cherokee Nation citizen since the age of 20. In addition to supporting ICWA for all Native people, I also felt that I was giving from the heart, from one Cherokee citizen to another, and to my tribe, in the spirit of gadugi.

Unfortunately, we did not get the outcome we had hoped for. I attended the hearing at the U.S. Supreme Court on April 16, 2013 along with Sandy, Gina, Christina White Eagle (another adoptee I had become friends with after meeting her at the Gathering for Our Children) and Leland Morrill, a Native adoptee from the Facebook group that I had interviewed for my Master's research. It was wonderful to reunite with everyone for such an important event. I was able to have dinner with Sandy, her husband George, and Gina the night before, and pack sandwiches for everyone to eat after the hearing. We "tailgated" with coolers and lawn chairs as we waited in line from the early hours to ensure that we got tickets to be in attendance at the hearing. Inopportunely, I began having pretty serious benzo withdrawal symptoms after we got inside the court building. My jaw was clamping shut and I felt like I had a high fever with severe sensory distortions. I could hardly walk into the courtroom, but I was able to make it through the arguments for the "adoptive couple" before needing to bail out. I completely missed the arguments in favor of Dusten Brown because I was in the nurse's station. It was all I could do to maintain some semblance of composure until the hearing was over and I could get to my car and then to the hospital. I had felt like I was going to drop dead so many times before since the withdrawal started, but that day was the scariest yet.

After all the stressful activity in early 2013, my health completely deteriorated. I didn't think my symptoms could get any worse after what I experienced in Reno and at the Supreme Court, but they did. I became so tired of being terrified for my life because of the physical symptoms I was having every day that I thought about ending my life. It wasn't that I was too depressed to live; it was that I was too scared. I felt terrorized, as if there was a voodoo doll of me and I never knew when a pin would be stuck in or in which body part it would be stuck. I didn't want to die in terror. My symptoms had become so bad that, by July, I was waking in the middle of every night, unable to breathe and having convulsions. I became so desperate that I began praying—something I hadn't done since I was a child. I prayed for divine help. I prayed that I would find a human healer to help me. I am not a Christian but I began visiting the "meditation rooms" at the hospital when I went to the ER. I also spoke with a hospital chaplain one time. I am beginning to believe that I had already started the healing and that what I was experiencing was a part of it. It was like I had to be completely torn down and decimated into a pool of quivering near-nothingness in order to be slowly and painfully reshaped and reformed. I'm still being rebuilt but I'm slowly becoming able to participate more in my reconstruction.

In July 2013, motivated by an authority on benzo withdrawal, I spent a lot of money to see a psychiatrist who specializes in functional medicine, in hopes of getting the right medical treatment for my condition. He took an extensive history of my personal background as well as my physical symptoms. Unfortunately he was completely ignorant of the severe, long-term damage benzos can cause. The visit might have been a complete waste of money had the man not recommend that I get involved in a 12-step program. He said that, given my background, I could use "a crash course in normality" and a 12-step program could deliver it. I had already stopped drinking alcohol (which is like a "liquid benzo" since it also acts as a sedative-hypnotic on the same neuroreceptors) by that point. So, I decided to investigate Adult Children Anonymous (ACA), a program for children who grew up with alcoholics or other dysfunctional parents. I had already been scheduled to start a three-day hospital stay for video EEG monitoring the day after my appointment with the psychiatrist because there was some concern that I was having cryptic seizures (I wasn't). I purchased the "big book" for Adult Children of Alcoholics and *Emotional Sobriety* by Tian Dayton to read while I was hospitalized. I was blown away by what I read. It was like the authors of these books had been spying on me and taking notes. The Saturday after I got out of the hospital, I attended my first ACA meeting. I've only been attending these meetings and making use of the concepts for six months now, but I have been exposed to some important things about relinquishing the standpoint of a victim, taking responsibility for what I can control, and accepting what I can't control. I also learned that I am codependent and began attending Codependents Anonymous (CoDA) meetings as well. Until I started attending 12 step meetings, I thought codependency meant that you were in a relationship with someone who was an alcoholic or an addict! But it is really about focusing on others instead of yourself. In relationships, the so-called "adult children" issues often manifest as either love/intimacy avoidance (e.g., for children who were forced to take care of their parents or were emotionally engulfed by them) or love addiction (e.g., for those who were physically and/or emotionally abandoned by their parents and consequently look to others for their validation and self-worth). I generally fall into the latter category. Love addicts/codependents and love avoidants are often drawn to one another like a hummingbird to nectar (or a fly to sh*t) with painful outcomes. This has been the dynamic in most all my significant other relationships to date. Only with my ex-husband was I the love avoidant; in the others I was codependent. What I am now learning is that, for the so called "love addicts," beneath the conscious fear of abandonment is an unconscious fear of intimacy that causes them to choose partners who become emotionally unavailable because it echoes their upbringing. The psychological theory is that we are subconsciously trying to recreate the patterns of our childhood in an effort to correct what went wrong. Well, I'm living proof that this subconscious strategy doesn't work. When you have learned maladaptive approaches to boundaries and control, you have to consciously recognize and unlearn those and then consciously learn more effective ways of doing things.

Without an understanding of boundaries, I had failed to protect myself with boundaries and also sometimes violated the boundaries of others by bursting in like a charging bull. As an example, for over 20 years, I had been trying to attach myself to my birth family in various unhealthy ways. I did not always know how to achieve healthy intimacy, so I sometimes took on the problems of my birth family members as if they were my own. One time, during that whole sh*tstorm (as I now call the meltdown/catalyst for catharsis that occurred from ages 38-40 years old), I called the Cherokee Nation tribal housing authority on behalf of my birth mom. Based on faulty information she had given me, I became very indignant with them for not helping her with her housing situation. After several phone calls and the housing authority taking time to look into her case, I learned that what my mom had told me was not the whole story. The housing authority staff had actually done their job to the best of their ability. I felt like a fool because I had been manipulated to act on her behalf and because I had made false accusations against innocent people. Another time, I sent one of my birth sisters money to keep her utilities turned on. When my birth mom learned of this, she told me that I had been fooled. Apparently, my sister was not in any danger of having her utilities turned off, the kids were not going to be cold, and my sister had other means of obtaining money at any rate. These are just two examples and, while there was dysfunction on both sides of these situations, I do not believe my birth family deliberately set out to deceive me or take advantage of me. Because of their own upbringing and circumstances since then, they have been just as unskilled in appropriate behavior as I have been. But I can only speak for myself. I have to acknowledge that my motives for "helping" were not entirely selfless. My reactivity, lack of personal boundaries, and codependence had me jumping at any chance to "earn my way in" to acceptance and belonging. I was trying to forge a family in whatever way I could.

I have now reached a point where I am maintaining healthier boundaries with my birth family as I develop my own inner strength. Since having this crash course in "normality" that the psychiatrist spoke of, when I hear my birth mom talk from the standpoint of a victim (e.g., when she is very depressed – and she actually HAS been victimized horribly) it is like holding up a mirror to the ugliness of the victimhood stance I had unknowingly espoused for so long. I want nothing more to do with a victim worldview but I am finding that it takes a lot of hard work and constant vigilance to recognize it and fight it when the tendencies rear. Some maladaptive feelings and beliefs are well ingrained and insidious. Awareness and mindfulness are key in overthrowing them, and it's hard to concentrate on making the changes in myself when I am snagged into a codependent dance with a birth mom I have habituated to trying to emulate for so long.

One of the most meaningful and gratifying things I have ever heard in my life is my birth mom's voice saying, "Meschelle, you're so much like me." I have been elated to hear that from her a few times over the years. Since my mom was a bit of a wild child in her teenage years and her 20s, and I got to know her when I was in my 20s, I had many occasions to show her my own reckless spirit and remind her of her "glory" days. Since she had depression and anxiety, I was actually okay with suffering from those too. Hell, even when I developed rheumatoid arthritis it was buffered by the fact that I had *inherited* it from my birth mom! But here's the thing. I have also had to wake up to the fact that I have at times let my mom's depression drag me down to the point where I was not taking care of myself.

Worse still, I have had to wake up to the fact that, over the years I have often "passed along" my overwhelm and emotional vomitus to my other family members (i.e. my adoptive mom), my friends, and my most recent (former) significant other. This realization has come as a result of the tremendous chaos of the past two years and reflecting back further in time. I'm still angry and disillusioned at the way this all happened. This whole sh*tstorm did not just happen to ME. Coming to terms with the repercussions of my stunted development, the frenzy of adult growing pains, and the nearly unbearable chaos, trauma, and emotional meltdown that stemmed from the terrifying health catastrophe occurring simultaneously with the most horrendous relationship breakup I have ever consciously endured, has affected my loved ones as well. Relationships with friends and family have been strained. In my panic and desperation over this whole crisis, I have reacted selfishly and *demanded* help and attention. I have peeled back the layers to see this and I am raw and exposed. I have even thrown salt and acid on my wounds since making some progress. It has not been just forward progress since "the big reveal." There have been setbacks and I have sabotaged my own progress a few times. I do not yet see a happy ending in my future and I remain impatient. I can have all the drive and determination in the world but I do not control time and process.

I have been telling my birth mom about some of the concepts of ACA, but I am mindful of not coming across as a "know it all" or pushing my new beliefs on her when I am only still learning and trying to incorporate them myself. Besides, this is all stuff my mom knows intellectually anyway. The goal is ongoing practice that gets the concepts to sink into the heart and spirit. I think we all need healing—my birth mom, my birth sisters, me, and others who were hurt by family dysfunction and adoption. It need not come from a 12-step group like ACA. My mom is a Christian, so she is more open to the actual format of a 12-Step program than I have been. I'm guessing that many of the concepts of responsibility for the self and healthy relating to others are found in the wisdom of many spiritual traditions, including traditional Native ways. I hope to expand my knowledge of the right way to get along in the world to include these traditions. I can already see overlaps in the approaches taught in ACA and CoDA with Buddhism, meditation, and mind-body healing.

May we all find the healing we need in whatever form we are able to embrace it. Wado.

32

Finding Peace, Coming Home

DEBBY PRECIUS POITRAS (Cree)

Debby

Fast forward to May 2011.

After a few months of communicating through the social worker, I have been in contact with my younger brother born in 1957. Brian contacted me through Facebook (FB) after an exchange through the Social Worker. His wife searched FB and found me; both of us were impatient with the slow process of exchanging letters. Brian and his fiancé were getting married in May and asked if we would like to attend. I shared the good news with Ted, Rick and Joseph. Soon after, Brian went to Regina to meet with Rick. What a wonderful reunion they had. Ted was unable to come from BC for the wedding; however Joseph, Rick and myself all planned to attend. The month of May soon arrived and I flew to Regina for a week. Rick had undergone a few more amputations, this time up to his knee. His diabetes was out of control and the wounds were not healing. A true Poitras, stubborn to the bone, Rick insisted on driving three hours with his prosthetic leg. Joseph drove from Calgary with his youngest son Matt. Joseph made it to Saskatoon the day before the wedding. We had agreed to meet for a coffee at the hotel where Rick and I were staying. A welcome addition to the reunion was our cousin Jannica who had flown in from Vancouver for the wedding also.

Jannica is known for her documentaries about native children forcibly removed from their homes and placed in Indian Residential Schools in Canada and abroad. Joseph was amusing when he arrived at the hotel. Knowing he was nervous, I made sure I was calm and collected on his arrival. Getting out of his car, he smiled for a brief moment walking towards Rick and me. Suddenly he made a 360 degree turn and headed the other direction. My heart sank!! Had he changed his mind? He stopped for a minute, tried to regain his composure and walked once again towards Rick and myself. Hugs and tears followed. To this day we laugh about that moment; he has no idea why he turned away or what he was planning to do. The next two hours were filled with tears, stares and many stories about our childhoods. Looking at Rick and Joseph, they are so alike in behavior but so different in size. Joseph is not much bigger than myself and Rick is the gentle giant. I learn over the course of the next week that we have so many similarities but we are all so different. Like Rick, Joseph and I are true brother and sister. You couldn't ask for a tighter bond. We breathe the same air and share the same thoughts. We are one.

Soon our family would be embracing one another.
Wedding day arrives. Running fashionably late, we arrived about 5 minutes into Brian's wedding ceremony. There was our brother at the altar, a man we'd never met with his bride to be. Cricket, Brian's fiancé, was the first to see us walk in. Nervous, Brian was concentrating on his vows. Within minutes the happy couple were pronounced man and wife. The bridal party continued to the lobby of the church. It was then that the four siblings were reunited. What a beautiful moment. We all held one another for a moment, a few pictures and the happy couple continued outside for congratulations.

In the week that followed, the family spent days exploring Lebret, Saskatchewan where our mother Nora grew up and attended school. We shared a telephone call with our eldest brother Ted and shared our joy wishing he were there to join us. We visited the Roman Catholic church that our grandfather Zachary helped build. We dined with cousins and shared yet more stories. On our last day together the siblings visited our mother's unmarked grave along with our grandparents and Aunt Doris. We performed a smudge ceremony along with drumming and prayers led by cousin Jannica offering bannock on each grave along with a rose from each of us. I promised my

Poitras family at wedding

mother on my initial grave visit two years earlier that I would bring her children home to her. At last we were healing and I know our mother was smiling.

Meeting THE big brother.

In October 2011, I received a phone call from my brother Ted. He asked would I be available to meet them while his wife Lynne was on a business trip to Toronto in November. I was elated. All these new siblings coming to light in such a short time and I'm going to finally meet the "Chief" of our Poitras tribe.

Ted is a gift from God. Four years earlier Ted had been diagnosed with emphysema and survived a lung transplant. He was in grave danger and Medical professionals told Lynne he may not be able to withstand the surgery. After many medical hurdles, he made it. Today Ted is doing well and probably healthier than the rest of the siblings. I thank God daily in my prayers that he spared Ted and gave him a second chance to be with us.

On the morning of meeting Ted, it was my turn to be nervous. Miss Social Butterfly had turned to jello. I had my two daughters attend the meeting with me to calm my nerves. Waiting in the hotel lobby, I paced for what seemed like an eternity. Local CBC television crews were there to film the meeting. Suddenly a handsome man in his late 50's turned the corner and smiled. *Debby, I'm your brother Ted.* We held each other for a few minutes unable to speak. I wish I could share the emotions that I felt at that moment. Some say their world has fallen apart. At that moment I felt like my world was coming together. My daughters stood there beaming, seeing their Uncle for the first time. We shared the afternoon together, walking, talking, joking and sharing stories. We visited Niagara Falls, enjoyed the views and took photos in front of the falls. Things we should have been able to do as a family many years ago.

We met Lynne, Ted's wife and what a lovely couple they are. To be married for so many years and to be so in love and respectful of one another! That truly impressed us. My daughters still glow when speaking of their Aunt and Uncle. My brother and his wife truly have what we all hope for in married life but very few of us are able to capture.

Loss

In the months to follow, Rick's health was failing. He had now been diagnosed with throat cancer and the diabetes was giving him a hard time during chemo. The wounds were clearly not healing and chemo was not making the situation any easier. Yet he stayed strong, being the true Poitras that he was, a warrior.

On March 5, 2012, I spoke to my brother on the phone. He was about to start another round of chemo. You could hear it in his voice, he was getting weak. Rick was frustrated that he had to endure yet another round of treatments and yet put on his warrior face and stated he was fine. A loss of appetite made him weak and he was not able to get around to cook a decent meal. Rick was always a joker making wisecracks throughout our conversation. Something didn't feel right that evening as I hung up the phone. Another sleepless night for me.

On March 6, 2012, I checked my Facebook account at lunch.

To my horror, Rick's roommate had posted that my brother had passed away that morning. It seems he had gotten up in the morning and suffered a heart attack. She found him hours later. I was devastated as were my siblings. We had so little time together. A memorial service was held in May 2012 and Rick's ashes were buried with his adoptive parents. The days to follow were difficult. A small piece of me died that day and my grief has not ended. I believe we never stop grieving when we lose someone so dear to us. Rick's adopted family still call for Christmas and birthdays. They are wonderful people and consider me their little sister. I love them all dearly like family. Two years later, Rick's death is not much easier to deal with but I am thankful that I was blessed to have him in my life. I know one day we will be together again. I envision him there with Mooshum, Kokum and Mom watching over us. I can hear him making jokes with all of them, giving trouble.

During the months preceding Rick's death, Ted revealed that he was raised with one of our other siblings, Danny. Two brothers placed in the same home and both adopted. Danny has not yet decided that he would like to meet his siblings and I can totally respect that. It's an emotional roller coaster ride. We are friends on Facebook but there is little communication.

I do believe that when the time is right we will reunite.

That leaves one sibling yet to locate, Patrick. At this point Patrick is aware that siblings are looking for him but he has decided not to pursue a reunion. No reason given, he is happy with his life. I congratulate Patrick for that. He has his personal reasons and if he is blessed in such a way that his life has been full without knowing his birth siblings, so be it. I make it my duty annually to contact the Post Adoption Worker to show an interest in reuniting. Nothing yet from him but for my own selfishness I hope one day his curiosity will get the best of him.

Many life changing events have happened throughout the years but nothing can compare to finding a birth sibling, almost knowing what that sibling is feeling or about to say. Finishing one another's sentences and laughing when it turns out to be exactly what they were going to say. We are connected without being raised in the same household. The land miles may separate us but our Poitras genes are very strong.

Aunt Doris and Nora Poitras

When I actively started this journey I was 28 years old, I am now 58. I have felt every emotion possible over the years but never had one regret, whether the news be good or bad. I am who I am and proud of my roots and heritage. I came from the strong bloodlines of Poitras/Parisiens and Peltiers. I believe this is the reason why I still have my warrior hat on to this day. I have never given up on my journey. I am a strong Warrior Woman and a Survivor.

The next task at hand will be to ensure our Mother, Nora Poitras, receives a headstone on her unmarked grave. The plastic flowers I left on my first visit 3.5 years ago were the only visible markings since I visited. I promised my mother at my first visit I would eventually bring each of her children home to her.

33

"Home at last, Thank God I am home at last"

THOMAS PIERCE (Menominee)

Wyomissing High School Graduation, PA

Friends, since I last wrote for the book, "Two Worlds," many things have changed in my life, mostly for the positive. My health overall has vastly improved. It took proper medical care and several operations to make this happen. My mobility and pain remain an issue. I suspect they always will due to my Military service days. I am a Proud Native Warrior and Healer and I have been granted a new lease on life. I am truly grateful.

My ability to reconnect with my family has gotten on well since my financial woes and health have improved dramatically. I can sit and drive for four hours without too much discomfort. That's how long it takes me to get to the

Menominee Reservation. My retirement accounts have kicked in so I can live comfortably without worries for the rest of my life.

My family life gets better and better. In the last few years we have really become close. My wish for family has come to fruition. We have become friends as well.

Now that I can again travel, I can be a full and loving Nephew, Brother and Cousin that attends birthday parties, weddings and sadly even funerals. I am still having problems keeping the names straight, especially nicknames. My Aunt Ava is more like a sister than an Aunt. There are so many Aunts and Uncles, eleven in all. My Aunt Ava is actually younger than I am, and we have gotten to be partners in crime, so to speak. My Aunt Verna is the Matriarch of the family. This is as it should be, because the Menominee Nation is a Matriarchal society as are many Native tribes. We are blessed to have such Great Women leading us all.

I am learning our language, which is an Iroquois dialect, and it is going slower than I had hoped but our history, which is easier for me, is full and vibrant. We are a not just a proud people, we are very civically oriented, as are most Native peoples nowadays.

This is normally a great thing, but as most Native Tribes, we were herded on to lands that European Americans didn't want and placed in the middle of nowhere with few jobs or prospects. This is why percentage-wise, more Native Americans have joined the military in droves as a way to better them selves and escape poverty. The Menominee as a people have fared better than most other tribes, but during the Civil War and the two World Wars, our tribe lost so many young men, our numbers suffered dramatically.

Many died while serving our country or were wounded physically and psychologically. Just in my immediate family, nine have served their country, including my biological mother. One suffered a death and one was severally wounded. Perhaps that is why I started writing a book on America's Indigenous people and the conflicted truths of loving and honorably serving a Nation that has not loved us back.

So in the immortal words of Poet Wilfred Owen, "Dulce et decorum est pro patria mori" or "How sweet and honorable it is to die for one's country." That being said, being a Warrior in a Native Society is practically a given and one that we as Native men can be PROUD of, and I, for one, am. I have finally come home and how sweet it is to have such a family.

34

Knowing You Are Not Alone

JOAN KAUPPI (Red Lake Anishinabe)

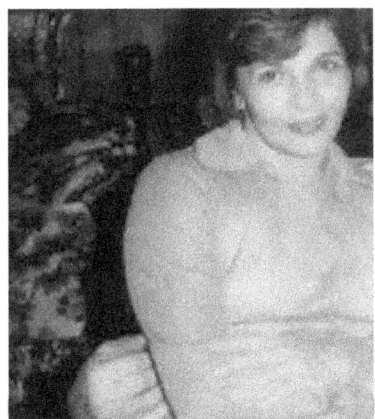

Joan's mom

Joan's mom and the children she raised

When we were asked to write an update reflecting upon the past year, it was more difficult than I had imagined. The year has sped by so quickly, so many things have happened but what was really important? Everything. Each experience, every moment, no matter how subtle or seemingly insignificant, are worthy of reflection and are as important to one's life as any grandiose occasion.

As a Split Feather, we are prone to bouts of depression and anxiety; I am no exception. Fortunately, I have a physician who is understanding and has treated my symptoms enough to mask the soul crushing darkness of which I am susceptible. The medications have allowed me to emerge from the sadness that overwhelms me to find peace while sitting outside and listening to the sounds of the Natural World. I find great joy watching a hummingbird feed and hearing its wings vibrate in the air. Catching the sight of a tarantula or a gecko scurrying across the patio, hearing coyotes howling in the distance or watching a single feather drift from the sky, I am truly happy. It is within these truly magical moments that I realized are miracles. I belong in the Natural World without pretense or action on my part. I do not have to think about, justify or defend my ethnicity; I am not American Indian, Caucasian or have a blood quantum. Immersing myself into those exquisite albeit brief segments of time, I simply am. My spirit is free.

The Creator has honored me to bring children into this world and now they are parents. There is nothing more amazing than being a mother and grandmother, at least in my eyes. My children are grown and have emerged into kind, thoughtful, caring and loving adults. They have their own trials and tribulations as we all do but they move through them with grace, courage, dignity and morality. It's a joy to watch them interact with their own families, each other and their sisters' children. There's a comfort and respect they share when they are together. I'm not saying they are perfect and don't argue, but the manner in which they do has matured as they have. When I am with them, there's a wholeness and tranquility. Even if I never find the total peace within myself, I know that being with them is a spiritual experience. I pray every day that I will be able to afford the move home soon. I am honestly a little afraid of the pain that the cold Minnesota winters will bestow upon me, but the emptiness without them far outweighs any physical discomfort. There was an added incentive of a new grandson Liam born mid-January.

Other than the self-realization I have enjoyed, I continue to write my memoir and Master's thesis. Not only is it therapeutic but it's an awakening of sorts; I've been able to equate my thoughts and experiences with those of other Split Feathers. Of course I am not happy that these kindred spirits have experienced being a Split Feather, but there's a certain comfort (for lack of a better word) knowing you are not alone or secretly harboring some sort of psychosis. I have read Trace's book *One Small Sacrifice* and *TWO WORLDS* multiple times and each time I recognize more of myself from my fellow contributors' experiences. That is a therapy that no one could find paying a counselor.

Due to the recent legal purchase, kidnapping and adoption of Veronica Brown, I have a renewed energy to have the voices of the Original Parents heard. I had considered asking the mothers about their experiences when their child was trafficked to a Caucasian family but why is it only the mothers' pain? The fathers must suffer as much. By asking only the mothers, it would only be half of the story. I understand what it feels like to have a child growing inside of you, there is a connectedness like no other. Mothers bond with their children while they are in the womb, we nurse them, comfort them and teach them. We are responsible for their health and nutrition, we feel their movements while they are inside of us; we understand their moods and needs.

Fathers love their children but cannot experience having a child grow inside your body. I had a realization that excluding the fathers' experiences was biased, based on my own motherhood. I want to explore what was happening in their lives at the time of the kidnapping, what the agencies told them (if anything), the tribe's response, how it impacted their lives and if they were ever to meet. I do not want to exclude anyone who lost a child, sibling, grandchild, niece or nephew—these stories need to be told. I am nearly 53 years old and time is quickly passing. Soon this history will no longer be available to those of us in the physical world.

This past year has been one of self-awareness and healing. I am grateful to Trace DeMeyer and all of the contributors to TWO WORLDS and CALLED HOME for opening up and sharing with us the wound of our adoptions. I continue to look at the positive aspects of my life so I may continue to move forward and join in the life which I have created.

Miigwetch.

35

Lost

ANDY MILLER HILL (Mohawk, Pawnee, Shawnee, British Isles ancestors)

Andy's self-portrait

OIE! Amend, amending, amended: all to work forward in a clear, concise and better manner in my review of LOST and the word's meaning. SO to amend my previous writing of my adoption story in *Two Worlds*, I need to reach down into my life and pull up my thoughts, actions and at times scars (whether *physical* such as the neglect of a few stitches needed in that knee at the age of four, or *emotional* when called fat while weighing in at 145 lbs, 5'9" at the age of 15.)

My visible attributes of being the adoptive daughter were: wearing a smiling face, and being kind even when unkindness felt like the way of life in the home. The small things when added up become huge and would mark how I would be as an adult and parent. For me I basically take everything mother Hill did and do the opposite. I am not lost in this aspect of living, loving, embracing my children for all their foibles, unconditional love as it should be with a parent child relationship, but never as it was with my Hill parents. In looking at this, all of it, my life as I remember balanced side-by-side with the photos I have saved, and I realize that truly I do not know who I am. I know parts of what make up this body, this vessel of my life's essence. What I don't know are the remnants of the lies that the family told themselves as to who I was and am within this family. I am lost in this; I have become lost where I had thought I had been found. Lived my life with a family that I called home and have finally faced that they were not what home has come to mean to me. There is a letting go of their falsehoods of that life and that me, that I have worn as a coat and mask allowing an embracing of who I want to be what I want to do without their restrictions that I still play in my head.

In writing the first part of my adoption autobiography in *TWO WORLDS*, I tiptoed and at times deleted my true feelings of growing up not knowing who I was, let alone why I was. I allowed that staged life with all its props to be my truth on paper while in my heart and head I was screaming *NO, NO, NO,* this is not who I was, this is not who I am, this was not my life! I coated my life's story, its memories in sticky gooey Grade A smoky maple syrup, forcing it to drip into all the dark hidden cracks and crevasses of that life. Instead of it becoming sweet to my tongue, it has become bitter darker, harder to swallow.

Andy (left) and a friend

I was up until a few months after my 2010 accident a hoarder of dates and words. A generic date book was used as my journal of life and living, thoughts at the end of the day, appointments and school projects. It was the finding of the 2009-2010 datebook and my small leather bound sketch book that has pushed me to come forward for myself and for those that may read these words. All that was written in the first telling of my life, adoption, finding family was true. What was deleted and not addressed had the truths becoming false by omission. Perhaps my not wanting to fully face the negative side of my life as an adoptee had me only telling the positive. But no one's life is filled with only positive, we grow from the negative life's lessons. I would not be the woman I am if I had had only happy times filled with all that one could ask for as a child, young adult and adult. I leave this self rant with two small pieces the first was written in 2009 addresses the interactions between myself and my sister through adoption and the needed care of our aging parents. The second was written in 2013 and was the end result of one of my rice bowls being dropped and caught, giving me a moment of clarity, along with a deep gash in the palm of my hand.

    I look forward to the day that I can place all my pain from the adoption and the losses that I felt while growing up in the palm of that hand to have the wind pick them up, scattering them to the four directions.

    I.
Door upon door upon door
closed in this house
a continuous shutting out

spirit wounded
life changes

one resounding click
reinforced
by a slam

conversations slashed

thoughts torn free
left to litter
the hallways' floors
I become
framed, viewed

watcher
guardian of the
door.

II.
Pure white
bright red

porcelain bowl
lies broken
hand above
the heart beats.

36

She Went Home

EVELYN RED LODGE (Sicangu Lakota)

As I stood atop a rancher's grassy hill on the Rosebud Indian Reservation where the Broncho Bill cemetery sits, I could not keep my eyes from my mother's casket.

I stood remembering our first meeting only four years prior with tears that seemed to be the same tears as when I found her. Such a feeling of loss engulfed me now, as it did then.

Then, something amazing would happen, and I would cry no more.

I stared at her casket remembering the first time I saw her after I was ripped away from her decades ago and adopted out to the sea of white. As if being in a tunnel, I saw nothing else around me. Thoughts flooded in again.

I found her in 2001 living in a nursing home in White River, South Dakota. Her eyes were teary as I neared her, for it had been roughly 37 years since we had seen each other.

I thought of those years wasted on hoping she would find me and love me long passed as I examined what was left between us. I, searching for simple acceptance while she, hoping to obtain the same.

There were no I love you's said, and I think time had erased much of the love we could have had for each other. After all, we were like strangers yet, a constant pull kept us searching for each other.

Although we didn't look alike, we were more alike than we knew. It seemed there were more things we could not say to each other than what we could. Deep down we both knew we suffered lives no one should.

I never did tell her about the insane adoptive mother who violated my body with beatings, my brain with trauma, and my soul with indignity of the worst kind.

She never asked about my childhood.

However, through one of our four meetings after I found her, I would find out my mother's childhood was as bad as mine.

My mother survived the beatings at St. Francis Indian School. For her at the time, the United States Government made boarding school her only option.

For me as a child in my time, it seemed the only two options were boarding schools, or adoption. The American Indian Adoption Projects were in full swing in 1965 when I was four years old.

As I stood there atop the hill, the summer sun shone high with a few clouds. Suddenly my friend nudged me and I looked up to see three eagles hovering. Unmoving they kept formation.

Then, feeling as though I was back in the tunnel, her casket was lowered. Tears engulfed me, and I could only concentrate on the shovelfuls of earth filling the grave.

Suddenly I was nudged again. This time I beheld the range horses that came from the southwest so quietly I hadn't noticed. They had made a sort of formation at the south end of the cemetery which was only about 30 feet from where I stood. They outnumbered the 15 or so people that came to the burial.

The four colors of horses filed in with one staying to the south. The others then walked single file past the one horse, turned back west, gave a look toward the grave, and moved on to the west side of the cemetery. It was as though the little ones knew what to do, also. They continued on until they all finished their ritual positioning themselves to the west side of the cemetery. I was awestruck.

After the grave was filled, the horses stayed around and even little bitty children came to feed them grass. No one was afraid.

I then retrieved my disabled daughter from the crowd, and stood near the horses. As I held her, the dominant male appeared in our faces, lifted his head, and neighed loudly to my little one. I noticed, the horse had an eye injury that left him blind in that eye. Was he telling us not to worry? That everything would be okay?

Then as suddenly as they came, they left.

As for crying no more, I was instructed that, in our family, once the last bit of earth is put on the grave, "we cry no more."

Less than a year later we moved 900 miles to live in South Dakota.

Evelyn is a freelance journalist in South Dakota.

Evelyn Red Lodge

37

I Am Home

LELAND P. MORRILL KIRK (Navajo Nation Citizen, Many Goats Clan)

Leland Morrill Kirk, Navajo adoptee (right) with Ft Lauderdale Mayor Jack Seiler, at Hyatt Regency Pier Sixty-Six in Fort Lauderdale, FL. Leland and other adoptees were presenting at the NICWA conference in Florida.

Much has transpired for me since the book "Two Worlds: Lost Children of the Indian Adoption Projects."

A big breakthrough came for me when my biological family, the Kirks, started to step in and help out. In March 2011 my biological cousin Matthew came to Los Angeles and offered to help. I was blown away. The same month the National Archives (NARA) came through as well. They were able to write a letter to me giving me the final links of information needed to provide to the Navajo Nation Vital Statistics. Also Matthew's dad, my Uncle Bob, also helped, along with his wife Ruth. We'd even discussed DNA testing, and found out the Navajo Nation Vital Statistics Office does not recognize this. We also discussed other ways of approaching the Navajo Nation to prove my need for a birth certificate. Uncle Bob went countless times to the Window Rock Navajo Nation Vital Statistics Office.

In January 2011, after becoming exasperated with the slow pace of the Navajo Nation Vital Statistics Office, I called Navajo Nation President Ben Shelly's office on January 11, 2011, the day he stepped into office. At that time I found out one of my relatives, Cyndi, worked in his administration in the Office of Constituent Services. Then I found out another "auntie" Gertrude worked for Navajo Nation Vital Statistics. It seems the Kirks were well-placed for my return.

On April 9, 2011 while I was attending a conference at the UCLA School of Law, around 2:00 p.m., Alicia Milford of the Navajo Nation Vital Statistics Office called to tell me that I had been granted a Navajo Nation Birth Certificate.

Finally. Validation. A sense of completion.

I no longer had to hear my adoptive mother say, year after year, **"Your birth certificate is your responsibility, not ours."**

This after my adoptive parents adopted an undocumented Navajo Nation child named Leland Kirk (me) on July 15, 1971, then moved out of the country to Burford, Ontario, Canada on July 16, 1971.

Yes, my adoptive parents both worked for the Latter-Day Saints (LDS) Church at the time. My adoptive father worked his entire professional career for the LDS/Mormon Church Education System. My adoptive mother worked several years at LDS Social Services. They still are in denial that they ever saw or did anything that was against the law. They removed me and my sister, also Navajo, from the Navajo Nation and moved to Canada the next day, and they also continued to adopt seven Ojibwe children (siblings) in Ontario. Then we moved back to the states to Rapid City, South Dakota, thus removing them from their culture.

The question remains open for me: Does this constitute Genocide? It does to me.

The United Nations defines genocide as the intentional "destruction of racial, national, linguistic, religious or political groups," "with the purpose of destroying it in whole or in part or of preventing its preservation or development," either "causing the death of members of a group or injuring their health or physical integrity," or interfering with their biological reproduction or also "destroying the specific characteristics of the group" through the "transfer of children."

My adoptive parents knew of the genocidal nature of what they had done. Another Mormon couple they knew in 1971 also adopted an undocumented Navajo child on the Navajo Nation when we all lived in Chinle, Arizona.

This is the email I received in September 2012:

"Alton Johnson called us today. You may not remember him, but they were our good friends in Arizona. When we lived in Canada, they came to visit us once. We also went to their house one night when they lived in Provo. Anyway, his daughter, Rachel, is struggling to obtain a census number. I told him about your experience, and he would really like to get information on what they can do to help Rachel get her ID. Could you send us a sort of step by step plan she can follow to get what she needs. Sounds like you're doing pretty good. Is your health still okay? I haven't heard you say anything about it for a long time.

Love, Mom"

So, you can see my adoptive parents walk a very thin line discussing genocide. (Without documentation, Rachel will have the same problem I did, having no birth certificate. Without that, you could be deported, according to the REAL ID ACT of 2005.)

Leland (grade school photo)

I did end up returning to the Navajo Nation in March 2012 with my Uncle Ernest after we met and enjoyed Christmas 2011 together. We went to Ganado, Arizona, where I met many relatives and had a tete-a-tete with my Uncles Bob and Ernest about what life would have been like, had I been raised on the Navajo Nation Reservation.

In my case, **discussing it after the fact**, there were some opportunities I may not have had if I stayed on the Navajo Nation Reservation. That is not to say the Kirk Family was derelict in staying in an impoverished state. In fact they evolved in leaps and bounds. Many of my Navajo relatives have gone on to obtain university degrees, had families, travelled the world and are living amazing lives. During discussions around Uncle Bob's dining room table, it was apparent Uncle Ernest and Uncle Bob and I have the same sense of humor and we relate to each other instinctively. I feel their presence. Not only that, looking at my biological relatives, it's like looking in a mirror. Behaviors, glances, the twinkle of an eye, the gestures we make, are some of what I missed over the past 40 years. Thanks to social media, cellphones and email, I am now able to communicate with my biological family where ever they reside.

Becoming an advocate for Native American adoptees and our Citizenship Rights has been one of the blessings, all from researching my own information.

Through an invitation by Korean "Vietnam Baby Lift" adoptee Bert Ballard, I attended the conference "Inter-country Adoption Orphan Rescue or Child Trafficking" in February 2013 at Pepperdine University School of Law. I was the only Native American pre-Indian Child Welfare Act of 1978 (ICWA) adoptee to present.

At that same conference I was able to speak with Ambassador Susan Jacobs who is in charge of the U.S.'s compliance with the Hague Convention on Inter-country Adoption. We discussed my lack of documentation and the impact of the REAL ID ACT on my life and the Baby Veronica case that was about to go to the U.S. Supreme Court. I shared my story with her, and the concerns of Native American adoptees in this country during a private meeting, a standing luncheon.

In February 2013, because of my work in film and television as an actor on *Savages, End of Watch, Rissoli and Isles, Crooked Arrows, Stand Up To Cancer*, etc., the Screen Actors Guild contacted me to be a guest speaker for "Honoring Natives in Entertainment Media Night," on March 23, 2013. I was able to tell my story and also discuss the book *Two World: Lost Children of the Indian Adoption Projects*. It was quite an honor to be recognized for accomplishments on this level.

In 2013, I was fortunate to be part of the Baby Veronica Case in the "BRIEF FOR AMICI CURIAE ADULT PRE-ICWA INDIAN ADOPTEES SUPPORTING BIRTH FATHER AND THE CHEROKEE NATION."

Because of the case, I raised the funds (making and selling my turquoise and silver earrings online) to attend the hearing on April 16, 2013. During the visit to Washington DC, I was also able to have a meeting with the Navajo Nation Washington DC office, set up through Jared King.

A fellow Native American adoptee Christine White Eagle, who let me stay at her family residence, also attended that meeting. We discussed my adoptions case and legal issues from Navajo Tribal Council, Tribal Policy on Adoption of Navajo Orphans and Abandoned or Neglected Children, 1960 (Adopted November 18, 1960 and CN-63-60 Resolution of the Navajo Tribal Council's Adoption of Members.) It was quite healing to be able to discuss this with representatives of the Navajo Nation and to make them aware of how I felt, and all the loopholes that had been used in my own adoption case in the Navajo Tribe Children's Court in 1971 in Chinle, Arizona.

Because of the amazing turn out of Native Americans for the Baby Veronica case, the National Indian Child Welfare office staff photographed many of us and featured Sandy White Hawk and me on their Spring 2013 cover of their newsletter, and it was quite an honor to be photographed with her, knowing what great work she does.

Being part of the Baby Veronica case was a great opportunity. Attending the U.S. Supreme Court argument, *Adoptive Couple V. Baby Girl*, watching the Justices question the attorneys, being around others who were part of the case was affirming that we were doing the right thing. The closure of the case on September 22, 2013 with Veronica being handed over to the adoptive couple at four years of age was heart-wrenching, especially for me as a foster to adoptive child at four years of age.

I can recall standing in Chinle Arizona Navajo Tribe Children's Court on July 15, 1971, being questioned by Judge Joe Benalley of the Navajo Nation and then our long drive on July 16, 1971 as my foster (now adoptive) sister Gin, also Navajo, were being driven away from the Navajo Nation to Canada. I remember that drive, not knowing where we were going to and resting my head in Gin's lap in the back seat of the blue sedan. We stopped in Chicago, first at my adoptive mother's sisters house, and then northward to Burford, Ontario.

My question to the world of adoption is: Will Veronica remember her adoption and the turmoil?

She has the added advantage of knowing many Native people from Tribal Nations across America and from other cultures traveled to the Nation's Capital on her and her biological father Dusten Brown's behalf. We live in an information age, so when Veronica is old enough to read, type on a keyboard, she will learn bits and pieces of the importance of her case. There are countless articles, briefs, court documents, etc., online that she will be able to access regarding her case where she will learn what a special child she is. So far, as of April 2014, we know little about the relationship Veronica Capobianco has with her biological father Dusten Brown. We do know Dusten Brown has seen her but that is being kept private as it should.

In another related case [No FA-20013-4 filed with the Nowata County Oklahoma Court Clerk] on November 1, 2013, *Adoptive Couple Planitiffs, vs. Baby Girl, a minor under the age of fourteen years, Birth Father and the Cherokee Indian Nation, Defendants*, the adoptive couple, Matthew Capobianco and Melanie Duncan, with their four law firms, are attempting to recoup total fees of $1,028,797 and $6,535.27 in costs as a result of the ongoing interstate adoption of Veronica Brown from Oklahoma to South Carolina and costs associated with going to the US Supreme Court.

These costs were supposed to be "pro-bono" (free). In any event, once Veronica sees "Baby Girl" as she is listed on this document, she will know it refers to her as a defendant and she will learn her adoptive parents entered the order on August 30, 2013. This legal document, as well as online news, videos on national television shows, and from her peers, she will learn and understand from their perspective who Veronica is in relationship to the Capobiancos which will help form who she will become. It is now the responsibility of the Capobianco's to supply her with truth, but Veronica will learn her own truth when it is best for her.

In September 2013, a few of us Native American adoptees were able to be part of a Reuter's news article "Baby Veronica's adoption case re-opens wounds for Native Americans" and I was able to use a Navajo photographer at Reuters for my photo. The reporter also asked if my adoptive parents would be willing to be interviewed. I gave her their contact information and they were part of the article. It was great to see mainstream media showing interest in our Native American Adoptee experiences. Giving us voice and letting us be part of the international conversation is a good sign.

I continue to volunteer with GLAAD, Gay & Lesbian Alliance Against Defamation, Human Rights Campaign, and NALEO Education Fund advocating, telling my story and also helping out with Citizenship workshops and assisting prospective citizens fill out the N400 forms for naturalized citizenship into the United States.

One thing I want to make clear is that I spent 22 years of my time doing research after work, on weekends, unending, lost time, years, decades. (Sometimes researching late into the night, the internet became part of my life in the late 90s to 2011.) I was writing letters to ecclesiastical leaders, hospitals, anyone who I could get an address for in Arizona and New Mexico. I used social media, fine-tuning research using keywords and names to find connections which prior to the internet did not exist. Accessing property records to find biological relatives, these were online and searching hundreds of relative names until finding the connection. This was risky and I don't know if I would suggest everyone else do the same but it worked for me.

So after 22 years: sometimes eight hours a night of research, sometimes 16 hour days. What is the cost of all those hours, years, decades, lost livelihood, freedom, a slave to research?

When I was in Ganado in March 2012, a grandma Margaret told me:

"We looked for you, we didn't know where you went. We had to move forward, we had other children. It is the Navajo Way to move forward."

So, all those years, I choose to let them rest and move forward and help others who need that extra push, learning and never forgetting the past, and sharing my experiences.

Citizenship is a blessing, and because of the Real ID ACT of 2005, a birth certificate is too. Mine is not issued by any of the 50 United States of America but the Navajo Nation. So first and foremost, I am a Citizen of the Great Navajo Nation.

I am home.

38

Fresh Flesh: Ronni and me

TRACE A. DEMEYER (CO-EDITOR) (Tsalagi-Shawnee-Euro)

Trace in one of the earliest photos (1957?)

As I watched the custody dispute unfold over the little Cherokee girl Ronni, or "Baby Veronica," I was horrified and very sad for this precious little girl. I understand her because I'm am her, just 50+ years later.

I was swept up and placed in a closed adoption with an infertile couple Edie and Sev DeMeyer, in their 30s. Veronica was swept from the hospital by Matt and Melanie Capobianco, an infertile couple in their 30s. (These couples want a fresh newborn; they incorrectly believe we babies are blank slates and they can write whatever they want on us. Like biology and DNA doesn't matter.)

Catholic Charities, the adoption branch of the church, never contacted Earl Bland, my birthdad, when I was born in 1956, nor did they need his permission to sign me away for adoption. When I finally found him years later, he said he would have raised me, had he known... But he didn't know because my birthmother Helen didn't tell him, just like Veronica's mom Christy didn't tell Dusten.

My dad Earl didn't have a chance to object.

What's better for Veronica is that her birthdad Dusten Brown did object and fought for her from the moment he found out what was actually happening. And it's not exactly a closed adoption since Ronni lived with her dad Dusten for two years and will remember him. I have vivid memories at age four, the same age Veronica was when she was removed from her father.

Most believe adoption is about orphans, right? It used to be adoption was for a child who had no other family or dead parents… Adoption has changed. It's now a marketplace for infertile couples who are willing to pay for fresh flesh, using unscrupulous adoption agencies who are literally trafficking in babies and children.

On my original birth certificate I am listed as illegitimate since my parents were not married. Veronica is also illegitimate since her parents were not married. Both of us were made into paper orphans although we both had two living breathing birth parents. We both had mothers who gave us up and fathers who wanted us.

On my amended birth certificate I'm renamed DeMeyer and my ancestry was erased. I do not have a copy of my original birth certificate from Minnesota even now. Veronica will also have an amended birth certificate, listing her adoptive parents as her biological parents. Thankfully she is enrolled with the Cherokee Tribal Nation and has a piece of paper to prove it. (Veronica will easily find him and reunite when she's older.)

Did Indian Country go on the warpath over this Baby Veronica case? Absolutely! It was like a nightmare all over again. Tribes remember the earlier Indian Adoption projects and government programs (via adoption and residential boarding schools) that traumatized hundreds of thousands of children. (Read the chapter **Baby V.**)

Some of the survivors writing in this anthology CALLED HOME found out how they were removed from their Nations, communities, and families and deliberately assimilated by adoption and by non-Indian parents.

Since 1978, the Indian Child Welfare Act (ICWA) was supposed to protect tribal nations against any ongoing efforts to forcibly remove Native children from their family, culture, and political birthright. Along with the era of tribal self-determination in the late 1970s, these policies have been central to revitalizing Indian Country. Remember that many tribes were decimated when up to 85% of their children were taken away… That's why organizations involved in these past adoptions/removals, like the Child Welfare League of America, apologized and now advocate for the rights of Native children. The CWLA and other national leaders were outraged when the South Carolina courts failed to uphold Veronica's rights and hold a hearing of best interest for her, and called this a civil rights violation.

What's even more troubling is that Veronica's adoption maybe a sign of what's ahead. Increasing pressure on adoption agencies to find adoptable children leaves Indian Country's children vulnerable once again to outside forces, and adoption agencies. And as a result there may be a new push by some to ignore federal laws like ICWA and commit fraud; all the more reason for ICWA to remain intact as a federal law.

There are many in the adoption industry and in religious institutions that value ICWA and follow the law. However, there were a number of red flags that became evident in Veronica's adoption case. Those advocating for the child's return to South Carolina, specifically, the Capobianco's supporters and fringe faith-based organizations, used a hauntingly familiar "Save the Native child" mission. In fact, these supporters are still actively working to erase ICWA altogether.

According to South Carolina court records, the biological mother Ms. Maldonado and the adoptive couple, the Capobiancos, were connected by the Nightlight Christian Adoption Agency —a Christian based non-profit with offices in California, Colorado, and South Carolina. According to the agency website "Nightlight provides domestic and international adoption services, to families in all 50 states, and embryo donation and adoption worldwide" while remaining "committed to carrying out our mission in a way that will bring glory and honor to our Lord and Savior, Jesus Christ." Faith is clearly a driving factor in this adoption effort. As Ms. Maldonado pointed out in her Washington Post op-ed, speaking publicly for the first time in years, she wrote that she chose the Capobiancos because she, "could tell they were people of strong faith, like me."

Adoption agencies like Nightlight rely on the ever dwindling "supply" of children for their livelihood, not just to achieve their religious mission but to make millions. That's why it's concerning that the adoption lawyers filed error-filled ICWA paperwork to the Cherokee Nation. Even the original South Carolina Supreme Court decision stated that though Maldonado alerted the agency of the father's status as citizen of the Cherokee Nation, "It appears that there were some efforts to conceal his Indian status."

If those efforts to conceal his status had never occurred, Veronica's father would have been notified of the attempt to adopt his daughter and she would have been with her father from the very start. Instead, without Mr. Brown's knowledge, Veronica was removed from Oklahoma to South Carolina just days after her birth. Mr. Brown was then notified of the adoption four months later, only days before he was to be deployed to Iraq with the United States Army. Meaning, he was subject to South Carolina laws for four months and didn't know it. However, before deploying to Iraq he retained legal counsel from military lawyers and from that day on he fought for his daughter.

The actions of the Capobianco's supporting cast during this should raise the greatest concern... The Capobiancos family friend and PR agent Jessica Munday, who has represented them in the media since the very beginning, has been working hand-in-hand with a group called the Christian Alliance for Indian Child Welfare to operate the **"Save Veronica"** campaign which gathers support and raises money for the couple's legal fees –$40,000 by the end of 2012. If the mission to "save" Veronica from her Cherokee family wasn't problematic enough, the Capobianco's supporters have stealthily created a new organization (CAICW) with other religious adoption interests to lobby Capitol Hill to end ICWA and its protections. And the Capobiancos violated gag orders and went on national media more than once. (The PR campaign was clever to use Ronni's blood quantum, which always infuriates white people who think Indians are privileged in some way they are not.)

When a forced removal happens, when you read the writers in this book, there is trauma, pain and grief. An adoptee feels confusion, loss and heartbreak. Adoption is something you live with your entire life! As "lost birds" have said repeatedly—our trauma is compounded by the institutional efforts to assimilate and alienate us from our culture, even our own parents. It is extremely hard to go back to your tribal nation when you are like a child and know nothing about the culture of your own people.

Veronica's deeper primal wound may not be evident at first. Later, when she realizes what happened, how her adoption is permanent, she'll feel distrust of her adoptive parents and the courts who handled her at such a young age.

Together the actions to keep Veronica's Native father in the dark, to keep him from his daughter, and his subsequent long stand against those trying to "save" Veronica made him the *David* in an all too familiar battle with a holier-than-thou *Goliath*. If anything, the history of removals in Indian Country should be better examined by the national media. If they aren't, you can be sure Veronica will read this book and others someday and she'll find answers on her own. She'll face the stark reality that ours was not a story told by the "Save Veronica" advocates to the national media of a white couple caught in a King Solomon custody nightmare.

One thing Veronica will have, that many of us lost birds never had, is a public record that her father and many others stood up for her and fought for her best interest.

I contributed a chapter in this new anthology ADOPTIONLAND

Orphans to Activists

New books like ADOPTIONLAND and others are changing the landscape and perceptions of adoption. Adoptees in this book CALLED HOME are not victims but survivors and warriors and activists.

In 2014, we know there is a growing infertility epidemic. You'd have to google what chemicals are causing this in both men and women. Infertility creates a demand for newborn infants. If we connect the dots, we'll see how this creates a population of people who wish to raise children despite their medical condition of infertility. The preferred way to remedy this will again be adopting an infant. That is how the adoption industry has grown for the past century, made billions and will still need to find a supply of newborns.

Data shows a rising scarcity of adoptable children. The trafficking adoption industry will react. The state welfare departments (and those who work in the billion dollar adoption industry) who handle these transactions and placements of these children will be hurt financially. They don't want that.

Demand in the U.S. for adopting "voluntarily relinquished" domestic infants (newborns) and young children (healthy and preferably white) remains high, while the availability of these children is very low and shrinking.

Estimates indicate that ten years ago less than 14,000 children were voluntarily relinquished in the U.S. each year due to an increase in women who choose to be single mothers. In addition, over the last decade the adoption industry has faced decreasing rates of international adoption prospects, primarily due to changes in policies by foreign governments, like Russia recently.

The new reality is that 62% fewer children are available from other countries than a decade ago. According to U.S. Department of State Office of Children's Issues a decline from 23,000 international adoptions in 2004 to around 8,700 in 2011.

The number of families and individuals looking to adopt is only increasing during this decline in options. As some in the billion dollar adoption industry attempt to remain afloat and making money, **Indian Country** and other Third World countries will once again be a primary target.

Some of this increase in adoption demand is driven by calls for capable families and individuals to adopt—especially in the faith community. Like the Southern Baptist Convention's 2009 resolution calling on its 45,000 churches and nearly 16 million members "to pray for guidance as to whether God is calling them to adopt or foster a child or children."

What I do know is my closed adoption literally and slowly destroyed me emotionally. I was trapped, told what to believe, told how to behave and had no choice but to accept that my adoption was sealed by law and I would never know who I really am or be able to meet my birth parents. I searched for answers, for people, for years. At age 38, in reunion with my birthfather, it hit me that I could never replace those missing years with my dad, my sister and brothers. Adoption destroyed years of my life. There was no way to get it back.

Being trafficked, I was adopted out when I had two living first parents. I was not an orphan. I was placed with an infertile couple who lost two children to miscarriage.

I was fresh flesh. I filled a need.

SOURCES:

Custody dispute unfolding: http://www.slate.com/articles/double_x/doublex/2013/07/baby_veronica_case_the_south_carolina_court_got_it_wrong.html

National outcry: http://www.ncai.org/news/articles/2013/07/31/federal-civil-rights-lawsuit-filed-on-behalf-of-veronica-brown

South Carolina court records: http://www.judicial.state.sc.us/opinions/HTMLFiles/SC/27148.pdf

Nightlight Adoption Agency: http://www.nightlight.org/why-choose-nightlight/

Maldonado op-ed:

http://www.washingtonpost.com/opinions/baby-veronicas-birth-mother-girl-belongs-with-adoptive-parents/2013/07/12/40d38a12-e995-11e2-a301-ea5a8116d211_story.html

South Carolina Supreme Court decision: http://www.judicial.state.sc.us/opinions/HTMLFiles/SC/27148.pdf

Save Veronica: http://www.saveveronica.org/

Christian Alliance for Indian Child Welfare: http://caicw.org/2012/12/24/consider-a-tax-deductible-end-of-year-donation/#.UWbEHVtKmi0

The Coalition for the Protection of Indian Children and Family: http://coalitionforindianchildren.org/our-members/founding-members/

39

The Path from Separativeness to Oneness

JOHNATHAN BROOKS (Cheyenne/Cree)

This chapter of my life story will show, I hope, a small beginning to my understanding of Lesson 79 in A Course in Miracles which says:

"Everyone in this world seems to have his own special problems. Yet they are all the same, and must be recognised as one if the one solution that solves them all is to be accepted... If you could recognise that your only problem is separation, no matter what form it takes, you would see its relevance."

Allowing wounds to become resources has been, I believe, a relevant and important step for me, out of separativeness.

In the first anthology 'Two Worlds', I started my chapter 'Two Worlds' with the quotation from Oscar Wilde.

'The aim of life is self-development. To realise one's nature perfectly—that is what each of us is here for.'

This remains my aim, but I would now describe my nature as needing to be realised on two levels:

<u>One being the psychological</u> —That is developing my potential for using my creative talents in my life and work, and in harmonising my relationships towards becoming my fulfilled personality self.

And the other...

<u>A spiritual level</u> when, I am told, I can lose all sense of separativeness, and know myself at One with Creation—as my Light (enlightened) Self.

So for this edition of the book describing my life journey so far, I have chosen two additional introductory quotations.

The first is from the Pathwork lectures channelled by Eva Pierrakos:

"Through the gateway of feeling your fear lies your security and safety...through the gateway of accepting the lacks in your childhood lies your fulfillment now."

This quotation may strike at the sensitivities of most children 'adopted out'.

The second is a Lakota prayer.

"Grandfather Great Spirit,
   all over the world the faces of living ones are alike.
   With tenderness they have come up out of the ground.
   Look upon your children that they may
   face the winds and walk the good road to the?Day of Quiet.
   Grandfather Great Spirit,
   fill us with the Light.
   Give us the strength to understand,
   and the eyes to see.
   Teach us to walk the soft earth as relatives to all that live."

Surely an aim for all mankind to realise.

LEVEL I THE PSYCHOLOGICAL

I have told the story of my early life and my physical journey across America to discover my roots and my birth family, and becoming an enrolled member of the Northern Cheyenne.

During this part of my life I saw myself as having been prevented from discovering who I was (Self realised) by other people's actions. As a child victim I had neither the strength nor insight to find any meaning in my situation and so my childhood wounds remained into adulthood as psychological problems, rather than the means (through the gateways) of transformation.

I had first to <u>identify</u> my specific wounds and confront them, instead of keeping my head down and enduring.

<u>RECOGNISING MY WOUNDS</u> (and beginning to do something about healing them)

1. ABANDONMENT

Whether it was true or not, I felt I had been abandoned firstly by my birth family, and secondly, partially, by my adopting family, leaving me later with feelings of insecurity in relationships, and hanging on when it was obvious they no longer had any value for either side.

I feel that one of the first steps I took as an adult in becoming less dependent was in choosing to take Landmark Education Forum, and exposing my hurt emotional little self to a room full of strangers. The participants having listened to my story, afterwards came up to me and told me that I had made their Forum. My further training in Neuro Linguist Programming, Cognitive Behavioural Therapy and other psychological techniques have led me to the satisfaction in the employment I have today of helping others with their psychological problems.

2. REJECTION

From my adoptive mother I felt a rejection of who I was. Why she felt I should keep quiet about being a Native American I could not understand. What was there about me that was so unacceptable in the culture in which we lived?

Fortunately my foster parents raised no such difficulties. They did not regard racial or cultural differences, as barriers to close relationships. They felt everyone has their own particular value. During my later childhood they encouraged me to build a sweat lodge in the garden, go to lectures by visiting Native American Indian Movement members who wanted to recruit me, go to British pow-wows and have my photograph taken in full Sioux chieftain regalia for the front cover of a local magazine, with an interview about my history.

Reading the stories of other 'lost children', I realise I was comparatively fortunate, but perhaps I took an interest into my history too far as I felt proud of being a Cheyenne who was part of the new generation born exactly one hundred years after the attempt by Colonel Chivington to annihilate all Cheyennes at the Sand Creek massacre in 1864. This perhaps made me feel separate and a bit special, in view of my birthday was in April 1964.

I began to feel my value lay solely in being of a indigenous minority race and looking different. After my first visit to Montana I decorated the back window of my car with a sticker saying 'I am Cheyenne and proud of it' which increased interest, but actually became a nuisance when people kept stopping me to chat.

I tried to make capital out of my different appearance by becoming a model for men's casual clothing, but this soon came to an end when the popularity for beefy, blue-eyed blondes took over, and my market as a Nick Kaman Levi TV commercial look alike came to an abrupt end. I then moved into acting when I was offered Native American roles, on both stage and film, as the real Native American. I was very successful in that niche market as I was able to add an air of authenticity to my roles. I later began to realise, after starting on my personal development path, I was no longer just a dark complexion, dark eyed, stereotype Native American. I was becoming a representative of everyman's problem of separation.

I read that we are born to parents (birth or adopted) who will provide us with the needed environmental and physical experiences, that, with the specific energies with which we are equipped before birth, can aid us with first, our personal life learning task, and when this is fulfilled we may go on to our world task—the gift of our unique talents for everyone. I realised I still had an awful lot of learning to find out about myself.

3. BEING LABELLED AN ASHMATIC

At an early age I developed Asthma and Hay Fever, badly enough for me to be hospitalised when my adoptive parents decided to send me away to school, abandoned and rejected.

The attacks lessened as enthusiasm and skill for hockey and other outdoor sports increased. I played first for school, then Sussex Schools and local regional teams and later founded and set up the Battersea Hockey Festival in London.

It was on the hockey field that I met my future wife, who is also adopted out of her native culture (South Korean) and knows the suffering it entails.

Although I had not heard then of Louise Hay, I think I was beginning to take on some of her new thought patterns.

For Asthma she wrote:

"It is safe now for me to take charge of my own life. I choose to be FREE."

And for Hay Fever:

"I am one with all life. I am safe at all times."

Much later Gill Edwards in 'Conscious Medicine' (2010) gave the underlying meaning of asthma as "suppressed grief and sorrow. Feeling suffocated (by a relationship or situation). Feeling unworthy to live—not even allowed to breathe" and of allergies she wrote, "Feeling unsafe. Not owning your power. Suppressed weeping."

I am still (naturally) working on these 'gateways' and although I have never really taken to camping or gardening, it is only at times of increased stress, and extreme weather conditions that I really suffer and feel life as constricting and hostile. The dates of these episodes usually coincide with the month I was given up for adoption.

4. BEING LABELED A DYSLEXIC

At about the age of ten I was diagnosed as a moderate dyslexic by a highly qualified world renowned educational psychologist. The tests were instigated by my foster mother, my school in those days having failed to recognise the condition. My adoptive mother who I only saw during holidays for a short time during the day (she never cooked a family meal) had the ultimate responsibility for my welfare. She not only refused to pay for the test, but also refused to allow me to have treatment.

She said it would 'mess up my brain'. It was only later that I realised she did not distinguish between psychology and psychiatry and preferred to think of me as educationally 'slow' rather than unbalanced as she most definitely was. I realise that my relationship with her was the instigating force for forgiveness that is an ongoing gift to myself to this day.

I feel this refusal to allow me to have treatment slowed up any talents I may have had in communication line, but in the end, by taking on a job of doing research for authors on a wide variety of subjects, I became skillful at computer speak, speaking in public and writing articles for magazines, and I began to realise my identification with the archetypal energies of communicator, were an important part of my life learning task.

From the lacks in my childhood I now feel fulfilled in my work, and also feel more sure of myself in relationships, especially since the birth of my daughter when I have had to take responsibility for someone other than myself now as an adult and parent and not as a child victim.

Was I truly slowly moving towards a greater union with "all my relatives" and, as Wyn Roberts (2010) calls it, Shape Shifting into Higher Consciousness?

LEVEL II THE SPIRITUAL

"Who are you? I am awake." ~The Buddha

"Awakening and the outgoing movement." ~Eckhart Tolle

With each challenge in life that has been dealt with, our identity enlarges and shifts; and some of the greatest challenges in our lives are said to occur around mid-life, which for me personally is around this particular time.

Now, must then offer great opportunities for shifting my consciousness beyond the life experiences I have known so far: From having been centered in my own problems, could I move into an unknown increasing inclusivity and awareness?

The Buddha and Eckhart Tolle talk of 'awakening' and a story which that describes an awakening for me, is told by Jon Kabat-Zinn in his book 'Mindfulness in Everyday Life', (1994). It is about the great Buckminster Fuller who, after a series of spectacular business failures was contemplating suicide. He felt his life was in such a mess it would be better for his wife and child if he were dead.

However, fortunately for the rest of us, rather than ending his life, he decided that instead of living his life for himself alone he would continuously ask 'What is it on Spaceship Earth (i.e. the planet) that needs to be done, that I know something about, and which probably wouldn't happen if I didn't take responsibility for?'

The rest, as they say, is a life history of great original creativity.

Few of us are of the caliber of Buckminster Fuller but I have begun to believe that as there is so much that needs to be done in the world that....

1. Every mundane task that presents itself to me is part of my process towards an eventual unification with 'all my relatives' and later with ALL THAT IS.

2. The circumstances of my birth and of those of all 'lost' children of traditional ways of living are of universal significance, and are part of a divine plan, whereby the ancient prophecy concerning the Eagle and the Condor 'peoples' (mind people and people of the heart and senses) will come together to learn and live as One.

Could it be that we the 'lost children' of North America are part of that spearhead directed towards unity?

'The path is the goal.' ~ Old Zen saying

'Walk in Peace;

Walk in Beauty'

Johnathan Brooks works as a cognitive behavioural coach, a facilitator, a trainer and careers management consultant for a large medical insurance company, and has taken an active interest in Native American wisdom for many years. He is an enrolled Native American from the Northern Cheyenne and Cree tribes of Montana, USA, dedicated to the interpretation of shamanic wisdom for today's ever changing world. His shamanic message is from the perspective that all things are alive and that we are part of a community of co-creative and potentially co-operative beings. The shamanic attitude is one of reverence and honour for all life in all its forms of manifestation and of responsibility to that community, and to unify everything and return to Source through the magnetism of Love. Johnathan has a postgraduate diploma from Kingston University, which he passed with a 'Commendation', is a postgradu-

ate in Cognitive Behavioural Therapy and is widely published, with highly insightful articles on how to use power animals to guide one through life's up and downs.
www.spiritbearcoaching.com

PART III

SEARCHING

The following are Lost Children, Lost Birds and are searching for their relatives and tribe.

40

Brit Reed

Brit Reed

Name: Brittany (Brit) Reed
Birthdate: December 5, 1988
Place: Parkland Hospital, Dallas, Texas
Mother: Diana Burghardt
Father: Unknown
Place of Conception: Miami, Oklahoma
Known tribe of decent: Choctaw Nation of Oklahoma
I was able to talk to my maternal family and visit my maternal uncle in Oklahoma. I'm no longer looking for my mother, we've not had contact yet, but I've had contact with my uncle, aunt, and grandmother via my aunt. I also had it confirmed via DNA tests and what my maternal family has told me in

person that the man listed in my adoption papers as my biological father (Michael Culver) is in fact not my father... just a friend of my mother's when she was in college there. I can only pray to get to the bottom of the full story and know who my father really was/is.. but perhaps this will be a step that helps.

My mother listed in my adoption papers that my paternal grandfather was a full-blooded Choctaw and that his wife (my paternal grandmother) was half white and half black. I'm not sure which information in my papers concerning my paternal side of the family is true and what are lies... but perhaps this is a piece that is a grain of truth about the man who is legitimately my biological father.

41

Kim Dupre

I am the daughter of an adoptee. I call myself *"Little Lost Feather"* because I am a fledgling born in my mother's womb but she had no knowledge or understanding of her tribal origin. Subsequently, I offer the following writing in honor of her memory:
My mother was abandoned at an unknown women's house, in Houston, Texas back in 1921. She was a tiny newborn who somehow made her way to the Gladney Adoption Agency, and at barely four-weeks old was adopted. She was born on October 12, 1921 and her birth name was Moreelle Shaw Duffy. At the time of her adoption she was given the name Edna Caroline Mosely and her birth date was changed from October 12, 1921 to October 19, 1921. (Funny all those years we celebrated her birthday one week late!) I had no idea that my mother was adopted until my early teens, and looking through the family album I noticed that there was no family resemblance between her and her parents. When I asked, she simply said, "I was adopted." Getting her to relate much more than that was tough. She told me that she accidentally found out about her adoption around the age of 16 years old when she was going through some papers in her parent's desk. She said she was extremely upset over the discovery. End of story.It was not until I was a young woman that I again asked my mother about her adoption and what she knew. She told me she did not know much at all and although she had attempted to uncover some of the mystery surrounding her personal history, she was unsuccessful. I respected her words but I could see a sadness in her a face that pricked my heart. My mother, the beautiful vessel that transported me into this world and made me her little lost feather, we needed to complete this circle of life and the only way was to discover the truth of her biological parents and my grandparents.She was an artist, a painter, with a gentle heart that loved animals of all sorts. She painted little girls, some Indian, all of whom were positioned in such a way that their faces were never the focal point of the painting. I sometimes wonder if her paintings of little girls as faceless was because she didn't know *all* of who she really was. Who were her ancestors, what blood ran through her veins?My mother and I were very close, she loved me well and I her. Sometimes amidst our laughter and tears I would tell her that when

she passes over she must come back and tell me that she is alright and to confirm the existence of the "other side." My requests were serious and somewhat thought out and since she loved birds so much I would tell her that in order for me to know it was really her on the "other side," she must do so through the birds.On May 3, 1996, my mother passed to the other side. It was a beautifully warm day with the sun peeping through the leaves of the trees in my backyard. I was treating myself to a massage and because the weather was so very nice I asked the masseuse to set-up her table outside in the backyard. After awhile a song bird started in and it was singing its little heart out, so much so, that I mentioned it to Althea, the masseuse. That little bird sang and sang with such joy and it was still singing when I was saying goodbye to Althea.

That day I was going out with my mother to pick out a baby shower gift and when I called her to confirm a time an unknown voice answered. It was the police department, "I'm sorry your mother is dead." I fell to my knees moaning saying "No, no, no." I told the officer I would be right there and hung up the phone. As I stood there in complete shock I looked up to see a little brown sparrow at the threshold of the partially open patio door ready to hop right in.

If that wasn't enough with the presence of birds, about seven months after my mother's funeral a bird reappeared. It was an incredibly tumultuous time in my life. Huge transitions were happening and everyday like clockwork a robin would light itself in the fichus tree just outside my office window and peck at the glass with its beak! I named him Einstein! He hung around pecking at that glass for about six months and for anyone wondering, there was no reflection to cause the pecking. Clearly, my mother's spirit comes to me through the birds. I believe that the singing songbird was my mother's spirit rejoicing and the little brown sparrow was there to express the existence of the other side. As for Einstein, I believe she really wanted to make sure that I got it and that she hears me when I talk to her. Still from time to time, a robin will light directly in my sight and when it does I smile and say hello.

She was an interesting character, my mother; she wore sterling silver bangles and earrings. Her hair was so dark brown that you could have possibly said it was black, her eyes were a golden hazel green. She has blessed me with so many gifts to wit the awareness of life around me, a love of the arts, animals, and love, so much love. It is out of that same love, that I search on her behalf to discover our ancestral roots.

The synchronicity that has occurred within the past four months of my life surrounding my quest to discover my mother's true birth identity has been uncanny. I received a gift of a psychic reading; out of that reading I was told that my mother was Indian and that she had one other sibling. From there, I started reading up on Indian adoptions and in searching on the Internet I came to discover Trace DeMeyer and her work regarding American Indian adoption. I contacted her via e-mail wherein she was so gracious to forward a name of someone who could perhaps help with my quest. I attempted several times to contact the referral to no avail. At that, I let the trail grow cold. Maybe the psychic was wrong.

The only information that Gladney Adoption Agency released was that my mother's name was Marcell Shaw, and that she was abandoned. Not much else there, but then it was discovered from a ship's passenger list that my mother's real birth date was October 12, 1921 and her actual name was Moreelle Shaw. However, it was my mother's original birth certificate that I needed and the only way for me to possibly see it was to travel to Houston, Texas, Harris County, and petition the court to release the document.

Now back to the psychic reading. Not too far in the recent past, I opened my e-mail to see a subject line all in upper case "THIS IS YOUR MOTHER'S BIRTH CERTIFICATE." I opened the e-mail and there it was, her birth certificate and it revealed that she had one other sibling. If that was not enough I looked to see who it was from and there below was a picture of an Kumeyaay Indian women (Karen Vigneault, Trace's contact) whose smile looked as if she knows many truths – sort of like the laughing Buddha. We e-mailed back and forth a lot that day; she helped find my great-grandparents as well and also discovered that my grandmother's name is on the Dawes Roll.

As it presently stands, I'm waiting for the results from a DNA test to get scientific confirmation of my Indian heritage, although my soul already knows that my mother was Indian; and also me, her little lost feather. To follow my on-going discoveries as they unfold you are welcome to contact me at littlelostfeather@gmail.com …I am happy to share and happy to help.

"Trees whisper to my soul, there is a calling, I feel the soul of our great mother earth and hear her languishing cries brought on by man's poison factories that pollute her waters and leach her soil. The mountain lion, coyote, wolf and bear sing woeful songs of disappearing land, forced out of their homes by the encroachment of blind corporations that seek blood money from the destruction of scared land and the life it sustains."

42

Catie Ransom

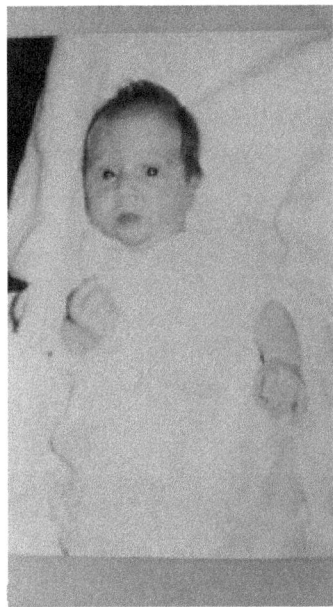

Catie Ransom

My given name was ANDREA LYNN before my adoption but no last name was ever revealed to my adoptive parents.

One unique thing about my birth is I was born on a Leap Year. I was born February 29, 1968. I was placed on July 25, 1968. My placement and adoption was done through the Hennepin County Welfare Department and I was born in St. Paul, Minnesota. The actual legal adoption went thru on March 26, 1969.

The information my birth parents have is limited:

The records said my father was one-half Comanche and Caucasian, 5 ft. 11" and 170 lbs. with dark blonde hair and a medium complexion. It also said his nationality was unknown(?). My birth mother was Polish, German and one- half- Russian, 5 ft. 2" and 109 Lbs. with brown hair and brown eyes.

That is all the info given to me about my birth parents. There was never any names revealed and the adoption was closed so I have not been able to obtain my original birth certificate from Minnesota and as a result have not been able to enroll with the Comanche Nation Tribe. I have not yet done DNA testing but I am looking into it.

Email: catieransom@yahoo.com

43

Drew RedBear Rutledge

Drew

Hau' Oyate. Honestly, I'm not sure where to begin, so I guess I'll start with the basics. My name is Drew Thomas Rutledge; I was born September 5, 1970, in Detroit, Michigan at Booth Memorial Hospital, at 7:36 P.M. My biological mother is/was Native American (tribal affiliation unknown) and Irish, almost 19 years old, she was 5'5", 125 lbs., dark brown hair, deep brown eyes, with olive complexion. She was of Baptist faith and the oldest of four siblings; sister age 16 (12th grade); brother age 14 (9th grade); and brother age 11 (6th grade). She had graduated high school and loved to read. (Her father was 46 and a high school graduate, and was employed as an inspector at one of the automotive plants.

Her mother was 41, also a high school graduate and not employed outside the home.)

Not much is known about my birthfather except that he is/was German and French, almost 18 years old (at the time of my birth), 6'3", 195 lbs. with brown curly hair and green eyes. He was a high school dropout and during her pregnancy with me, he was suspected of using drugs and was abusive towards her, and was employed as a carpenter. They also had one child previous to me as well. His mother did not allow them to marry because he had lied about his age, stating he was older than he was. My birthmother was not financially or emotionally able to handle another child, so I was put up for abuse (adoption.) Their parental rights were terminated September 27, 1970, and I was placed into the adoptive home in October that same year, with the adoption being finalized November 2, 1971.

When I was about 24, I decided I would try and look for my biological parents. Getting only a non-identifying information packet, I still was shocked to see what it said. My biological mother was Irish and Indian, tribal affiliation was unknown. Thinking I was English, Irish, and Welsh, this was a HUGE shock, and I remember almost falling over. Calling the adoption services agency, I tried to find out which tribe I was from, but to no avail. Hence, my search for answers started. Christianity was a part of me then, but after reading a few Native books, Black Elk Speaks, John Fire Lame Deer, and a couple others, I began to question my life.

I'm still searching for my biological family, as I always will, but for now, I'm content and I will keep writing. Alcohol and drugs do not play a role in my life, I've gone back to school and I'm living a good honest life. At times emotions still get to me, as life hasn't been the easiest, and I get into moods and places I don't want to be in, but again, through prayer, friendships, and especially my daughter, I am surviving.

Mitakuye Oyasin, Aho.... We are all related... (Drew RedBear contributed song lyrics in the anthology **TWO WORLDS**.)

44

Karla Mena

Karla Mena

All I know is that my original birth records were destroyed or can't be found. I was adopted as a baby, and my parents are believed to be Irish [mother] and Cherokee [father]. No birth searcher has been able to locate any information about my birth right.

All I want to know is my Tribal heritage. I was born in 1961, not even sure the birthdate on my 'fake' birth certificate is accurate.

45

Lisa Bos

email Lisa: adopted1966@gmail.com

Michael Pintozzi

My Birthdate: July 9, 1968
 Adopted name: Michael Robert Pintozzi
 Adopters name: Robert and Claire Pintozzi
 I was born in LaCrosse, Wisconsin. All I can think of is this was done through Catholic Charities.
 EMAIL: mpintozzi@gmail.com

47

Marylyn Jean Chrismer

Marylyn Jean Chrismer
   Birth Date: 02/01/58
   Birth Place: Rosebud Reservation

My first name is Marylyn, middle name Jean, names given to me at birth and keep after adoption. I was adopted with my biological sister, Louella Rose. I was 4 or 5 years old, she was 7, or 8. I am 55 years old and have just begun looking for my history.

Until recently I always believed that my birth parents must be horrible people because good people do not get their children taken away. Right? Well, I found out I was wrong. A good friend of mine asked, as 100's of other people had, if I had looked for my birth parents. I briefly told her my story and she told me that what I believed was not necessarily true, and, that in that day children were being taken away from their parents in what was thought to be the childrens' best interest. I had never heard this. I went home and searched the internet and found it to be true. I read many persons stories and read articles and found "me" in those stories.

Since then, I'm searching. It's only been about 3 months, I've got patience and I won't give up.

One story I overheard when I was young was that I always called every women I saw, Mom. My heart breaks every time I think of that little girl and the fact is, is that I never did find a "Mom" as my adopted mother never had it in her heart to love us.

If you know of two little girls named Marylyn Jean and Louella Rose, please let me know.

My email: chrismer.marylyn@yahoo.com

48

Doreen Evelyn Sinclair

I am hoping to find my sister Doreen Evelyn Sinclair
DOB 9/16 or 10/16/68
Born in Selkirk Hospital, Manitoba
Birthparents:
Darlene (Asham) Sinclair…but now last name is Hill (DOB 9/16/48)
Samuel Sinclair (DOB 9/22/38) Deceased…
    My info is:
Sheryl Lee Sinclair
DOB Jul 4/67
Born in Selkirk Hospital
Adopted in 1972
Live in New Jersey US since my adoption.
    My email: cher7467@aol.com

49

Mary Thompson

Female 3-22-1955, Casper, Wyoming

My name is Mary Thompson. I recently celebrated my 59th birthday. I have always known that I was adopted from a very early age. I was born in Casper, Wyoming but adopted in Butte, Montana. I petitioned the District court in Montana in 1989. My file was unsealed and I was given my original birth certificate with my birth parents listed. My birthmother's name is Mary Walks Alone Reed and my birth father's name is Arthur Inman. I was the eighth child my mother gave birth to. I recently received non-identifying info from the State of Montana Department of Family Services. The information I received was my birth mother stated she was full blooded Cheyenne. I have contacted the Northern Cheyenne to be enrolled. I have yet to hear back from them. My birth mother also stated that her mother died when she was 5 years old. I sure would love to be reunited with my parents and or siblings. [Email Trace if you have any information: tracedemeyer@yahoo.com]

50

Amelia Cagle

Amelia

I am in search of my birth father. I have all of my adoption records but the information I've obtained has lead to a number of dead ends.
I was born Jennifer Dyann Mitchell on February 23, 1973 at University of Tennessee Memorial Hospital (currently referred to as UT MEDICAL CENTER) in Knoxville, Tennessee.
I have a lot of information on my birth mother but very little on my birth father—and I can't seem to locate either. I'm not even certain my birth father ever knew of the pregnancy.
It doesn't give me any information on my birthfather except he was of the American Indian decent—no name, location or anything on my birth father.

However it does state he was 23 years old (in 1973), 6'2, large build, black hair, brown eyes, dark complexion. He was interested in his vocation of construction work and interested in horses and cars.

According to the information in my records my birth mother's name is Shelia Marie Mitchell—the middle name Lorena is written but marked out and replaced with Marie so I'm not sure of the actual middle name. There's no birth date listed for my mother with the exception she was 18 (on one paper- 18 1/2 on another paper) when she had me in 1973 putting her approximate age being 59-60.

The information said she lived in another county other than Knox County (Tennessee). It refers to her living in Blaine which is part of Grainger County, Tennessee. The information in the records advised that she quit school—although it doesn't indicate what school—when she was in 10th grade due to both parents being killed in an auto accident—but it doesn't say specifically where.

The information I have from the department of welfare describes her as redheaded, fair skin with freckles and beautiful straight white teeth. On my birth certificate (mother's copy from hospital) it has Susan Kelley listed as next of kin but no other information is given on her.

I do not want to disrupt my birth father's life—I have children of my own but we have no background or medical information from my side. Of course if I found him and he wanted to meet me, I'd love to meet him and introduce him to his beautiful grandchildren.

Any help you can provide will be greatly appreciated! EMAIL: born02231973@yahoo.com

51

DNA: The New Normal

By Trace A. DeMeyer

These adoptees are the heart of what I do. They are the reason there is a blog AMERICAN INDIAN ADOPTEES and this book. In 2014 Karen Vigneault and I are working with 20+ adoptees who are trying to find their families. Because of the adoption laws in the USA, the "**New Normal**" is adoptees doing a **DNA test**. They have no other choice or option with the laws not allowing adoptees to access our own names, our parent's names and our tribal nations, and we are still denied our basic rights as human beings and citizens of sovereign nations and denied our legal documentation. Some states charge crazy fees to be "confidential intermediaries" or they charge adoptees to be on registries or they create "no contact clauses" for birth parents—it's feels like they are always sticking it to us, or profiting off us, or only making it harder.

Our adoptive parents who raised us may or may not realize that we **NEED** information and our ancestry and medical background. Many adoptees tell me they are afraid to search because of their adoptive parents! That fear has to stop because if you wait, you may never get to meet your mother or father!

Alice, one of the adoptees in this anthology, wrote about finding new cousins who are trying to figure out who her mother is. This is the new normal. It's not right but because of the adoption industry and archaic laws and no contact clauses, this puts adoptees at the bottom of the totem pole as far as our rights.

I don't know how many times I have said to an adoptee: do not delay your search. If you do get a name or phone number, make the call. Have a friend with you to keep you calm. Write a set of questions. Just make contact then offer to send a letter explaining what you know about your first family. Send them your phone number so they can call you back. Give people time to adjust to the truth that you are definitely one of their family members.

If you do get your DNA results, which is the new normal, make contact with cousins who share your DNA! Give them your birth date and let them help you try and figure out how you are all related.

The new normal isn't fair but we'll use DNA tests until the laws change.

From CALLED HOME contributor Mary St. Martin Charles:
Being an adoptee, originally I just wanted to know my ethnicity. To confirm what I felt in my heart, I never had access to the truth. I was told my birth father was 1/4 Aleutian Indian from Alaska. At the time, the DNA company also offered medical evaluation to help see if you may possibly carry genes to hereditary diseases. The government stepped in and laid that service to rest. I literally had no concept of having a relative who shared DNA with me. I didn't even hope to find anyone when I submitted my spit.
So, I spit in the cup and sent if off last fall. My results were astonishing. My DNA read 51% European and 49% Native American and Asian. That was news.
The biggest shocker was a 25% DNA match that the company connected to me, suggesting that I was this man's aunt. We had the same exact birth date only a year apart. He was 99.9% European and an adoptee as well. I did my little chromosome research and quickly concluded that he was my **half brother** although every search angel, friend and even my half-bro could not believe our connection. I went with my instinct, we made quick friends and he helped me out. At some point, he was given the name of our birth mother and some notes from Catholic Charities about her.
It took a few months and I did locate her which was also confirmed through another 2nd cousin on my DNA listed from her family tree. But, this is where making connections and contacting your closest cousins on your DNA list comes in handy. Also, contact cousins who have taken the time to make family trees and have a genuine interest in genealogy. E-mail as many as you can. Some will be so happy to help, others you will hear nothing. When you get names, just send quick emails like, "Hi cousin, do you have so and so on your list?" Friend them on the social media as well.
In time my birth mother furnished me the name of my birth father and acknowledged she did indeed adopt out my half brother a year later. When I posted my fathers name on the social media, it flew like a wildfire. In a matter of hours I had a gazillion Alaskan Native relatives who wept, called me on the phone and sent photos of my father who died in 1992. They know about us. They do want us back.
I am now in the process of doing even more DNA tests with my relatives. The State I was born in still has closed records and are still defiant. When I sent for my non-ID, they would not provide me with any information on my birth father when I specifically asked for his ethnicity. Concluding, they are **still** trying to keep us unaware and I find it so very racist. Insidiously handing me the white card, they think it's OK. My father was full blood Koyukon

Athabascan. My birth mother has since told me that the hospital asked her what my ethnicity was because they were not sure if I was half "black" at the time. She told the hospital my father was full blood Native and to this very day are still trying to hide it by not providing me with my records. Records they probably falsified anyway by lowering his blood quantum and changing his tribal lineage. Man, wish I could sue their asses.

OK, back to DNA... my family in AK and I have submitted DNA to provide lineage. The tribe understands that the government won't be of help and will accept our DNA samples for enrollment purposes. I am waiting results. Like I said, go for it. They want us home.

On 23andme I found my half sibling plus other cousins. Since my mother was white and my father native, I could definitely distinguish by haplogroup which side my cousins came from.

I also did FTDNA which yielded no close cousins and the ethnicity had me Mayan. I did this one in Dec. 2013 and still no new relatives.

AncestryDNA is where I hooked up with the more genealogy-minded cousins and was able to friend them on Facebook. That was how I was able to find out who my father was. Also for adoptees searching, looking at the map locations of cousins helped me to figure out what tribe location I'm from. All my native cousins are located in native villages up and down the Yukon River.

For those who are apprehensive about searching and being non-loyal to your adoptive folk: Get your wings on. Your life is about you. You cannot be the best person in this life unless you fulfill your inner calling. Take control of and start the path your feet are ready to walk. There you will feel fresh wind in your hair and lift your wings to take flight.

Please share this book so the whole world can be made aware of Native American adoptees. We are taking a stand, reaching out, supporting and learning from one another. The first thing I did when my DNA results revealed "Native American" was surf the internet for Native American adoptees. The link I was found was a blog by Trace DeMeyer called American Indian Adoptees (www.splitfeathers.blogspot.com.) For the first time in my entire life I was made aware of other people like me, and the very real history that laid there waiting for me to find. With this blog, I found the validation to find my Alaskan Native family. I believe we are making a permanent mark in history. Peace and Love to all.

Image Credits

Cover and story photos were provided by the adoptees. Some are posted on Facebook.

Newspaper sources for Operation Papoose and The Rainbow Project are linked on their page.

Adoptees on the book jacket include: Anecia O'Carroll, Lawrence Sampson, Terry Niska Watson, Samantha Franklin, Johnathan Brooks, Drew Rutledge, Elizabeth Blake, Cynthia Lammers, Andy Hill, Suzie Fedorko, Debby Precius-Poitras, Mary St. Martin Charles, Ani Chosa, Joan Kauppi, Thomas Pierce, Lynn Grubb, Janell Loos, Evelyn Red Lodge, Janell Black Owl, Gail Huggard, Jessup Neubert, Leland Morrill, Meschelle Linjean, Mark Heiser, Patrick Yeakey, Trace DeMeyer, and Patricia Busbee.

Cover Design: Kim Pitman (Firefly Inx)

Acknowledgments

From Patricia:

I would like to acknowledge and thank my ancestors. Without them my daughters, Hannah and Leigha would not have been born. My darling grandchildren, Taj and Mairead would not be growing and thriving. I am thankful for my ancestor's guidance and for calling me home. Thank you to my grandmother, Alta Fletcher. I believe it was her unseen hand that guided my searching. Thank you to my husband, David Victor Busbee for supporting and loving me when I felt most unlovable.

I am grateful for my adopted parents, Helen and Edmond. My adopted mother was an artist. She taught me to see beauty in the most mundane places. My adopted father gifted me with the love of learning.

I want to thank Trace DeMeyer for her support and encouragement. She is a true sister and friend. Without her vision and trust in the Great Spirit this book would not have come to fruition. A special thank you to Blue Hand Books.

A heartfelt thank you goes out to all the adoptees. Their stories are soul gifts to the reader. I understand what it takes to wrestle with what is stirring inside and birth it onto the page May each adoptee continue to heal, grow and integrate. May those that are still seeking find the much-needed missing pieces and may each adoptee understand their true worth in this lifetime.

From Trace:

I would not be able to do this work without the love, patience, and support of my soulman, my best friend husband Herb. He has endured 10 years+ with me writing at all hours and many moods which can get pretty dark doing research, blogging and writing. Words are not enough but I love him and I thank him.

I thank Patricia Busbee for being a light, a constant source of love, and for being a brilliant writer and editor. Working with you is a dream! I love you and thank you, sister!

Thanks to the Native American publishing collective Blue Hand Books.

I thank Karen Vigneault for her first email in January 2014 which changed lives, including mine. Her ability to locate lost relatives for adoptees, without charging money for all her time and work, I cannot possibly thank her enough. Karen, beautiful you, you define the word ANGEL.

For the Adoptees/Lost Birds/Lost Children/Split Feathers, I thank you and applaud you for your courage to write your own story and share your feelings and truths in this anthology. With you all, we change history. Your writing is truly incredible, powerful and life changing for all of us. The writers in this book and in Two Worlds are some of the most extraordinary people I have ever met!

For adoptees still on the journey home, who keep in touch with me on Facebook and in emails, I send you love, good thoughts and keep you in my prayers.

To my family, all of you, siblings, nieces, nephews, aunts and uncles, cousins, all my ANCESTORS, all of you, I love you and thank you.

To Creator, Great Spirit, I am your grateful servant.

About the Authors/Editors

Baby Patricia

Patricia is an emerging author/editor/teacher and graduate of Evergreen State College and Goddard College. She has an MFA in creative writing. She received her education later in life. She enjoys the process of fusing fiction and non-fiction with poetry, art, and photography. Patricia is an adopted woman. She is also an adoptive parent. Standing on both sides of the fence continues to be a learning experience. She is of Cherokee-Shawnee, Irish, Welsh and German mix. Her family is multi-cultural. One of her daughter's is African American. Patricia's grandson is Turkish, Egyptian and Native American. Patricia is still in the process of reuniting with siblings, family members and places where her ancestors lived their lives. Patricia firmly believes that healing happens when we reconnect to ourselves, when we are truly heard and when we share our stories.

Trace's memoir ONE SMALL SACRIFICE: Lost Children of the Indian Adoption Projects is a ground-breaking exposé on the systematic removal of American

Baby Trace

Indian children from their mothers, families and tribes for adoption to non-Indian families and she weaves in her own personal story. Known for her exceptional print interviews with influential Native Americans such as Leonard Peltier and Floyd Red Crow Westerman, DeMeyer started research on adoptees in 2004. Her discoveries and research culminated in a fact-filled book she published in 2010, then a second revised edition in 2012. Her adoptee journey takes her around the country, finally meeting her birthfather in 1994 and learning about her Cherokee-Shawnee-Euro ancestry. She is also French Canadian with ancestry from Ottawa and Quebec.

Trace is former editor of tribal newspapers the Pequot Times in Mashantucket, Conn. (1999-2004) and Ojibwe Akiing in Wisconsin (1996-1999). Her chapter HONOR RESTORED on Sac and Fox Olympian Jim Thorpe won critical praise in the 2001 book *Olympics at the Millennium* (published by Rutgers Press). She read from her highly-anticipated memoir at the Wisconsin Book Festival in October 2008. In 2009, she started her blog about American Indian Adoptees: www.splitfeathers.blogspot.com. Her memoir was chosen as Native America Calling's Book of the Month in March 2010.

In 2014, Patricia and Trace co-edited and published TWO WORLDS: Lost Children of the Indian Adoption Projects, using the Blue Hand Books as its publisher. This ground-breaking collection of adoptee narratives and its contribution to American Indian and First Nations history is a major accomplishment and the editors were invited to present on a panel at Brock University in Ontario in 2014.

Trace has contributed to new adoption-themed books *Adoptionland*, *Adoption Reunion in the Age of Social Media*, and the *Lost Daughters* anthology.

She teaches social media and blogging at Greenfield Community College and operates Blue Hand Books as a collective with other Native American writers/authors.

Trace has changed her name to Lara Trace Hentz. She lives at the foot of the Berkshire Mountains in Massachusetts with her husband Herb.

Come Home

JUDI BRANNAN ARMBRUSTER

To all that hurt because of culture lost
I have felt your pain.
To all who are angry because the connection seems broken
I have been there too.
To all who are still reaching and searching
I offer these words:
The dreams and the songs live in the earth;
Come Home.
Even if most are assimilated,
Even if some that dance are not worthy,
Even if you have to stop romancing the culture,
Come home.
Come and let go.
Stay open even through the heartache.
Walk the land with clear eyes, and ears.
If there is language, learn it.
Because perhaps it is you
That will "catch" the song and bring it back.
Do not ever give up on your culture
In spite of the hardness of those that are left.
I have been through all of these things,
And I will not go away.
There will be more generations to come
And then we will be the Elders.
What will you remember
And what will you pass on?
    03-04 JArmbruster

Judi Brannan Armbruster, is a direct descendant of Ah Ish Ka'a, Full Blood Karuk of northern California. In the mid 90's, she returned to ancestral territory to find some connection and instead found the threads of her poetic voice. She is 65 years old, married, and the mother of one daughter. Her poetry is

Judi Brannan Armbruster

found on the internet, in literary magazines and anthologies. Judi's poetry covers the journey out of an abusive home, through two abusive relationships, and finally to healing as she connected with her Tribal roots and grounded herself in Nature. *Come Home* is a part of the journey to claim her place in the world. www.judibrannanarmbruster.blogspot.com

www.ingramcontent.com/pod-product-compliance
Lightning Source LLC
Chambersburg PA
CBHW060820050426
42453CB00008B/515